...opy of "Manuskripte" ...

...just weird! It's got ...

...invariably has nega...

...embers to "Manuskripte" cant be that ...

...he U.K. - let alone contributors.

... - but then, on second thoughts, there's

... should have.

<u>Berlin</u>

...have that feeling I'm more at home in a wa...

...aking another language.

...d the other day? He thought I should ...

...fusing the insights I've gained from

...me and abroad

...ries of times past, the journey over

...se years ago and the encounter with

...k dress

Ariadne's Thread

In Memory of W.G. Sebald

Philippa Comber

Foreword by Iain Sinclair

propolis

*The publisher wishes to acknowledge and
is grateful for, the support of Mr. Dolf Mootham*

Norwich

UNESCO *City of Literature* ™

First published in 2014

by Propolis Books
The Book Hive,
53 London Street,
Norwich, NR2 1HL

COVER: Studio Medlikova
front: photograph by Tim Atherton
back: diary extracts by the author

The right of Philippa Comber to be identified
as the author of this work has been asserted by
her in accordance with the Copyright, Designs
and Patents Act, 1988

A CIP record for this book
is available from the British Library

Printed and bound by
TJ International Ltd, Padstow, Cornwall

Theseus, the tenth king of Athens ... having possessed himself of Ariadne's affection, who was Minos's daughter, received from her a bottom of thread, by which he conducted himself through all the crooked and inextricable turnings of the labyrinth, made in all like that of the city of crocodiles in Egypt; by mean[s] whereof, having slain [the] Minotaur, he found a ready way to return ...

Sir Walter Raleigh, *The History of the World*, 1614

Contents

Acknowledgements

I am indebted to Richard Sheppard for having first made the suggestion that I write a memoir of Max Sebald.

It was via Max – after his death – that I was to meet and form lasting friendships with a number of people, amongst whom I should particularly like to mention the poet and translator Adam Czerniawski, and the poet Stephen Watts.

In 2008 I had the good fortune to be put in touch with Jean Boase-Beier at the University of East Anglia and through her, with Ada Vigliani in Turin. Ada, the guiding spirit behind the international forum for translators of Sebald, has been a constant source of inspiration.

Special thanks go to Carole Angier, Hanna Blösser, John Faulkner, Amanda Hopkinson, David Lambert, Richard Trim, Andrea Voss, Helga Williams, Janet Wolff and Kate Wood for kindly agreeing to look through initial drafts; to Richard Hibbitt for putting me in the way of relevant documentation; and to Ulrich von Bülow and his colleagues at the German Literature Archive for having made me welcome in Marbach and offering valuable assistance.

Above all, I should like to express my gratitude to those whose far-sightedness and dedication to the project made things happen, Henry Layte and his team at the Book Hive in Norwich.

Lastly, sustained rounds of applause for my partner, Barrie Hesketh, who has gone with me every step of the journey.

Manchester, March 2014

Ariadne's Thread: A Response
by Iain Sinclair

The essential mystery of a writer is the residue left on the printed page, the permitted labyrinth of words. Philippa Comber, thinking of Sebald, quotes Wittgenstein: 'The limits of my language are the limits of my world.' Our fetish for biographies of these enigmatic personalities, their masks, gestures, loves and affections, is an abiding one. That final rank of books, arranged by death, reaches out towards the great audience of unknowns; shadowy tiers of readers hunched in their communal privacy.

Comber employs the metaphor – so attractive to Freudians and poets – of Ariadne's thread: the gift of a dangerous woman, an unspooling of self, to a man. Her potential suitor and chosen violator. The fearless hero who will penetrate the maze of mirrors. As Comber's vivid memoir, recovered from unmediated diaries, digresses with all the subtle swerves of her chosen mentor, it becomes clear that W.G. Sebald is more Minotaur than Theseus. Max (as his friends knew him) haunts corridors of elective darkness, arguing with pain and memory, dreaming of a healing garden. Comber facilitates this alchemy of process: how we read in order to write, how we remake ourselves from the prose models we most admire. The contemporary diarist pays her respects to Norwich by way of John Evelyn's visit to Sir Thomas Browne – with a nod at the way Browne's fecund *bricolage* inspires and entraps Sebald. There are no accidents here, every street collision is a significant element in the detective story. Three sentences rescued from a random past are a complete autobiography: 'Felt in a better mood today. Cleaned my bike, cooked an ox-tongue and put it to press. Then, after a gin and lime, got out my cello.'

* * * * *

Women are absent in the Sebaldian terrain of railway hotels and microwaved culinary disasters. Men are spectral Xeroxes of other men who step, obligingly, out of the woods and cities to repeat their tales. Comber reveals a passion she shared with the Norwich-based German academic: European art cinema. 'Going to the cinema with Max was a treat.' They discovered a mutual delight in the Resnais/Robbe-Grillet puzzle from 1961, *L'année dernière à Marienbad*. A formalist nightmare in which operatic mannequins from discrete narratives engage and re-engage with fixed architecture and a set of dissolving instructions from psychosexual limbo. 'I was beginning to recognise,' Comber said, 'that when it came to confidences, Max was extremely sparing – at most, he'd drop hints. It wouldn't do to press him.'

Cinema – and Sebald made the classics of the silent era, Fritz Lang, Murnau, Wiene, part of a necessary history – was an antidote to the demands of academic life, that ponderous weight of reference, the authorities to be honoured or challenged. In another life, the images Max embedded in his published texts would have flickered into movement. Sebald, as a filmmaker, would have solved the riddle of autobiography and confession. In his treatment for an unrealised project, *And Now the Night Descends – Scenes from the Life and Death of Immanuel Kant*, he stated: 'Women appear very little in the piece and, for that reason, are of central importance.' They must have an aura. And silence.

Comber's memoir presents Sebald as a benevolent absence: the hesitant caller at the door, the deep voice on the phone at bathtime, repairer of sash cords. Accident-prone driver of imported cars. A lover of the house as much as the woman, Max was a compulsive collector of unregarded trifles from car-boot sales and Norfolk junk pits. He assembled his cabinet of curiosities – while threatening, in moments of crisis, to be swallowed into *The Cabinet of Dr Caligari*. Sympathetic listener and trained therapist, Comber cannot accept Max as a suitable subject for analysis. Not while he is still alive and tending the garden of the Old Rectory at Poringland, bringing her baskets of vegetables. But the analysis, the book Max pushed her to write, is now delivered, with considerable tact: posthumously. We should value it as much for the diversions into Comber's own legacy, her European journeys, the acts and coincidences of a rich life, as for serial revelations of the Sebaldian persona.

'He took a very dark view of the redeeming power of heterosexual love,' Comber tells us. A moment of crisis arrives. She calls on him, solicits his presence. 'Max would have been aware of the heightened sexual desire that so often accompanies feelings of grief, especially the grief of a woman for the death of a father she has loved.' Sebald declines. He has to walk the dog.

The relationship is a romance about which we are told exactly as much as we need to be told: a literary friendship, a ritualised courtship of oblique and never-quite-connecting needs. An alliance based on long conversations, letters, years of silence. The resulting book is a portrait that can be endlessly flipped: private impressions of a public author (and the cost it required to achieve that status) superimposed over an account of the spiritual and cultural evolution of the woman who is keeping the record. And constructing, in careful language, the film of a life that Sebald was never able to realise.

Prologue

... Et pulsae referunt ad
  sidera valles –

    ... Et pulsae referunt ad
      sidera valles –

Zu Pythagoras aber gehört das
  Geheimnis er
Sei in der Lage gewesen die
  Sterne zu hören
Die Täler von Bleston haben
  kein Echo
Und es wendet sich nicht mehr
  mit ihnen
Wort ohne Antwort fil
  d'Ariane...

It was Pythagoras however
  of whom it was said
He possessed the secret of
  listening to the stars
The valleys of Bleston do
  not echo
And with them is no more
  returning
Word without answer fil
  d'Ariane...

W.G. Sebald
Bleston: A Mancunian Canticle – IV Lingua Mortua, 1967[1]

It's a hot summer's day in 2009 – Monday, 18 May – and I'm at the top of the house, my special retreat. From the desk by the window, there's a view of the eaves and, through the trees at the bottom of the garden, a glimpse of the railway line.

Over the years, I've got so used to the rumble of the trains I scarcely notice it any more – at least not during the day. If, on the other hand, I wake at dawn and creep upstairs to do some reading or writing, it's a different matter. The 4.32 breaks through the silence – bearing two and a half thousand tons of limestone from the Tunstead quarries near Buxton in the Peak District to Brunner Mond, the chemical firm in Northwich, Cheshire. The walls of my house tremble and shake, calling to mind chthonic deities.

The space up here has become hopelessly crowded – stuffed full of boxes, books and papers. For months, I've been dreading this moment: the house is in urgent need of a new roof and the builder has insisted that the old one be stripped to the rafters. So, with the house open to the skies, there's nothing for it but clear the attic of valuables and shift them elsewhere.

I've made a start, not looking for anything in particular – indeed, doing my best not to look at all, just get on with the job. And then, out of the blue, I come across some loose sheets of paper in one of the files. At first glance they look like diary entries, except they're not in a diary. I extract a sheet at random and read:

> New people – encounters...
>
> Had a phone call, quite unexpectedly, from Max Sebald – that friend of Walter's who lectures at UEA who joined us at the cinema last Saturday evening. After the screening, we got talking in the bar about all kinds of things: favourite films, nineteenth-century literature, psychopathology...

This stirs memories and puts me into a fair old turmoil. I decide not to pursue it – not for the time being. In any case, I reason, my priority is to have the roof replaced, press on with the clearing.

* * * * *

Summer has melted into autumn. The leaves have fallen and, yet again, the clouds over Manchester are spoiling for a downpour – though with a brand new roof over my head, why should I care?

I return to that sheaf of notes. Timidly at first – it's the last day of October,

All Hallows Eve, and, well, there are bound to be ghosts. Also, there's that boxful of old diaries – proper diaries – that have been sitting under the rafters for years now, right at the back of the loft. I brace myself, climb in amongst the trunks and tea chests, eventually digging out diaries for the relevant years.

I go downstairs and make myself a strong cup of tea, which I take back to bed along with the diaries. Start reading. By dawn, I know what it is I have to do: get something down on paper and see where it leads...

PART ONE

A MAN CALLED MAX

A strange picture we make on our way to our Chimæras,
ceaselessly marching, grudging ourselves the time for rest;
indefatigable, adventurous pioneers. It is true that we shall never
reach the goal; it is even more probable that there is no such place;
and if we lived for centuries and were endowed with the powers of
a god, we should find ourselves not much nearer what we wanted in
the end. O toiling hands of mortals! O unwearied feet, travelling ye
know not whither. Soon, soon, it seems to you, you must come forth
on some conspicuous hilltop, and but a little way farther, against the
setting sun, descry the spires of El Dorado. Little do ye know your
own blessedness; for to travel hopefully is a better thing than to
arrive, and the true success is to labour.

Robert Louis Stevenson,
"El Dorado" in *Virginibus Puerisque*, 1881

I

... I must restore that missing link, and since the recollection
of it has recurred so clearly to me I must fix it in these pages
before it fades or is submerged again under the pressure of
other waves of events and memories ...

Michel Butor, *Passing Time* [*L'emploi du temps*], 1957[2]

In August 1980, I went on a journey that took me across northern Europe
– from West Berlin to East Anglia. I'd been offered a job as manager of a
psychiatric day centre in Norwich.

East Anglia is a part of the British Isles I first got to know properly as
an adolescent. During the school holidays, my father, a keen yachtsman, had
taken me sailing along the Suffolk coast – those stretches where the elements
intermingle, where land is indistinguishable from water.

Such places have a distinctive appeal, though are not for the faint-
hearted. I remember countless sleepless nights, lying at anchor in some
godforsaken creek, willing my father to stop snoring, listening to the
wind as it hissed through the reeds and played tunes in the rigging. I was
terrified; but not daring to forego my status as his "favourite crew", I
said nothing.

Many years later, I fetched up in another watery landscape; the lakes on
the outskirts of West Berlin were surprisingly reminiscent of the Norfolk
Broads and it was in this "island city" that I spent the best part of the
seventies, studying psychology and training as a psychotherapist.

We – that is, my husband and I – lived in Charlottenburg, halfway between the Kurfürstendamm and the S-Bahn station at Savignyplatz, an area that had seen better days – as had the flat we rented on the first floor of an old tenement block.

The flat consisted of an enfilade of three interconnecting rooms with high ceilings and stucco decoration; temperamental tiled stoves to provide heat in winter that devoured peat briquettes, letting off noxious fumes in the process; and a balcony where I used to keep pots of basil and thyme in summer.

Whilst extremely run down and in urgent need of re-plumbing, it represented "home" in a way that nothing had ever done before. By the start of 1979, however, the marriage had begun to founder and we agreed to separate: he returned to England and I stayed on for another year and a half.

When the time came for me to leave, it was with very mixed feelings. I hadn't had the heart to give up the flat and it was not until I had been in Norwich for several months that it dawned on me: in order to stop living in an emotional limbo, I needed to go back to Berlin, wind down the flat and make a clean break.

By chance, I had another reason to visit. A friend of mine, Barbara Heinisch, had recently got in touch – she was a performance artist who had once used me as a model in one of her action paintings. She had let me know about a forthcoming event in Berlin for which she'd been asked to submit a "visual contribution" and wondered if I'd be interested.

Wide-ranging in scope and subject matter, the conference organisers were aiming to attract a polyglot audience. The title was captivating; translated literally, *The Return of the Body* might sound spooky, even a bit daft. But in the context of Berlin in 1981, *Die Wiederkehr des Körpers* had about it the ring of utmost academic respectability. In addition to the native scholars, a posse of Frenchmen were coming from Paris for the occasion: Michel Tibon-Cornillot, René Scherer, Bruno de Panafieu and the urban theorist Paul Virilio; the sociologist and cultural theorist Jean Baudrillard had been invited to inaugurate proceedings. I didn't hesitate to enrol and make travel arrangements.

At the end of the first day's presentations, there was to be an informal reception hosted by the installation artist Margaret Raspé. I had first met Margaret during the early years in Berlin and been intrigued by her video work; she had made a name for herself by devising something known as "the camera helmet" with which she recorded herself on Super 8 film, often as a vehicle for exploring anthropological themes. One slightly unnerving example featured Margaret dissecting a chicken on her kitchen table.

It was to this same table that she welcomed us that Monday evening. I took a seat opposite a tall, bespectacled man who, despite his youthfulness, was completely bald – in effect, a Michel Foucault look-alike. I took him to be French, since this was the language he was speaking with those on either side of him, without trace of an accent. After a while, he leaned across the table and introduced himself to me – in dignified German – as Uli Raulff. That's strange, I thought: "Uli Raulff" didn't sound at all Gallic.

After the feast, I went and consulted my programme, noting that the following day, Uli was scheduled to deliver a paper with the tantalising title *Chemie des Ekels und des Genusses – The Chemistry of Disgust and Pleasure*. Like everyone else, he had been allotted the standard thirty minutes to make his presentation. Taking as his starting-point a quote from the Austrian writer Alfred Kolleritsch, he proceeded to reference three or four centuries of Western European thought, sweeping us along from one set of complexities to the next: from "gastrosophy" to transubstantiation; Kant to Lévi-Strauss; Brillat-Savarin to Julia Kristeva – for good measure, Joyce's Leopold Bloom was awarded a star role. Uli had engaged his audience with enviable suavity.

After the conference, we agreed to meet again. Uli continued to display an astonishing range of interests – suggesting, for instance, that we spend an afternoon at the zoo – in the reptile house. He said he wanted to observe the snakes close up.

The rest of the week turned out to be just as exhilarating – but also heartbreaking. My stay put me in mind of all the things I would continue to miss by having accepted the job in Norfolk. Saying farewell to the flat in the Knesebeckstrasse for the last time proved almost too much. On the flight back to London and from there by train to Norwich, I found myself in a quandary: had leaving Berlin for good been a dreadful mistake?

The ensuing lively correspondence with Uli helped get things in perspective. We covered a lot of ground – including, somewhat surprisingly, Uli's fascination with the way the media were handling the story of the rise to stardom of Lady Diana Spencer. He wrote that he would like to come and see me in the summer – timing his trip to coincide with the celebrations for the Royal Wedding.

On 30 July, the day after the wedding, Uli made his way to Norwich, catching the train from Liverpool Street Station – a detail that continues to carry special personal significance. My earliest encounter with the outside world had also involved a train journey between Liverpool Street Station and East Anglia. Exactly thirty-five years previously, in 1946, having been discharged from the London Hospital, Whitechapel, my mother had returned with me, her first-born, to the calm and safety of my father's family home in Hutton, Essex.

The week with Uli was brilliantly sunny, the mood festive. Time off work meant time to slacken the pace, take the bus out into the Norfolk countryside, explore the park and garden at Blickling Hall, eat crab from the shell on the esplanade in Cromer and join the funfair in Great Yarmouth. In memory, it passed like a dream – a dream that couldn't last. Uli was as reluctant to return to Berlin as I was to go back to my patients – he was tempted to cancel his ticket. But he didn't. And the story, in which he would later play a vital role, was shortly to take an unexpected course.

Throughout my life, chance encounters have been a key factor. One of the people I happened to meet soon after my arrival in Norwich in 1980 was Rodney Foster. Rodney was an Ulsterman who had been working on his doctoral dissertation for a great many years – more than he cared to recall. Realising they were likely to have interests in common, I had introduced him to Uli. Two weeks later, Rodney returned the compliment by inviting me to meet a German friend of his, Walter Bachem, currently on a visit to look up some of his former colleagues at the University of East Anglia.

Walter hailed from Bochum in the Ruhr district of Germany – I remember him affectionately and alliteratively as "*Bachem aus Bochum*" ("Bachem from Bochum"). Hearing about my previous life in Berlin, he suggested I would have much to share with one of these colleagues, another German who lived in Poringland, a few miles outside Norwich.

And so it was that on a warm Saturday evening at the end of August, arrangements were made for a group of us to meet at the Noverre Cinema for a showing of Polanski's 1979 movie, *Tess*. There were five of us: Walter and his girlfriend Angelika; Rodney and me; and Walter's colleague – introduced quite simply as "Max".

II

... there runs through Ottilie's journal a thread of
affection and inclination that binds everything together and
characterises the whole. It is this thread which turns into
the peculiar property of the writer of these observations,
thoughts ... and whatever else is there, and makes them
significant for her. Every single passage we have selected
bears indisputable testimony to the truth of this.

Johann Wolfgang von Goethe, *Elective Affinities*
[*Die Wahlverwandtschaften*], 1809[3]

What with the long queues for tickets beforehand and the general hub-
bub in the bar afterwards, the situation didn't lend itself to ease of conversation. No matter. What struck me at once was Max's demeanour – kindly,
yet somewhat aloof and formal; and when I managed to catch what he was
saying, it was couched in perfect, slightly dated English, spoken with a
distinctive South German lilt.

Six days later, out of the blue, I received a phone call. It was Max.

He was ringing now, he said, because he'd like to see me again. I told
him which days I'd be around next week but it seemed he'd already
decided he wanted it to be this evening, after a meeting... He assured
me he'd be able to find his way to the house, didn't need directions...

Friday, 4 September 1981

Max uses the expression "potty" a lot – has all sorts of ideas about
what constitutes "the marginal"; also, regarding parallels between
natural history (especially disasters – floods, earthquakes and so on)
and man-made history (war, genocide etc.). There's a great deal to
talk about. I like him...

At this time, I was still living in rented accommodation – indeed, in the
space of a year, I had made no fewer than seven moves. Even so, I was an
unconvincing nomad and had left a trail of belongings with long-suffering
friends. What I needed was a place of my own.

The previous month's searches proved successful: contracts had finally
been exchanged on a small terraced house in a pleasant pedestrianized street
within easy walking distance of the city centre – a stone's throw away from
the old Norfolk and Norwich Hospital – the same hospital to which, twelve
years later, Max would be admitted "in a state of almost total immobility"
as he described it in *The Rings of Saturn*[4], subsequently having to undergo a
four-hour operation for a shattered disc.

During the week, running the day centre – managing referrals, providing
individual and group therapy, devising activity schedules and supervising the
volunteer workers – took up most of my energy. By the time I finished work
on Friday evening, I was ready for a change of scene. Up to this point, I had
spent as many weekends as possible away – often in London, catching up
with friends. Now, however, there was an incentive to stay put: the property
required substantial renovation.

Wednesday, 9 September 1981

Shortly after I got back from work this evening, there was a soft tap at
the door. I opened it and did a double take: it was Max again! Smiling,
without a word, he handed me a selection of vegetables: courgettes

and tomatoes from his garden, sun-warmed and fragrant, arranged on a bed of chard leaves. I invited him in. He said he couldn't stay – but would be back again another day...

The following weekend, with the help of friends, I began shifting my things out of the rented accommodation into the new house: this included several loads of books, the sewing machine and my Bavarian cello, safe in its fibreglass case and swathed in an ancient blue candlewick bedspread for extra protection.

In the meantime, Max had been in touch for a progress report. He wanted to know architectural details, when the house had been built and what repairs needed doing. With mock gravity, he said he'd be coming round soon, whilst the evenings were still light, "to make an inspection".

Tuesday, 15 September 1981

I feel quite "mellow" these days – just as well in terms of my work. If I'm not relaxed, things go haywire and that invariably has negative repercussions for the patients... I know next week's going to be a tough one; all the more important to take things one step at a time ...

Max arrived this evening to look at the house, along with the builder he's recommended. I caught myself blushing, a bit flustered – couldn't disguise it. And yet I feel at ease in his company in a way that's quite rare for me; perhaps I'm falling in love with him ...

Actually, he seems quite in love himself – with the house! He said he could imagine me being settled in it along with my cello ... remarked that I looked like a cellist. He's brought me more vegetables – home-grown, beautifully fresh, tied in little bundles with green string. I'm deeply touched by the gift – by his manner in general. He's very discreet, careful not to pry.

He talks about what he likes doing in his spare time, "pottering about" at home and in the garden, fixing things, mending things ...

I was discovering that Max was eminently practical – the embodiment of *metis*, that quality that combines hands-on wisdom with skill and inventiveness. At the same time, he seemed to have something of Autolycus about him – Autolycus, the roguish peddler in *The Winter's Tale* who describes himself as "a snapper-up of unconsidered trifles".

In the true spirit of the *bricoleur*, Max had a habit of keeping an eye out for bits and pieces in junkyards and second-hand shops, making good with the help of an assortment of found objects. As I was shortly to recognise, this tendency was also apparent in his literary tastes – for example, in the manner of writing of those he most admired – and which would later find its way into his own writing.

In an essay published in 1983 concerning the Bavarian writer and film-maker Herbert Achternbusch, Max draws on the notion of the *bricoleur* to describe a particular literary style. Acknowledging his debt to both Johan Huizinga and Claude Lévi-Strauss, he puts forward the idea that primitive man, the creator of new ideas of the universe ("cosmogonies"), pieces together a view of the world from "the remains of previous constructions and destructions"[5] – in other words, a form of *bricolage*.

The *bricoleur* – *Bastler* in German – works with odds and ends; with the debris, fragments and fossilised remains of individual and societal history. Whilst this might seem to be at variance with the way the specialist or "engineer" goes about his business, the difference, according to Lévi-Strauss ...

> *... is less absolute than it might appear. It remains a real one, however, in that the engineer is always trying to make his way out of and go beyond the constraints imposed by a particular state of civilisation while the 'bricoleur' by inclination or necessity always remains within them. This is another way of saying that the engineer works by means of concepts and the 'bricoleur' by means of signs ...*[6]

At the time of writing his essay, it was of greatest importance to Max that the meaning of *bricolage* had been extended to include a specific form of intellectual pursuit; and could now be applied to a style of writing.

I suppose that I, too, had been something of a *bricoleuse* – "collector" is too grand a term for it. Ever since childhood, I had amassed great quantities of stuff – mostly things of no intrinsic value or interest to anyone but me – a hoarding instinct sustained by the illusion that "you never know, one of these days it might come in useful". One example of this inanity was the piles – later to become leaning towers – of *Vogue* magazine.

I'd been a regular subscriber since 1963. As a collection, the *Vogues* had something talismanic about them – serving as an ongoing record of my adult life. They were to accompany me everywhere, becoming heavier and more unwieldy with every move. The first few years' worth were a simple matter – they fitted neatly on a shelf in my bedroom cupboard; by the time I'd left university and gone to live in London, however, the logistics of transport and storage were daunting. For all that, nothing and nobody could have persuaded me to part with the collection.

Saturday, 19 September 1981

Despite glorious, bright sunshine, I felt disconsolate when I woke up this morning. Resolved to do more packing but ended up lazing about before going out shopping. Came home, ate doughnuts with coffee, then started wrapping up *Vogues* by the year-load in old copies of *The Sunday Times Business News* ... Later, made a few phone calls, including one to Max. He wasn't at home. An hour later, he rang back and came round, bringing with him an umbrella plant for the house, as well as a folder containing a typescript ...

He was impressed by the quantity of newspaper strewn around the front room and intrigued to know what I was doing with all these copies of *Vogue*.

Having confessed to my squirrelling habit, we picked up the conversation from where we'd left off the time before.

Things had begun to take on a more personal tone, I noticed. Still decorous in his questioning, Max was curious as to what had first sparked my enthusiasm for literature and writing; and how come I was so interested in languages, he wanted to know – specifically, this fondness for German. I hesitated – not because I didn't want to tell him but because I was nervous; it had been barely three weeks since we'd met and I didn't want to jeopardise the friendship by saying something out of turn.

I looked at Max. He smiled, which I took as a cue to carry on.

III

... the main things about a man are his eyes and his feet.
He should be able to see the world and go after it.

Alfred Döblin, *Berlin Alexanderplatz*, 1929[7]

By the time I reached adolescence, I knew there were certain topics that could not be talked about freely at home: sex, madness, the Suez Crisis – and "the Germans". My parents, both decent people – in common with many others of their generation and class – had harboured a vague, generalised antipathy towards Germans and Jews. Mostly, such sentiments were kept politely suppressed, though they did leak out on occasion. In retrospect, I realise I could quite easily have grown up to do likewise: automatically, to hate the Germans and be anti-Semitic. What happened was the exact opposite...

I paused and glanced at Max, wondering what he was making of this. He seemed unperturbed; so I started to tell him about the first German I had ever got to know: Christine.

Christine and I had met as teenagers under somewhat unusual circumstances, in the household of one Cecil de Sausmarez. As I said the name, the thought occurred to me that Cecil was exactly the sort of person whose idiosyncrasies Max would relish. I went on.

Cecil was born in 1907 in Rawalpindi in the province of Punjab, the son of a soldier.

He was educated at Winchester, followed by Oxford. In 1932 he became an assistant master at Wellington College, a boys' public school in Berkshire...

I interrupted myself again, this time to add that after leaving the army in 1945, my father had also accepted a teaching post at Wellington – indeed, it was there that I'd grown up.

Returning to the subject of Cecil, I told Max about his special gift as a linguist: he could make himself understood in half a dozen languages, including – when formalities required – Norman French. On the outbreak of war, he was selected to go to Brussels where he'd worked as press attaché at the British Embassy. Over the following two years, his knowledge of Belgium, together with a fluency in Flemish and German, had proved crucial in securing him work at the Ministry of Information, first in the anti-rumours office and then as a specialist on Belgium. In 1941 he had moved to the Political Warfare Executive as regional director for the Netherlands.

Amongst his other accomplishments, Cecil was a natural at public speaking – and then, it emerged, at broadcasting. He'd been the first to announce the D-Day landings on the wireless in Flemish and was one of the originators of the "V" sign. In 1944 he'd returned to Brussels with the restored government, where he served as first secretary at the Embassy until 1946...

At the mention of 1946, the year I was born, I hesitated. Looking across at Max, I realised I didn't know when he had been born – it hadn't felt necessary to ask him and I'd simply assumed we were of the same generation.

"Where was I? I seem to have lost the thread!" I faltered.

"On the contrary," said Max, keeping a completely straight face, "it's always a good thing to include the historical context." Licence enough for me to continue.

Cecil stayed in Belgium until 1951, at which point he returned to Britain to work as a tutor at Wilton Park, the organisation set up by Winston Churchill after the war to promote good relations between England and Germany – a cause dear to Cecil's heart. And then, in 1959, as Seigneur of the Fief de

Sausmarez, he went with his wife and family and settled in Guernsey. Two years later, he was elected people's deputy to the island's Parliament, where his experience was an added bonus in helping establish links between the Channel Islands and the European Economic Community.

Since its creation in 1957, Cecil had taken a lively interest in "the Common Market", as it was known at the time. Amongst the various schemes he devised, one in particular stood out: to encourage understanding between the member countries. He did this by opening his home to groups of young people during the summer. In the informal atmosphere of Sausmarez Manor, students on residential courses could debate issues of cultural and political importance whilst building their English language skills.

By chance, in the spring of 1961, Cecil had been invited back to Wellington for a term in order to deputise for his old friend and fellow-Wykehamist, Rupert Horsley – Rupert had fallen ill and had had to abandon his teaching duties to go on sick leave.

My mother had always had a penchant for the unorthodox. To her, meeting Cecil was a breath of fresh air; right from the start, they got on famously. One weekend, she invited him to dinner – an occasion that promised to be all the more relaxing because she wouldn't have to do the cooking. "Whenever we have guests, I leave the cooking to Philippa," she told him. It would also mean that she and Cecil could concentrate on discussing the posters he'd asked her to paint for him: three simple line drawings representing Tradition, Anarchy and Politics – or was it Philosophy? – to take on his next European lecture tour...

Max looked puzzled. "What *were* they talking about?" he wanted to know. "And how come you were left doing the housekeeping – surely you were still at school?" "Yes," I replied, "still at school but loathing every minute of it – barely able to wait for Saturdays to come round when I would go to Joy's – Rupert Horsley's wife – to learn cooking and Italian."

Joy, a friend of Elizabeth David's sister, was an inspirational cook and a fluent speaker of Italian. It was she who had first instilled my love of cookery

– no doubt helped by the hoarding instinct and the fact that, since the age of eleven, I had collected recipes from every available magazine and newspaper. It followed that I had grabbed any opportunity to try out new dishes on the family – and were there a dinner party to cater for, so much the better. This had come as a huge relief to my mother, for whom domesticity in any form was a grinding chore; she would far rather use the time for painting and music-making.

Days in advance, I had set about devising a menu. Knowing that Cecil came from Guernsey, I decided on something tomatoey as an opener – a sherry-flavoured *consommé madrilène* – to be followed by veal escalopes *en papillote* as a main course and lemon syllabub for dessert. Cecil was very appreciative – and showed it on the spot by inviting me to come to Sausmarez Manor in the holidays to help out with his summer school.

"And what happened when you got there?" asked Max. "Did you spend your time in the kitchen, preparing three-course meals every day?" "No, not exactly," I replied. Admittedly, I had cut up an awful lot of vegetables and prepared dozens and dozens of tomato salads. But that hadn't been the whole story.

Cecil had been keen for me to engage the students in English conversation whenever possible, something most of them were singularly disinclined to do. Mealtimes were a case in point. Cecil was deaf. Here at home, he communicated by means of an old-fashioned ear trumpet and, much to everyone's amusement, would sit at one end of the long baronial table, bellowing out questions and pretending not to hear the answers unless delivered in perfect, idiomatic English.

That year, there were about twenty teenagers on the course, all a bit older than me: French and German, but mostly German – one of whom was Christine. Up until then, being painfully shy and generally scared of my contemporaries, I'd never had a close friend. On Guernsey, however, away from school and family, I felt much freer. From the word go, Christine and I got on like a house on fire and it wasn't long before we struck a deal: in exchange for help with her English, I would start learning German. I couldn't have had a more sympathetic teacher.

By the end of the holiday, we had agreed to invite each other to our respective homes. Christine would come and stay with me the following summer; I would go and stay with her the year after that.

In the meantime, I set about broadening my knowledge of German by taking up a course for beginners on the BBC in the hope that, when the day came, this would be enough to get me across Europe. In July 1963, armed with a dictionary and phrase book and a huge amount of luggage, I caught the train to Dover, took the ferry to Ostend, and from there made the journey by rail through Belgium and along the Rhine. This allowed plenty of time to have dire fantasies about what would happen when I arrived in Munich: would I have enough German to get by? And would Christine be standing on the platform to meet me as promised?

She was not. I was about to panic – wondering if I should look for a taxi – when suddenly, as if out of nowhere, she appeared; casting black looks at the number of suitcases, she began talking very fast, in German. Getting home involved two tram-rides and a longish walk at the other end. By the time we arrived, I was exhausted – but then, completely bowled over.

The house was a modern Bauhaus-style villa set in its own grounds; indoors, the ceilings were in rich-coloured slatted wood, the floors tiled in white ceramic. Christine explained that we were a stone's throw away from Munich's famous park, the Englischer Garten – handy for bike rides! The reason they lived here, she put in as an aside, was so that her father could be close to his work at the Max Planck Institute. This information meant nothing to me – in any case, there had been so much to take in, I wasn't going to start asking questions now.

It wasn't until 1964, during Christine's second stay at Wellington, that further details about her father began to emerge. Naturally, my parents were aware of her surname. But apart from mentioning that she was the sixth of seven children, she had remained extremely cagey concerning her family.

And then one day, my father happened to be chatting with a colleague in the staff common room – a physics master who also had a daughter called Christine.

The conversation had gone something like this. Rex Strachan to my father: "Well, Peter, who is this German girl you've got staying with you again – a friend of Philippa's, I understand? What's her name?" "Christine – Christine Heisenberg." "Heisenberg! Heisenberg, did you say! You know you really ought to find out if she's related to *Werner* Heisenberg... that chap who got the Nobel Prize in 1932 – the physicist who came up with the Uncertainty Principle!" My father was nonplussed; by nature somewhat otherworldly, he wasn't *au fait* with developments in the natural sciences. None the wiser for what Rex had just told him, he nevertheless came home and put the question to Christine. "Yes," she replied, with customary reticence, "it is my father."

Without batting an eyelid, Max urged me to go on.

The fact is, neither Christine nor I had thought there was anything particularly remarkable about each other's circumstances – for example, that I lived in a boys' boarding school, or that most evenings Christine's father and other members of the family would assemble to play chamber music and discuss philosophy over wine from the cellar. In my innocence, I had taken it on trust that this was simply the way they did things in Germany. For me, the contrast with life at home was of much greater significance; above all, the kindness and level of acceptance shown to me by Christine's parents. Having been admitted as a kind of honorary member of the family, that sense of belonging, of well-being in the company of Germans, was to remain with me.

Max took stock, observing that whilst this would explain my interest in things German, it hadn't answered the other part of his question: my preoccupation with literature. By now, the light had begun to fade. "Might be better to save it for another time," I ventured. But this wasn't good enough for Max. "Just give me an idea," he came back with.

I had always been an avid reader – reading provided a necessary escape from parental rows and sibling rivalries. I was for ever jotting down words, making lists: anything from the names of flowers and trees to types of seaweed; the colours of boat sails to snatches of vocabulary overheard in conversations between our Danish au pair, Grethe, and her friend Gitte – all in tiny, spidery handwriting.

This prompted another comment from Max. "Benjamin, Walser..." he intoned. The gloss was lost on me and it wasn't until later that I appreciated what he'd meant. Walter Benjamin had been an inveterate list-maker and, like the Swiss writer Robert Walser, in the habit of filling his notebooks with handwriting so minuscule, it was often indecipherable.

I cited the diaries I'd kept, sporadically, since the age of nine. Their only real value was their usefulness as source material when we'd been set "composition" for homework. Writing essays was the only aspect of school I'd ever really enjoyed. Everything else – the other girls, outdoor games, geography, maths – was an ordeal; and though most of the teachers had long since given up on me, I was – in secret – a terrible swot. Desperate to get shot of the place but leave without loss of face, I had set my sights on passing as many O-levels as possible. What would happen after that, I hadn't a clue.

Considering my father was a schoolmaster, his views on education – education for girls, at any rate – were hard to stomach. He'd pronounced me "far too neurotic" to think of trying for A-levels, let alone university. His idea of a suitable preparation for life was for me to enrol on a secretarial course. We reached a compromise: I would endure six months of shorthand and typing and, in the meantime, prepare myself for A-levels in English and languages. My results were good; despite the fact that this cut no ice with my father, they were enough to secure me a place at Exeter University to read English.

My degree served as the springboard for a somewhat haphazard career, starting as an assistant librarian at the Inner Temple Law Library, followed by a series of jobs as an apprentice editor with various London book publishers.

Thinking this would suffice to put Max in the picture, I paused, hoping he'd reciprocate with something about his own past life. But it didn't happen – at least not in any obvious way. Within the comparatively short time I'd known him, I was beginning to recognise that, when it came to confidences, Max was extremely sparing – at most, he'd drop hints. It wouldn't do to press him.

With a somewhat sly expression, he handed me the folder he'd brought with him, referring to it as his "Kant script" – a potential screenplay, he explained, something he'd been working on in his spare time. He said he'd like me to read it and if I had any suggestions as to where to send it, so much the better.

I mentioned that I still had one or two contacts in the media in West Berlin – including a producer who worked for the radio station, Sender Freies Berlin – that I could try and chase up. Alternatively, it might be worth getting in touch with Peter Stein, the guiding spirit of the Schaubühne Theatre Ensemble. I promised to do what I could and, with that, he left.

> Max's charm makes me think of Vienna ... An image sticks in my mind, the image of a waltz: I am dancing with a man and we're in formal evening dress. We whirl round and round – keeping time. The music stops – but we go on ...
>
> The prospect of living in an "owned" house for the first time in my life is exciting – a very different story from the Berlin days and all the years before that. Maybe my values are changing ...

Tuesday, 29 September 1981

> Incredibly on edge at the moment ... Just too tired to get on and finish the last of the packing tonight – almost too tired to cook or eat. It'll require a big effort to keep up with what's going on at work at the same time as sorting out the house ... All this moving from one place to another – the story of my life! Roll on the day when I've got things unpacked, restored to a semblance of normality ...
>
> ... what I would most like to do is just fall into someone's arms and forget about the whole business ... Feel like chucking out most of

my wardrobe whilst I'm at it and buying a whole lot of new clothes; dressmaking days seem miles away. Rang the builder: it looks as though the work could be done in four weeks and within the budget, £6000 ...

The house had come with a uniquely ghastly front door – a door that couldn't easily be replaced because of its unusual, non-standard measurements. The sash cords on the window frames also needed attention; as it was, even a gentle breeze would cause everything to rattle alarmingly.

Max came to the rescue. He told me about a place near Bungay where, amongst other oddments, I'd be most likely to find a door that would both fit and be in keeping with the period features. At the sight of the sash cords – which were indeed in a sorry state – Max's eyes lit up. Without hesitation, he volunteered to replace them for me.

Max has just rung to say he'll come on Friday to fix the sash cords ...

IV

Early on, I learned to disguise myself in words,
which were really clouds. The gift of perceiving similarities is,
in fact, nothing but a weak remnant of the old compulsion to
become similar and to behave mimetically. In me, however, this
compulsion acted through words. Not those that made me similar
to models of good breeding, but those that made me similar
to dwelling places, furniture, clothes.

Walter Benjamin, *Selected Writings 1935–1938*[8]

The sash window is a peculiarly English invention whose original design is attributed to the scientist Robert Hooke – the word "sash" deriving from the French *"chassis"*, meaning "frame" – and for Max, sash windows exerted a peculiar fascination. He'd go to any lengths, he said, adjusting the new cords, to have a sash window in good working order.

He was also very partial to the writing of Laurence Sterne and, in this context, I'd be prepared to bet that a passage that would have tickled his fancy was the description of Tristram Shandy's "accidental circumcision" by sash window:

'Twas nothing, – I did not lose two drops of blood by it – 'twas not worth calling in a surgeon, had he lived next door to us – thousands suffer by choice, what I did by accident. – Dr Slop made ten times more of it, than there was occasion: – some men rise, by the art of hanging great weights

*upon small wires, – and I am this day (August the 10th, 1761) paying part
of the price of this man's reputation. – O 'twould provoke a stone, to see
how things are carried on in this world! –The chamber-maid had left no
******* *** under the bed: – Cannot you contrive, master, quoth Susannah,
lifting up the sash with one hand, as she spoke, and helping me up into the
window-seat with the other, – cannot you manage, my dear, for a single
time, to **** *** ** *** ******?*

*I was five years old. – Susannah did not consider that nothing was well
hung in our family,– so slap came the sash down like lightning upon us; –
Nothing is left, – cried Susannah, – nothing is left – for me, but to run my
country.*

*My uncle Toby's house was a much kinder sanctuary; and so Susannah
fled to it.*[9]

Some months later, when we were talking about the hazards of literary
translation, Max homed in on "sash window" as an instance *par excellence* of a
phrase – and concept – so embedded in the vernacular, you'd be hard put to it
to find an equivalent in another language; what was more, he'd insisted, even
if you were to land on a reasonable approximation, it wouldn't do justice to
the original.

Max savoured words for their own sake – held them in the greatest
respect, irrespective of language. His pleasure often related to idiosyncrasies
of function – as is clear in his description of the "teas-maid" (sic) in *The
Emigrants*:

*... Mrs Irlam knocked at my door. Apparently by way of a special welcome,
she brought me, on a silver tray, an electric appliance of a kind I had never
seen before ... [it] was both an alarm clock and a tea-making machine.
When I made tea and the steam rose from it, the shiny stainless steel
contraption on its ivory-coloured metal base looked like a miniature
power plant, and the dial of the clock, as I soon found as dusk fell, glowed a
phosphorescent lime green ... as if it was that weird and serviceable gadget,*

with its nocturnal glow, its muted morning bubbling, and its mere presence
by day, that kept me holding on to life at a time when I felt a deep sense
of isolation ... Very useful, these are, said Gracie as she showed me how
to operate the teas-maid that November afternoon; and she was right ...[10]

The model in the accompanying photograph, the Goblin Teasmade, was the very one my grandmother had had by her bed throughout the sixties. I, too, had been fascinated by the way it worked.

In English, words that had a particular appeal for Max often had as much to do with their sound as their meaning or dictionary definition: "potty", for example, the word I'd noticed him use a lot when we first met.

Before long, I began to detect a distinct penchant for phrases denoting mental instability – or just plain loopiness. With no regard for political correctness, he took huge delight in peppering his stories with expressions like "off his trolley", "thick as a brick", ditto "as two short planks" or "put in with the cakes and taken out with the buns".

There was also that other great preoccupation of Max's: ways to describe chaos and disorder: "topsy-turvy" or "higgledy-piggledy", not forgetting "at sixes and sevens". Increasingly, it seemed to me, his visits were coming to represent an opportunity for indulging in that speciality of his, the rhapsodic complaint – he knew he could bank on being met with a willing audience. The trick never failed to work, particularly the finale when, with feigned exasperation, things were pronounced "AN UTTER MESS" – the technical term he applied to a wide spectrum of situations and behaviours, from the conduct of committee meetings to persons in breach of a promise.

* * * * *

By now, we were on the threshold of autumn – enjoying an Indian summer. I hadn't yet heard from my German media contacts but, wanting to keep my word with regard to Max's "Kant script", I decided to drop a line to Uli – just the person to come up with helpful ideas.

At this time, Uli was working for the Berlin publishing firm Merve Verlag and as a regular contributor to the cultural magazine *Tumult*. He wore his learning with enviable lightness and, from the outset, had struck me as the embodiment of the *flâneur* – in the Benjaminian sense. Indeed, he loved all things French, which, remembering Felicité's parrot in the tale by Flaubert[11], had earned him an affectionate nickname: for me, Uli was "*le grand Loulou*".

Here's an extract from my letter, dated 8 October 1981:

> *... a small request! I wonder if you could send me the new address of the Schaubühne am Lehniner Platz. There's someone here in Norwich from Southern Germany called Max Sebald – extremely imaginative; alongside his academic work (he teaches at the University), he writes plays and film scripts. He's already in contact with people at RIAS and SFB – but would like to try his luck with the Schlausteiner...*
>
> *Please find enclosed some 100% GENUINE DUST from 28 Ampthill Street, Norwich about which I trust the German postal service won't get itself into a fluff. Amongst other things ... don't go into a TUMULT panic because, if you do, I'll have to invent even more ways to distract you from your work...*

This is fairly typical of the way Uli and I had conducted our correspondence over the preceding six months. From time to time, along with the letters, we'd send each other "surprise packets" – an assortment of old photographs and postcards, a newspaper cutting detailing some bizarre discovery or other, a miniature wooden toy.

As often as not, Uli's parcels used to come with samples of his writing – what in German would be described as *Belletristik*. One such was a lyrical meditation entitled *Glass. Silver. Dust.* that had appeared in an art magazine earlier in the year. This is a representative passage:

> *... dust exists through dance, floating at the slightest touch; it is borne along on the air or rather, by the sunbeams. Wherever it comes to rest or seeks*

to settle, it has to fight for its survival; because even the tiniest droplet of water is enough to reduce it to common muck. And that is why it loves all things hot: fire, the dry seasons of the year, summer and early autumn. Its finest time is an Indian summer. That is when the specks of dust go a-dancing, come together and exchange vows: as soon as the wet, rainy days of November or February are over, the dust will be back and here to stay... [12]

It was largely on the strength of such exchanges that Uli had come to visit me the previous July; and it was shortly after his return to Berlin that I'd been introduced to Max. In the light of subsequent events, it strikes me as poignant that the two of them had missed meeting each other in Norwich by a matter of just three weeks. In 2004, Uli was appointed Director of the *Deutsches Literaturarchiv* (German Literature Archive) in Marbach-am-Neckar; and, as such, headed up the institution responsible for the purchase of the Sebald Literary Archive the following year.

Whether or not the two of them got to know each other subsequently, they will always remain linked in my imagination by certain similarities of taste and outlook – and surely none more endearing than their predilection for house dust. What they admired above all was the tendency of dust to accumulate – for preference, the kind that had been allowed to remain undisturbed for a long, long time.

Dust was to play an important role in all Max's writing: the literary essays and meditations; the poetry; and each of the prose works from *The Emigrants* through to *Austerlitz*. It is granted special status in the story of Max Aurach (Max Ferber in the English edition), the painter who is drawn to the city of Manchester by its soot-blackened chimneys and who deliberately "creates" dust as part of his artistic technique.

I would hazard a guess that for Max, the peculiar charm of my house in Ampthill Street lay in the fact of its dusty state. The floorboards had never been replaced – they squeaked and groaned at every step; no attempt had been made to block up the fireplaces, either upstairs or down; and as for the cellar...

It was in surroundings like these that Max found true contentment, something he was to confirm sixteen years later. During an interview in 1997, he was invited to expand on the subject of dust. Having first alluded to its allegorical and biblical significance ("dust to dust, ashes to ashes"), he explained that he felt himself to be "one of those people who feel a sense of discomfort" in houses that are "tidy, well-kept, constantly looked-after", where "a sort of cold order is maintained".

He went on to illustrate the point with a personal experience. Round about the time he had been working on the story of Max Aurach, he had gone to London to meet a publisher at his home in Kensington. On arrival, since the publisher wasn't yet ready for him, Max was invited to wait upstairs. He was shown to "a sort of library room" at the top of the house, a room full of books and covered in dust – dust that, over the years, had settled on the books, the carpet, the windowsill – everywhere, in fact, except for a path between the door of the room and a single chair. It was

> ... *like a path through snow ... you could see why there wasn't any dust there because occasionally somebody would walk up to the chair and sit down and read a book. And I have never spent a more peaceful quarter of an hour than sitting in that particular chair. It was this experience that brought home to me that dust has something very, very peaceful about it.*[13]

For both Uli and Max, dust is benign. More than that, it is precious: dust contains memory – and history.

V

I have doffed my identity in order to pass for a
conventional spook and steal into realms that
existed before I was conceived ...

Vladimir Nabokov, *Speak, Memory*, 1966[14]

What made the conversations with Max so invigorating was the way they tended to proceed: there was usually a main thread, but round and about was intertwined many a good strand – in effect, labyrinthine. And as with all good yarns – for example, *The Histories* of Herodotus, which Max greatly admired – it was this very wandering from one topic to another, the digressions and pauses, that served to heighten our awareness of the interconnectedness of everything: people, places and historical events.

Amongst the subjects to which we returned over and over again was the theme of exile and emigration; also, more subjectively, a sense of displacement. When he'd first visited Britain in the 1960s, Max hadn't set out to stay for more than a couple of years; the fact that he'd eventually settled here for good, he told me, had been purely accidental.

With characteristic disingenuousness, he claimed that when he arrived to take up his post as a language assistant at Manchester University, he knew hardly any English at all. Nonetheless, whilst conscious of his status as a foreigner, it was in Manchester – a city with an established tradition of welcoming and integrating people from diverse cultural and ethnic backgrounds – that he felt comfortable. The individuals he met, he liked; what impressed him above all was the atmosphere of tolerance.

In 1968, he'd returned to mainland Europe for a teaching job in French-speaking Switzerland; ultimately, however, he'd decided against permanent residence there and come back to England. His sentiments about living abroad chimed with my own – albeit "in geographical reverse" so to speak. Neither of us had *had* to leave our native country; for both, it'd been a matter of choice.

On the subject of enforced exile, I had another story for Max. This was about someone close to me – a story of emigration that had been prompted by political events of the most turbulent kind. Neither "accidental" nor voluntary, this was an exile that, in one sense, was still ongoing.

My godmother, Elisaveta, was a White Russian, the granddaughter of Mikhail Morosov, one of the merchant art collectors whose brother Ivan, along with Sergei Shchukin, had been responsible for amassing the famous collections now housed in the Hermitage in St. Petersburg, and the Pushkin Museum and Tretyakov Gallery in Moscow.

Following the 1917 Revolution, her family had been forced to leave Moscow and seek refuge in Paris. In the winter of 1920, at the age of seven, Elisaveta and her little sister, Marina, fled with their mother, travelling to France by way of Constantinople and Potsdam. Over and above a small number of suitcases, the children were allowed to take with them just one possession. For Elisaveta, it was her beloved doll.

During the early years in Paris, whilst adoring her father, she'd harboured growing resentment towards her mother. By her mid-teens, having discovered that her father kept a mistress and her mother had a lover, she turned against both parents – doing so with a vengeance. In an effort to temper her daughter's fury – for reasons I'd never been able to establish – the mother had ordered Elisaveta to attend regular Sunday services at the city's Anglican church. It was here that she was spotted by a fellow worshipper – a very devout, very wealthy English spinster.

As chance would have it, this lady, Miss Boydell, was just then engaged on a somewhat unusual mission. Having reached a stage in life when she no longer wished to spend the rest of it on her own, she was looking to take on a young woman as a surrogate daughter. It would have been difficult for Elisaveta, aged seventeen, not to attract notice: with her thick, coal-black hair, deep grey eyes and high, Slavic cheekbones, she could not help but turn heads. Intelligent, beautiful and impressionable, the girl fitted the bill to perfection; she, for her part, was eager for any opportunity to break away from what she perceived as the hypocrisy of the parental home.

Negotiations bore fruit, bringing with them another emigration, this time to England – to a house close by the church in the village of Great Shelford, outside Cambridge.

It would not be long before those astonishing good looks and strong personality proved a questionable asset, serving as they did to make Miss Boydell all the more determined to keep Elisaveta under her thumb – and in the case of male attention, firmly out of reach. In other words, this was the start of another, equally stifling relationship.

Fortunately, Elisaveta possessed the strength of mind to liberate herself from the clutches of Miss Boydell by going and getting herself a university education. In due course, with two first-class degrees in French and Theology, she took up a series of teaching posts, one of which led to a lasting friendship with my mother.

I read Max an extract from a letter my mother had written me in which she recalled their first encounter:

... After a year came Elisaveta – from Benenden [School]. She never stayed in a teaching job long but at least I enjoyed her company for a year and a bit. She was the proverbial breath of fresh air in a fairly stuffy staff community ... The stables had been converted to accommodate the younger teachers and this is where Elisaveta joined us at night. That winter was freezing; we had one tiny heater that was supposed to keep us warm ... but what I remember most were the endless midnight chats with Elisaveta,

she talking about T.S. Eliot and religion (at that time she was a confirmed Anglo-Catholic) and anything else of interest that happened to come up. I knew I had found a friend for life. She quickly grew bored with the teaching regime ... she told me a lot about her family – her parents and sister Marina – and about how she'd been taken up by Miss Boydell and gone along with her patronage before eventually making her escape ...

By the time Miss Boydell died, Elisaveta was into her late forties. And whilst finding herself the beneficiary of a considerable estate, her new-found freedom came at a terrible emotional cost. She began to experience a level of despair so profound that it led her to the brink of breakdown; at one point she was so traumatised that she lost the power of speech.

Nevertheless, against all the odds, she managed to maintain a core of resilience. It was round about this period that she abandoned Anglo-Catholicism – her adopted faith – and became interested in psychology and psychoanalysis. She read everything she could get hold of on the subject and started to toy with the idea of turning this to her advantage by training as a psychotherapist and embarking on a new career. To this end, she sought the advice of the psychoanalyst Anthony Storr, then in his late thirties. Much to her chagrin (though also, retrospectively, to her amusement), he was not encouraging. At the end of an exhaustive interview, he pronounced her "far too intelligent to consider training in psychoanalysis" and suggested she would do better to go off and enjoy herself! What she needed, she realised, was not therapy but a change of scene.

At the mention of mental breakdown, Max showed particular interest and asked me to expand. I told him that wasn't easy because Elisaveta had never gone into detail about how the crisis had manifested itself – she wasn't one to talk about personal pain. All I could say was that, over and above the physical symptoms such as loss of voice, she'd taken the situation as a cue to try and rebuild her life by a form of self-silencing.

Max, listening intently as always, seemed to "disappear" for a moment. After a pause, I continued – saying that for a very long time, Elisaveta had resolutely avoided mentioning anything to do with her history, her Russian roots or her grandparents' generation. She had even refused to use her native tongue except when there was no alternative, such as in the company of fellow Russian exiles in the South of France. Might this have been a variant of internal migration? Max speculated. A state of mind that didn't necessarily entail leaving one's country but could be a means of coping with the pain of homelessness and deracination, actual or spiritual? As we both knew, *innere Emigration* was a concept with which dozens of writers and intellectuals had been familiar, notably amongst Germans and German Jews during the 1930s and 40s.

It seemed we had hit upon a common interest. Whilst on the topic, I explained how, towards the end of the 1970s – indeed, with Elisaveta's encouragement – I had become sufficiently interested in the psychology of exile and emigration to consider staying on in Germany to pursue doctoral studies in that field. Hearing this, Max expressed no surprise – it was as though he'd known what was coming or expected just such a twist in the tale.

It was getting late and I still hadn't finished telling him about Elisaveta. What had become of her after the old lady died? he wanted to know. A summary was called for.

Following the sale of Miss Boydell's property, Elisaveta had set about making a recovery by moving to London, installing herself in a spacious top-floor flat in Devonshire Place. For the first time in her life, she started to afford herself "luxuries": carefully chosen *objets d'art*, items of designer furniture, sets of LPs of Italian opera, lots of books. Things had begun to look up – and in 1966, reached a peak.

One afternoon, she met a gentleman – a quintessentially English gentleman, as she thought of him – walking his dog in nearby Regent's Park. It was an instant rapport, a *coup de foudre*. Though by now into his third marriage, there was no question in John's mind: he was for Elisaveta and she was for him. Without hesitation, he left his wife and moved into Devonshire Place. The relationship continued to flourish for the next nine years; and then, one evening in March 1975, John suffered a sudden, fatal heart attack. Once again, at the age of sixty-one, Elisaveta's life was shattered.

She had borne these vicissitudes with enviable dignity; and, fortunately for me, although she had long since given up on the idea of drawing comfort from religion, she had taken her responsibilities as godparent extremely seriously. As my mother had put it in the letter:

As soon as you were born, there was no question in our minds: it was Elisaveta we should ask to be your godmother. She was delighted and, in fact, outside the family, she was the very first person to be allowed to hold you in her arms...

It struck me – this is how I phrased it to Max – that, metaphorically speaking, Elisaveta was still holding me in her arms. What's more, I told him, she was now living in East Anglia, in Bury St Edmund's.

On Friday, 6 November I had been to see her in her new house.

Monday, 9 November 1981

I'd just finished having a bath when there was a knock at the front door. I grabbed a towel, rushed down the stairs, managing to catch my heel on an exposed nail in the process, leaving a small trickle of blood...

It was Max. Whenever he comes round, I find myself with butterflies... though once we've started on the stories and got chatting about this and that – anything that's irritated or amused us – I feel OK again. We always seem to take up the thread from where we left off last time and then the dialogue just flows – what Elisaveta had referred to on Friday as "a game of tennis"... something to do with being on the same wavelength, kindred spirits...

By this time, I'd begun to notice how, when Max came to the door, he would salute me with a gentle "*Grüß Gott!*", the greeting commonly used in Southern Germany. And as he took his leave, somewhat shyly and formally, he would bid me "*Adé*". I always found this incredibly thrilling – partly, no doubt, on account of its romantic associations: it put me in mind of Ludwig Rellstab's poem "*Abschied*" ("Farewell") in the Schubert song cycle *Schwanengesang* (*Swan Song*).

Friday, 13 November 1981

Elisaveta's birthday today. Max came round again this evening. We went along to Cinema City to see Fritz Lang's *M*, opting for this rather than the lecture on cubism at the Castle Museum. Good to do something I had *not* planned – *especially* good not doing the usual, i.e. go out on my own ...

Going to the cinema with Max was a treat. Not long before this, when talking about films, it emerged that there was one that had always held a particular fascination for both of us. This was Alain Resnais' *L'année dernière à Marienbad* (*Last Year in Marienbad*). Its appeal lay as much in the hypnotic quality of the cinematography and soundtrack as the enigma at the core of its narrative. Maybe this predilection dated us; but then, we were children of the sixties – of the Continental sixties.

I looked back to see when it was I'd first met Max.

Since the end of August, he's been round ten times. Not sure about the dynamics of this relationship or where we are with one another ... but we love telling each other stories ...

Clearly, the story-telling had become a habit; nor was it entirely a one-way process:

... and I love the way he tells his! His wry sense of humour is irresistible ...

The friendship had gathered pace remarkably quickly; indeed, it had begun to take on the appearance of an old-fashioned courtship – there was something slightly archaic about it. At the same time, I realised that, other than the fact that he was a couple of years older than me, there was a great deal about Max's life, past and present, I didn't know.

The diary entry for that day goes on:

> ... we seem to be at pains to keep at a slight physical distance from one another, avoid touching ... I've become aware of a groundswell. Delicately woven into the conversation, Max gives frequent indications that he's looking for some sort of escape: from material concerns, social responsibilities, pressure of various kinds. It wouldn't take much, I think, for him to act on impulse – except that something's holding him back ...

Monday, 23 November 1981

> A phone call from Max. He wants to see me.

Tuesday, 24 November 1981

> Max came round this evening with a glorious bottle of wine – too good to open straight away. Fortunately, I'd just made some punch and this helped put him at his ease ...

It would appear that Max hadn't yet developed his alcohol allergy – at any rate, it hadn't yet been diagnosed.

> ... He began talking about himself a lot more; says he feels torn between a need to depend on others and a sense of moral responsibility towards them. There are times, he added wistfully, when he'd just like to disappear ...

Wednesday, 25 November 1981

> ... I thought about what Max had said last night: how he both wants and doesn't want other people on whom to depend. I responded from the opposite point of view, admitting that, since living on my

own, I've found it extremely hard to imagine going back to being dependent ... He's loaned me some books, amongst which there's Thomas Bernhard's *Verstörung* that he's keen for me to read.

Despite the fact that Max had taken to dropping in on a fairly regular basis, his reasons for doing so were far from transparent. There was an undeniable frisson between us that I'd been predisposed to interpret as "romantic" – a delightful fantasy but most probably not what was driving Max. In any case, I had no wish to be the source of domestic embarrassment.

The more I thought about the situation and read the Bernhard novel, the more I began to believe that Max's views on love – any kind of love – were along the lines of those expressed by Prince Saurau in his lengthy monologue:

> *With justification, one might describe my character as loveless. But it is with equal justification that I describe the world as utterly loveless. Love is an absurdity and in no way part of nature.*[15]

If this was right, then how hopelessly naive I was being, how slow to register! It was not amorous adventure Max was after; what he sought was consolation.

VI

A time of expectant hopes encourages one to think
of oneself as unflinching. Everything needs to be faced. The only
danger seems to be evasion or sentimentality. Harsh truth will aid
liberation. This principle becomes so integral to one's thinking
that it is accepted without question. One is aware of how it might
be otherwise. Hope is a marvellous focusing lens.
One's eye becomes fixed to it. And one can
examine anything...

... In a period of revolutionary expectation [i.e. in 1963],
I saw a work of art which had survived as evidence of the past's
despair; in a period which has to be endured, I see the same work
miraculously offering a narrow pass across despair.

John Berger, "Between Two Colmars", 1973[16]

Thursday, 3 December 1981

... Max rang: he doesn't sound at all happy ...

Saturday, 5 December 1981

Max came round – twice in the morning – and then to tea. He had
on a brown tweed suit – cuts quite a dash; and takes great care over
his appearance ... He continues to keep at a slight physical distance ...
when we talk about books and ideas, the mood is extremely animated;

as soon as the conversation turns to personal matters, however, it changes ...

Though I'd begun to suspect that Max's frequent visits were not prompted by a need for romance, I couldn't help hoping I was wrong. I decided I must bide my time. Being by nature honourable, perhaps he was simply acting with caution. However that might be, what first struck me on this occasion was his appearance. I complimented him, which prompted a revelation of a very personal kind.

> Max showed me something he always keeps in his pocket – a little brush for the care of his moustache that he inherited from his grandfather ...

Just as I'd told him about my godmother, Elisaveta, he now began talking about Grandfather Josef. Max's happiest early memories were of the times he'd spent in the company of his maternal grandfather – it had been the deepest attachment of his childhood, he explained. And then, a month before his twelfth birthday, Josef Egelhofer had died – a loss with which he had never been able to come to terms.

Of particular significance to Max, who laid great store by the importance of dates, was the fact that his grandfather had died on 14 April 1956, i.e. the birthday of the Swiss writer Robert Walser and, as it happened, within four months of Walser's own death.[17] In an essay Max wrote many years later, "Le promeneur solitaire: zur Erinnerung an Robert Walser" ("The Solitary Walker: in Memory of Robert Walser"), he points to the striking parallels between Josef Egelhofer and Walser, including a marked physical resemblance and the way the two men had worn their hats.

For now, it was enough that Max had felt able to share his sorrow with me. But then he went on and, as he did so, I began to detect something other than the expression of unresolved grief – a fundamentally dark view of the world that seemed to verge on the pathological.

Max admits to feeling very disillusioned – "tired of life" is how he puts it. He says he has no ambitions and wishes he could return to the way things used to be – "a rather incompetent, idle, withdrawn existence" as he describes it! Not a picture that fits with what I know of Max and pretty difficult to believe (except if taken with a large pinch of salt). Even so, I think I understand what he means when he says he finds himself becoming intensely irritated by the pace of academic life and the compromises this entails ...

After the visit, I wondered whether Max's despondency had been triggered by anything in particular – indeed, what conflicts might have been brewing and for how long. I was left with the impression of a contradiction: here was a person who presented himself to the world with meticulous attention to outward detail – as far removed from signs of self-neglect as it was possible to be; yet who was in the grip of a dejection so profound that I began to worry for his safety. Was I being invited merely to listen and try to understand? Or was he looking for a more overtly "clinical" intervention? I lay awake that night, at a loss for an answer.

* * * * *

A month or so after arriving in Norwich – and still without a satisfactory place to live – one of the volunteer helpers at the day centre had introduced me to Julia – Julia Boswell. Realising that I felt like a fish out of water in my new surroundings, she had taken pity and offered me a room in her house where I would be able to stay for the next ten months. We enjoyed each other's company and became firm friends; even after I'd moved to other accommodation, we would often meet, go to the cinema together or share a meal.

Sunday, 6 December 1981

Spent the day with Julia who came for brunch: a good excuse to procrastinate with more sorting of books. I'd put together some muesli followed by bacon and eggs; afterwards, although we'd meant to go and see the Lucie Rie Exhibition up at UEA, we got so immersed in conversation, we lost track of time ...

After she left, I went on with the books ... Just then, there was a knock at the door: it was Max ... Things started off quite light-heartedly, chatting about this and that ... then it began to sound as if he had something on his mind – something he wasn't quite ready to talk about ...

Thursday, 10 December 1981

Max has brought along a copy of his study of Alfred Döblin, published last year – a slim, olive-green volume with a very long title and, inside, chock-full of learned footnotes. I took another look at the cover and noticed the author's name: "W.G. Sebald" ...

This stopped me in my tracks. "Is that you?" I asked him. "I thought your name was Max!" He went very quiet, which of course made me all the more curious. I persisted. "So what does the 'W.G.' stand for?" Somewhat sheepishly, he explained that though he'd been christened "Winfried Georg", he hated both names for different reasons: "Winfried" was archaic, too Teutonic and Wagnerian; and "Georg", his father's name, too Catholic and saintly; which was why – "mainly for academic purposes", as he put it – he'd settled for initials only. So what about "Max"? I got a laconic reply: this was the name he preferred, the one with which he felt able to identify.

Friday, 11 December 1981

I had arranged to meet Julia for the Fellini film at Cinema City – *La città delle donne.*[18] After I got home, Max rang and said he'd like to join us. Julia's friend Liam had also decided to come along. Following the screening, we went to the bar. There we were, Julia and I, sandwiched between two delightful men, rather giggly, talking nineteen to the dozen about the merits of the movie: in praise of women, full of bombast, double bluff and outrageous fantasy. Some critics had claimed it was a dig at feminism – but that's not how *we* saw it ...

Max was on top form. His reaction was typical of him. Keeping a completely straight face, he announced, somewhat portentously, "Well, I don't know; I don't suffer from this male paranoia of being eaten alive by women ..."

Whatever else, there'd been plenty of comedy within the film – and just as much in the real-life situation: the four of us sitting there in the bar, harking back to our schooldays, recounting old stories ... I've come home feeling quite carried away ...

Saturday, 12 December 1981

It was a gorgeous morning – sunny and full of snow – and I felt extravagant ... Went to collect my shoes from the menders and buy a few Christmas presents, including something for Max. Books are a safe bet as long as they're ones he doesn't possess already ...

In town, I gravitated to the Hungate Bookshop and took my pick. It was a motley assortment but each volume was chosen for its specific appeal. I remember four in particular. The first was *Period Piece*, written and illustrated by Gwen Raverat (the granddaughter of Charles Darwin), an account of her Cambridge childhood. It is, pre-eminently, a book to dip into, without a straightforward start-to-finish narrative; its brief preface announces the scheme as follows:

This is a circular book. It does not begin at the beginning and go on to the end; it is all going on at the same time, sticking out like the spokes of a wheel from the hub, which is me. So it does not matter which chapter is read first or last ...

Such an idea had always attracted me and would, I felt, do the same for Max.

Then there was Don Marquis's book of verses, *archy and mehitabel*, purportedly dreamt up by archy the cockroach and dedicated to his muse, mehitabel the cat, all set out in lower case because archy can't manage upper case on the typewriter. Interested as Max was in the niceties of textual composition, I imagined this would raise a smile.

I also included a book recently recommended to me by Julia, herself Norfolk-born. *Love Among the Butterflies: Travels and Adventures of a Victorian Lady* is an autobiographical account by Margaret Fountaine. Born in 1862, Margaret was the daughter of the Reverend John Fountaine, rector of South Acre, a hamlet about twenty miles away from Norwich. Rejecting her conventional upbringing, she dedicated her adult life to pursuing her passion for butterflies. An intrepid traveller, she journeyed all over the world, amassing a vast collection, which she had left in her will to the Norwich Castle Museum. Not long before, Max had chanced to tell me that for him – as for Nabokov and, indeed, for Kafka – the lives and habits of lepidoptera held a peculiarly strong fascination.

Last but not least, I slipped in a copy of John Berger's latest book of essays *About Looking*. Containing several pieces on the subject of photography – including one dedicated to Susan Sontag – it also had an article that had originally appeared in *The Guardian* which I envisaged as likely to strike a chord with Max: written in 1973, following his second visit to Colmar to view Matthias Grünewald's *Isenheim Altarpiece*, Berger comments on the psychological effect of the ten-year gap since he had last seen it. I had long been a devotee of John Berger's work – in particular, his art criticism – and didn't doubt that Max would feel the same way.

Satisfied with my choice, I took the books home, packed them up with a note inviting Max to dinner some time before Christmas and posted them off to "Dr. W.G. Sebald" of Poringland.

VII

Few people love the writings of Sir Thomas Browne,
but those that do are the salt of the earth ... For the desire to read,
like all the other desires which distract our unhappy souls, is capable
of analysis. It may be for good books, for bad books, or for indifferent
books. But it is always despotic in its demands, and when it appears,
at whatever hour of day or night, we must rise and slink off at its
heels ... Locked up in *Urn Burial* there is a quality of imagination
which distinguishes it completely from its companions ...

Virginia Woolf, "Sir Thomas Browne", 1923[19]

The parcel arrived safely and Max rang to say he'd like to come to dinner the following Friday. Knowing he was partial to cheese, I walked into town and made a beeline for Alan the Cheese Man. Soft-spoken and looking as though he was of Dutch ancestry, Alan Trower had held a stall in the Norwich Market for many, many years. He possessed a fund of knowledge about all aspects of cheese-making and cheese-buying, which had brought him a great reputation throughout the region; it also inspired fierce loyalty in his customers. Max was one of them.

Friday, 18 December 1981

Max to dinner – the first time he's taken up an invitation rather than coming round on spec. I prepared a Burgundian *gougère* inspired

by Elizabeth David's recipe, using the finest Gruyère Alan
could supply...

As so often, the conversation swiftly turned to books.

The mood was one of high hilarity – paradoxical, perhaps, in the
light of what we spoke about at the start of the evening: the nature
of melancholia and the theory behind the humours. Max says he
regards himself as "melancholic" (in the sense used by Robert
Burton); he'd been born when Saturn was in the ascendant – the cold
planet, heavy and dry – so thought that might have something to do
with it. This led to reflections on *Hamlet*, death and dying; and then,
Sir Thomas Browne...

One of the highlights of my degree course at Exeter University in the mid-
1960s had been reading English seventeenth-century prose – above all,
the writings of Sir Thomas Browne. Browne was born under the sign of
Saturn and had spent a large part of his life in Norwich. It was here that he
had written two of his most famous works, *Hydriotaphia: Urne Buriall* and
The Garden of Cyrus[20]. Max, also born under Saturn, wondered which of
Browne's works would be a good one to start with. Seizing the opportunity
to share my enthusiasm, I suggested the treatise on urn burial.

Not long afterwards, Max must have taken me at my word and gone
and got himself a copy. A couple of years later, in 1983, he was to publish an
essay, "Konstruktionen der Trauer» ("Constructions of Mourning»)[21], which
takes as its starting-point the 1967 book by the psychoanalyst Alexander
Mitscherlich and his wife Margarete, *Die Unfähigkeit zu trauern* (*The Inability
to Mourn*). Max argues that, with one notable exception, post-war German
authors had failed to use their writing either to acknowledge the crimes
committed in the name of National Socialism or to mourn those who had
died in the Holocaust. All the more poignant, therefore, that he took as his
epigraph this line from the third chapter of *Hydriotaphia*:

... And if the burthen of Isaac were sufficient for an holocaust, a man may carry his owne pyre ...

The surrounding text in Browne concerns a discussion of funeral practices: cremation as distinct from burial – specifically, the great variation in the rate at which individual corpses tend to burn. No doubt Max had picked out that particular line for its use of the term "holocaust"; but also, I believe, for Browne's special brand of humour, what the critic M.R. Ridley – in the Introduction to my old Everyman edition – had described as "the sparkle of the deft turn of phrase ... the half-humorous perception of an incongruity, which twinkles out from the graver background".[22] In other words, not unlike Max's own.

Within the family, from adolescence onwards, I had come in for a fair amount of teasing regarding my "over-serious" tastes – in reading as in other things. Neither could I forget a recent pronouncement of Elisaveta's, delivered in that inimitable French accent of hers: "Philippa is much too solemn; she needs to be frivolised!"

With Max, there were no such quibbles; indeed, my relationship with him had begun to release something qualitatively different: we seemed to move between the serious and the light-hearted, the solemn and the preposterous, with the greatest of ease.

It was in just this spirit that, after we'd finished eating, I went and fetched my grandfather's handwritten *History of the Comber Family*. I remembered it contained some first-rate stories; and, seeing as we'd been on the subject of burials, I selected a passage near the beginning concerning the will of John Rivers Comber of Sedlescombe, Sussex, dated 17 February 1557, seven weeks before he died:

"... to be buryed in the Churchyard of Sedlescombe. I will have at my buryinge day two masses and Dirges and the bred of a bushell of wheat and another bushel of bere and at my moneths day one mass and it be in lent to bestow amongs the poure breade and drynke & herryng pyes ...

Herring pies! The detail delighted Max.

Leafing forward, I found something in a rather different vein. This was the story of my great, great grandfather, Peter King.

Peter King had been born at Musselburgh, near Edinburgh, in 1800. Following his education in Edinburgh, he migrated to Brazil and thence to Chile in 1818, returning to Scotland in 1826 to marry Jane Finlayson Graham, a descendant of the Grahams of Claverhouse. In 1827 they returned to Chile where Peter King worked first for Anthony Gibbs & Co., a silver nitrate business, then as agent for the Pacific Steam Navigation Company and British Vice-Consul in Iquique. He was a well-loved character, known by all as "Don Pedro".

According to my grandfather, Peter King was in Iquique in 1854 – the year of a great earthquake and tidal wave. (I hadn't been able to verify the date; but the available records show that on 24 December 1854, there was a massive quake in Japan, the Ansei-Nankai Earthquake. This quake had reached a magnitude of 8.4 and given rise to a damaging tsunami.) The highpoint of the story was yet to come, I told Max, and proceeded to read on:

His wife and family being temporarily in the South of Chile on holiday, Peter K. was lying in bed in a room above his office overlooking the Bay of Iquique, recovering from typhoid fever. He felt the shock and, looking out of his window, saw the sea receding as far as the island situated about two miles off the mainland. Realising that the sea would eventually return, he jumped from his bed and ran up the main street leading to the hills at the rear of the town, calling to everyone he saw to make for the hills as the sea was coming. Few people followed his advice; seeing him attired in his nightclothes and knowing that he had been suffering from fever, they thought he had taken leave of his senses.

Iquique lies on a narrow strip of ground for about two miles to the base of the high hills, rising 3000–4000 feet above the town. At the foot of these hills, Peter K. had come to the cemetery when he was overtaken by the tidal wave that now reached to his knees ... Out of a total population of 4000 people, only about 30 were saved and these few were completely isolated for five days, subsisting on what they were able to recover from the wreckage of the town ... Being a town entirely of wooden buildings, it was wiped out by the receding sea. Peter K.'s safe from his office on the original sea front was subsequently recovered from the island two miles out, where it had been deposited by the force of the returning waters ... His wife and (youngest) daughter Margarita went to his aid as soon as possible from the South of Chile; when they first met him, he was still wearing the nightgown in which he had made his escape ... None the worse for this hair-raising experience, he settled down to work to rebuild his fortunes. He had lost heavily through the tidal wave ...

Max broke in with a remark about the story starting to remind him of two novellas by Kleist of which he was especially fond, *The Earthquake in Chile* and *The Betrothal in Santo Domingo*.[23] I read on:

Peter K. prospered in business and made a considerable amount of money out of the Huantajaya Silver Mines – the same mines that years later yielded a colossal fortune to John Chase ... About 1865, he purchased a property at Olmué in the vale of Limache, at the foot of the Campana Mountain ... He did not settle for long at Olmué but continued to wander over Chile and Peru until 1882, when he went to live there permanently.

By 1885, he had started to feel lonely so came to join my father and his family in Iquique ... In 1889, when we returned to England for good, Peter K. remained in Quilpué, looked after by two old family servants and, living nearby, his granddaughter Margarita. As a widower, however, he continued to complain of the loneliness of his life and in 1894, another of his granddaughters, Edith, travelled from England to bring him back. On my father's sudden illness in 1895, Edith was recalled by cable. "Don Pedro" did not wish to be left behind but said he would go back to England on one condition: that, were he to die there, his body should be returned to Chile. Thereupon, he made an arrangement with the Pacific Steam Navigation Co. to undertake the voyage with his coffin ready under his berth, arriving in England in February 1896...

At this point, I caught Max's eye and got the giggles. Dabbing at the tears, it was all I could do to carry on to the end:

One day, Peter K. insisted on going to watch the skating in Lammas Park, Ealing, deciding to venture on to the ice himself. He contracted a chill, which he was unable to shake off and which led to his death the following month, aged 96. His body was duly returned to Chile in the designated coffin.

This completely hit the spot with Max. In the four months since we'd met, I had certainly witnessed him giving expression to amusement, but had never heard him laugh out loud.

VIII

Ernst stood still, turned to me as though we were
both actors on stage, and in a theatrical manner uttered
a statement which appeared to me as if he had committed it
to memory a long time ago: That is a very fine sound,
borne upon the air, and uplifts one's heart.

W.G. Sebald, *Vertigo* [*Schwindel. Gefühle*], 1990[24]

The evening had ended on a light-hearted note – more so, perhaps, since I had managed not to bother Max with the latest news of my divorce proceedings: a few days earlier, I had received a copy of the decree nisi.

Before he left, Max explained that for part of the vacation, he would be in the States. He enquired how I was going to spend Christmas – surely I needed a break from work? I told him I had toyed with the idea of going to Berlin but then decided in favour of a trip to Devon to see my parents.

The following Tuesday, I caught the train to Totnes and, from there, took a taxi along the narrow, twisting lanes as far as Harberton, the village to which my parents had retired.

By curious coincidence, Harberton features in Bruce Chatwin's 1977 book about wandering and exile, *In Patagonia*:

From Ushuaia it was a thirty-five mile walk along the Beagle Channel to the Bridges's estancia at Harberton ... coming into Harberton from the land side, you could mistake it for a big estate in the Scottish Highlands,

with its sheep fences, sturdy gates and peat-brown trout streams. The
Rev. Thomas Bridges's settlement was strung out along the west shore of
Harberton Inlet, shielded from the gales by a low hill. His Yaghan friends
chose the site and he named it after his wife's Devonshire village ...[25]

Max was spellbound by Chatwin's books – *In Patagonia*, particularly. His
essay "The Mystery of the Red-brown Skin: An Approach to Bruce Chatwin"
first appeared in the year 2000 and was later included in the posthumous
volume *Campo Santo*.

I was greatly relieved to find that on this occasion, despite the tensions
that had built up over the preceding years between me and my parents, they
were genuinely pleased to see me: the visit seemed to represent some kind
of "return to the fold".

No doubt this had to do with the impending divorce. My mother, even so,
was less forgiving than my father. From the outset, she had been fond of my
husband; and in the past, when it came to the crunch, she had always leapt to
his defence rather than mine. It was now clear that she regarded the failure
of the marriage as something for which I alone was responsible.

Friday, 25 December 1981

Ma keeps on referring to my "wasted years". Why, I wonder? Maybe,
without saying so, she has in mind her own marriage – she didn't have
the courage to leave. But then neither did my father ...

Saturday, 26 December 1981

On Boxing Day, my father and I took a long walk along the River Dart.
We talked a good deal about marriage – his as well as mine; it seems that
openness about my situation enabled him to be frank about his own – no
longer so weighed down by moral scruples and his sense of Christian duty. I
remember it as one of the most important conversations I ever had with him.

That night, I noted in my diary:

> ... a few pangs of sadness as I reflect on past Christmases – many of
> the recent ones spent in Germany ... from time to time, my thoughts
> turn to Max; I wonder what he's doing ... and what it is he sees in
> me. Is it the fact that I'm a relative outsider, not part of the academic
> community at UEA? And does he like the talk about books and
> the storytelling because that way, the focus isn't on him? There
> is *something* on his mind, though; but what it is exactly, I've yet to
> discover ...

I returned to Norwich to find that whilst I'd been away, a whole pile of post
had landed through the letterbox. Amongst the last-minute Christmas mail
was a largish item in a cardboard wrapper with an Austrian postmark –
instantly recognisable as the latest issue of *Manuskripte*, a literary magazine
produced in Graz.

I'd been a regular subscriber since 1976. Initially, this had been
prompted by my enthusiasm for the exquisitely eccentric films of Herbert
Achternbusch and the fact that Volume 52 contained the full text of one of
these: *Die Atlantikschwimmer* (*Swimmers of the Atlantic*). The actors speak in
Bavarian dialect and, as always with Achternbusch, the impact is surreal. It
stars Herbert himself and, in a small cameo role, the beautiful Margarethe
von Trotta as a swimming instructress. My fondness for the film was also
on account of the locations. The Starnberger See – which stands in for the
Atlantic Ocean in the film – was one of the lakes I had got to know in 1963
during that first memorable holiday with Christine and her family.

Monday, 4 January 1982

I've just opened the copy of *Manuskripte* that arrived this morning ...
now that's just *weird*! It's got something in it by Max ... surely
individual subscribers to *Manuskripte* can't be that thick on the
ground in the UK – let alone contributors ... He never said anything –

but then, on second thoughts, there's no real reason why he should have ...

So here it was, an essay entitled "Kleine Traverse – über das poetische Werk des Alexander Herbrich" ("*En Travers*: the Poetical Works of Alexander Herbrich") – Alexander Herbrich being the *nom de plume* – or alter ego – of Ernst Herbeck.

One of the key points Max raises in the piece is the difference between writers whose concern is the act of writing itself, using whatever material comes to hand, and writers who consciously set out to "create a work of art", generally with a view to publication and posterity. Taking Herbeck as an example of the former, Max cites liberally from his verse. It's idiosyncratic – striking – and one line in particular caught my eye: "*Die Dame ohne Unterleib ist die Liebe in Berlin ...*"

Bizarre! Literally translated, the line would go something like this "The lady without private parts is love in Berlin". It seemed to me, however, that no English translation would be able to capture either the linguistic complexity or the acoustic play on words of the original.

In fact, I now remembered how, in the course of early conversations – whilst on the subject of psychopathology – Max had told me about his trip to Klosterneuburg the previous autumn. (Klosterneuburg was where, in 1924, Franz Kafka had died and therefore of particular interest to Max.) It was here, too, that Max had met Herbeck, whose story had continued to exercise his imagination. This is the gist of it:

Ernst Herbeck was born in 1920 in Stockerau, a town in the district of Korneuburg, Lower Austria. Having received a standard secondary school education, he spent a short time at business school before taking various jobs – working for a removals firm, for example, and in a munitions factory. In 1944, he'd been called up to serve in the army, only to be discharged six months later. Between the ages of seven and eighteen, he had undergone a series of operations to correct a deformity of the gums, and from the age of twenty onwards, suffered frequent bouts of mental illness – schizophrenia.

In 1946, following three short-term admissions, he was finally admitted as a long-stay patient to the Niederösterreichische Landesanstalt für Psychiatrie und Neurologie, Gugging, the regional psychiatric hospital near Klosterneuburg, outside Vienna. It was here that he attended Leo Navratil's Zentrum für Kunst und Psychotherapie (Centre for Art and Psychotherapy) enabling him to pursue his passion for writing.[26] Thirty-four years later, Herbeck had been discharged from the hospital and allowed to move into a home for pensioners situated in the town.

Max was to return to the story a decade later, in *Vertigo*. Here he describes the meeting – in October 1980 – during which he and Ernst take a train to Altenberg and walk to Burg Greifenstein, a fortress overlooking the Danube:

When I arrived ... he was already standing waiting at the top of the steps that ran up to the entrance. I waved to him from the other side of the street, whereupon he raised his arm in welcome and, keeping it outstretched, came down the steps. He was wearing a glencheck suit with a hiking badge on the lapel. On his head he wore a narrow-brimmed hat, a kind of trilby, which he later took off when it grew too warm for him and carried beside him, just as my grandfather often used to do on summer walks ... Now, on that bright October day when Ernst and I, sitting beside each other, savoured that wonderful view, a blue haze lay upon the sea of foliage that reaches right up to the walls of the castle ... At times, Ernst was very far away ... he smoked another cigarette in silence, and when he stubbed it out he repeated, as if in amazement at his entire past life, that single word "Argentine", which possibly struck him as far too outlandish. That morning, I think, we were both within an inch of learning to fly, or at least I might have managed as much as is required for a decent crash. But we never catch the propitious moment ...[27]

IX

'Even in the midst of laughing there is sorrow'
(as Solomon holds): even in the midst of all our feasting
and jollity ... there is grief and discontent. In the midst of our
enjoyment something harsh chokes us; for a pint of honey thou
shalt here likely find a gallon of gall, for a dram of pleasure
a pound of pain, for an inch of mirth an ell of moan ... these
miseries encompass our life, and 'tis most absurd and ridiculous
for any mortal man to look for a perpetual tenor of happiness
in his life. Nothing so prosperous and pleasant, but hath some
bitterness in it ... it is all bitter-sweet, a mixed passion ...

Robert Burton, *The Anatomy of Melancholy*, 1621[28]

The New Year had got off to a promising start. I had continued reading my copy of *Manuskripte* and been inspired by Max's piece on Herbeck: eager to talk about it, I was wondering when I might hear from him. But then:

Tuesday, 5 January 1982

More post today – that's nice! I thought as I picked up the letters
and took them into the kitchen to read ... there was one long one I
decided to leave till last ... it came with a postscript telling me that
last Saturday, George Rapp had had a final, fatal heart attack. The
news has knocked me sideways ... to think I had been on the point

of phoning the Rapps before Christmas to ask whether they'd mind
if I dropped in on them on my way back from Devon – but had then
written a card instead ...

I can visualise George immediately – the twinkle in his eyes, his
mellifluous voice, his jokes and anecdotes ... George has always
been an important person in my life; it was to him I turned so
often for advice ...

George Rapp was an outstandingly gifted German Jew who had emigrated
from Berlin. Having worked for Reuters, he later set up a scrap metal
business and subsequently co-founded the publishing company, Rapp &
Whiting. Here, he was instrumental in promoting the careers of numerous
young writers, including the Liverpool Poets. Amongst his friends had
been the Austrian poets Ingeborg Bachmann and Erich Fried; and the art
critics Edward Lucie-Smith and John Berger. George had two families
(in succession) and two homes (simultaneously) – one in Hampstead,
a comfortable house on several floors once inhabited by the painter John
Constable; and one in Sway, near Lymington, on the edge of the New Forest.
It struck me as poignant that George, the emigrant, had died on a cross-
Channel ferry, midway between the Continent and his adopted country.

Saturday, 9 January 1982

... there was an eclipse tonight, and a full moon. Some difficult days
recently ...

The following Thursday, having arrived home from America, Max had got in
touch and been round. A lot had happened since we'd last seen each other
– so much, indeed, that we weren't sure where to begin. In any case, I must
have come across as fairly self-absorbed – something Max was quick to pick
up on.

Friday, 15 January 1982

Although Max probably accepts how I was yesterday, I feel the need
to account for myself. I'm rather ashamed about not having given
him a proper welcome ... At the best of times, sitting on those hard
Berliner *Jugendstil* chairs of mine isn't conducive to relaxation; but it
wasn't just that: I know I was more tense than usual ...

He commented that I "somehow looked different" but I couldn't
bring myself to tell him why. Instead, I asked him what it'd been
like in the States. He began by describing a desolate American
landscape: "interesting, though ultimately depressing," he said he'd
found it ...

What was I doing at Easter? was his next question. He was
planning to go to Germany...

Frequent references to his sense of disillusionment – which I
decided not to take up. Had I done so, it might have helped bridge
the gap – the cautious distance – between us; on the other hand,
in my current dithery state, I don't feel I have much to offer by way
of comfort ...

Under the circumstances, I was relieved when Max got in touch again the
next day – to confirm when he'd be free to drive over to Bury St Edmund's.
Some time before Christmas, having told him about my godmother, I'd hit
on the idea of introducing them to each other. I felt sure they'd get on: they
had interests in common – exile, for one – and nineteenth-century French
literature. Elisaveta was agreeable and suggested lunch on 27 January;
adding that the trip would be a good opportunity for me to collect some
items she wished me to have. In particular, there was that miniature chest-
of-drawers. It was Georgian, most probably the work of an apprentice
cabinet-maker – a piece I instinctively knew would appeal to Max.

Whilst I was looking forward to the occasion, it continued to bother
me that I had been so cagey the previous Thursday; that I had held back on

the subject of the divorce and the death of George Rapp. Better to spill the beans before we go, lest it cast a shadow over the day.

On 21 January, I wrote to Max, half in German, half in English:

I thought it best to write. Wednesday 27th suits perfectly ... I've told my boss that I have to attend a funeral. I don't want people at work knowing what I'm about in the middle of the week ...

It turns out that that "white lie" isn't as improbable as it might seem. I had rather a bad conscience about how I was last time you came round, failing to explain why I not only looked different, *as you pointed out, but felt different as well. Indeed, I was very nervous, as you also suggested. Following the initial relief about the news that my divorce had been decreed absolute on 2 January, I began to feel quite vulnerable.*

As it happens, on the very same day – evening, rather – a close friend of mine died, mid-English Channel: the person who was largely responsible for bringing me and my husband together twelve years ago and who had in fact advocated the marriage.

I'm writing all this because I find it quite hard to talk about; had I told you last week, I fear it would have made matters worse. Despite all this emotional turmoil, I'm looking forward to our trip. It'll be soothing, refreshing.

Monday, 25 January 1982

No word from Max. Idiotic thoughts about his not having received the letter – could something have happened to him? Wanted to get home quickly in case he rang ...

But it wasn't Max who phoned this evening; it was Elisaveta. She'd enjoyed her weekend in London, telling me that in the end she'd decided against the "sad" blouse and worn Marina's [her sister's] beautiful lace one instead. She went on to describe the performance of Brahms's *German Requiem* she'd been to, how she'd had her hair done –

unlike the female cellists in the orchestra, she said, with a light laugh – it had looked lovely. Then, all of a sudden, came "I'm afraid I can't offer you lunch on Wednesday..." followed by a long pause. I asked her if there was anything wrong. I could hear her drawing breath before she went on. She'd been to see Piggy [the nickname she gave her Harley Street consultant] – indeed, that had been the main reason for her visit to London. Then she reverted to speaking in French. He'd told her she had breast cancer and would have to go into hospital immediately. At this, she'd protested, insisting that she wanted to enjoy the rest of the weekend first. She hadn't wanted to tell me all this, she said, but in the light of my visit with Max, felt she must. She asked me not to pass on the news to my mother – says she's spoken to nobody other than me and doesn't want anyone else to know. She hates the idea of being shown pity or sympathy; and begs me not to be upset.

I assured her that I much preferred having been told. Even in her present state of shock, she joked about Piggy's use of the tape measure followed by "a horrifying speech", informing her what the surgery would involve ... the very thought of having to be in hospital " ... considering how healthy and good-looking I've been all these years – it's disgraceful!" The distancing of pain through humour.

The news is shocking – deeply shocking...

It wasn't until after I'd put down the receiver that I came to my senses and realised I hadn't asked – hadn't had the nerve to ask – whether this meant a mastectomy. But of course! Why else had she mentioned that she wouldn't be able to use her right arm... "I shan't be able to scrub my floors any more!" she'd quipped.

My thoughts turned to one of the pictures Elisaveta had hanging in her bedroom: a charming, slightly risqué eighteenth-century print of a young woman sitting on the edge of a bed in a state of semi-undress with a little dog at her feet looking up at her adoringly. It bears the inscription *S'il m'étoit aussi fidèl!* (*If only he were as faithful!*).

Elisaveta had never been given to sharing intimate details about her past, including the happy years with John. It was a measure of her distress that she had just confided the following: John would have been heartbroken – he had always loved her breasts.

Wednesday, 27 January 1982

Spent the evening at Julia's – showed her the two silk blouses I've just bought: one white and one black, the black one very discreet with a high collar. No particular occasion in mind but it's bound to come in useful ... We talked about having fun – and she gave me a bunch of flowers.

I left at around 5.00pm and was halfway down Ampthill Street when a girl ran past me in floods of tears. I was on the point of offering to help when I thought I heard the sound of a phone ringing. Ringing, ringing, ringing, on and on it went – it seemed to be coming from the other end of the street. By now, the girl had already disappeared round the corner. Are the two things connected? I wondered. I continued towards the house and, as I reached the garden gate, realised the phone that was ringing was mine.

I unlocked the door, stumbled in and picked up the receiver. It was Elisaveta. Her voice was trembling ... she was in tears. I've never heard her in tears before. She said she'd been trying to reach me all afternoon. My mother, believing me to be in Bury St. Edmunds, had tried phoning me at Elisaveta's. Elisaveta had undertaken to pass on the news: my father has died.

In a sort of stupor, I went upstairs, removed the little gold-coloured cloth from the bedside table and replaced it with the Cambridge University Cruising Club scarf my father gave me at Christmas – a month ago.

The evening's worn on – I'm losing track of time. I need to talk to someone face-to-face, someone nearby. I know I'm in shock but I still have my wits about me – enough to remember that this is the day Max and I were supposed to have gone to Bury St Edmunds. He should be at home – and even though it's getting late, I don't think he'll be surprised to hear from me ...

I've rung Max. He was there but said he couldn't come now – he had to walk the dog! Couldn't I find someone else?

X

Fear means unhappiness but it does not follow
from this that courage means happiness; not courage ... but
fearlessness with its calm, open eye and stoical resolution. Don't
force yourself to do anything ... And if you don't force yourself,
don't hanker after the possibilities of being forced ...

Franz Kafka, *Diaries,* Entry for 18 January 1922[29]

Max had backed off and it's only with hindsight that I worked out what was likely to have been going on with him. For the previous ten years at least, he had been greatly preoccupied with the writings of Franz Kafka and, in particular, with what he refers to as "the landscape of death" in the novel *The Castle.* In 1972, Max had published an essay "Thanatos – Zur Motivstruktur in Kafkas Schloß" that was to appear in English translation the same year as "The Undiscover'd Country – The Death Motif in Kafka's Castle". From the placing of the words in the titles of the two essays, one could say that the German version emphasises the psychoanalytic idea of the death instinct, whereas the English version attaches significance to a quote from *Hamlet* – the lines from Act III, scene 1 with which Max concludes the essay:

The undiscover'd country, from whose bourn
  No traveller returns...

Over the subsequent decade, Max prepared yet another version for inclusion in his 1985 collection of essays *Die Beschreibung des Unglücks (The Description of Misfortune*), entitled "Das unentdeckte Land – Zur Motivstruktur in Kafkas Schloß"; in other words, it substitutes "Thanatos" with the German translation of Shakespeare's lines followed by the second half of the original title. So what? one might ask. Why should this be important and what has it to do with the sequence of events at the end of January 1982?

On first getting to know one another, Max had assumed – understandably – that as a psychologist and therapist who had studied and trained in Germany, I would be well acquainted with the works of Sigmund Freud. But, as I explained in the course of our autumn conversations, this was not wholly the case.

By fluke rather than by choice, I had managed to get myself enrolled at the Psychology Institute within the Faculty of Philosophy and Social Sciences of the Free University, one of three departments of psychology in West Berlin at the time. It had been set up in 1968, in the wake of the student movement, thereby launching a radical new discipline known as Critical Psychology. All students "lucky enough" to acquire a place at the Institute were expected to devote the first four semesters of their five-year course gaining a solid grounding in the ideas of Karl Marx and Max Weber, author of *The Protestant Ethic and the Spirit of Capitalism*; furthermore, to eschew psychoanalytic literature unless for the purpose of critiquing its "bourgeois" content; and to demonstrate their grasp of the true meaning of the class struggle by taking part in protests, strikes and marches at every opportunity.

For me, brought up in a "nice" middle-class home, virtually apolitical, this experience had more than broadened my horizons; it was a revelation. Moreover, it wasn't until my final years in Berlin that I had dared pursue alternative interests – including the study of texts not sanctioned by the Institute. Thus it would appear that whilst I was still trying to get my head round Volume Three of *Das Kapital*, Max had been busy absorbing large portions of Freud.

It is in *Jenseits des Lustprinzips (Beyond the Pleasure Principle)*, first published in 1920, that Freud outlines his concept of the two primal instincts to which the human being is subject: Thanatos, the death instinct (*Todestrieb*) and Eros, the life instinct (*Lebenstrieb*). What is interesting about Max's essay on Kafka is that, whilst he alludes to these drives, it's not in terms of their fundamental opposition. Rather, he highlights the idea of Thanatos and Eros as one and the same: both destructive, both ultimately deadly. He goes on to illustrate the prevalence of the Thanatos motif throughout *The Castle*, including how it's reflected in the erotic relationship between the protagonist K. and his lover Frieda.

What this tells me about Max and his personal as well as scholarly preoccupations at the start of 1982 is that he took a very dark view indeed of the redeeming power of heterosexual love. And whilst he had experienced the pain of grief vis-à-vis his grandfather, faced with the same intensity of emotion in someone else – in this case, my grief over the death of my father– he felt compelled to withdraw. Furthermore, I maintain that as a sensitive person, Max would have been aware of the heightened sexual desire that so often accompanies feelings of grief, especially the grief of a woman over the death of a father she has loved; and that were he to attend to such neediness there and then, he would be putting himself in a compromising and, to him, unwelcome position.

No doubt the situation was further complicated by Max's negative feelings towards his own father – a father who'd been largely absent for the first three years of his son's life. Kafka, too – with whom Max identified in so many ways – had been at odds with his father throughout his life.

It looked to me that Max had been so overwhelmed by his own emotional conflicts, he had had to protect himself by keeping his distance: being the kind of man he was, he could hardly have done otherwise.

Whilst he remained much in my mind, I didn't hear from him again for two weeks.

XI

In the autumn of 1945 in a small town north of the Harz,
teaching has resumed. According to the school curriculum of
the 1940s, the subjects History, German and National History
(*Heimatkunde*) can no longer be taught. One can make suggestions
along the lines of what the British, the Americans and the Soviets –
the occupying forces in this part of the world — consider desirable.
Schoolteacher G., who has taught History for the past 36 years,
feels confused. He certainly has ideas about Germany, and about
German history. He advises his headmaster that for the time being,
the subject of History should be struck off the curriculum.

Oskar Negt and Alexander Kluge, *History and Obstinacy*
[*Geschichte und Eigensinn*], 1981[30]

I got in touch with my mother; she sounded reasonably steady. Apparently,
the last thing my father had said before leaving the house to post a letter the
previous afternoon was: "When I get back, I must write to Philippa. She's
organised, like me!"

A fair amount of organising lay ahead of me now. From experience, I
knew that this time of year – the dead of winter – is a particularly taxing
one for people with severe mental health problems. My patients were no
exception, which made it all the more important to do whatever necessary
to try and dispel the seasonal gloom that had settled on the day centre over
the previous couple of weeks.

Reluctant though I was to put in a request for more days off work, I had no choice but to get in touch with head office and arrange to take compassionate leave.

Friday, 29 January 1982

Left for London, where I'll be staying over the weekend ...

Saturday, 30 January 1982

I've developed acute pain in my left hip, making walking hard ... tried to put it to the back of my mind by going to Bond Street and buying a hat in the Yves St Laurent sale – a very becoming toque in black astrakhan (imagined the pleasure it would have given my father had he seen me in it). In the afternoon, went to the Edwin Lutyens Exhibition at the Hayward: it included a scale model of Lutyens' study, decked out in black, white and a stunning shade of emerald green. Gave me ideas for decorating my tiny library at home ...

Sunday, 31 January 1982

In the afternoon, met up with Mary Z. at the Riverside Studios for a reading by Italo Calvino. Surprised and delighted when he mentioned Ortega y Gasset's essay on love.[31] An amazing coincidence! I was re-reading that only the other day ...

This wasn't the only coincidence. I had gone to the reading with Mary Zuckerman, a friend of my ex-husband's from university days. Mary was a young relative of Sir Solly Zuckerman, the zoologist who, between 1969 and 1974, had taught at the University of East Anglia. It was here he was involved in setting up a school of environmental sciences, after which he had remained in Norfolk in retirement.

During the war, Zuckerman had been engaged on various research projects for the British government, including one to measure the impact of bombing on people and buildings. After the end of the war, he agreed to put together a report for Cyril Connolly, editor of the literary journal *Horizon* – a report to be entitled *On the Natural History of Destruction*. As part of his preparations, Zuckerman visited Cologne; he had been overwhelmed by the nature and scale of the devastation – so much so that he found himself unable to write the report.

Max took a great interest in Zuckerman's work and, as he told me, had made personal contact with him the previous September. Specifically, he wanted to know what Zuckerman might have included in the report had it been written. As Max was later to describe at the end of his first Zurich lecture, Zuckerman offered two abiding images of Cologne: its cathedral soaring from the ruins and a severed human finger in the rubble.

This would have resonated with Max's own sense of loss. A great cathedral left untouched, a beacon to bombers; the Christian message of comfort amidst so much destruction, a cruel commentary on the hollowness of religious symbols. Such images would also have been a sickening personal reminder: his father Georg had been part of the very system that had brought about that destruction.

It was when it came to the planning of an English-language version of *Luftkrieg und Literatur*, which included additional essays on Peter Weiss and Jean Améry, that Max had the idea of adopting Zuckerman's title.

He had first addressed the topic of large-scale, man-made destrustion in an essay published in 1982: "Zwischen Geschichte und Naturgeschichte. Über die literarische Beschreibung totaler Zerstörung" ("Between History and Natural History – On the Literary Description of Total Destruction").[32] Re-reading this now, it's clear that Max took a consistently dim view of writers who, through the medium of fiction, had tried to capture the impact of the aerial bombing of German cities in the Second World War.

In his opinion, those who had succeeded had done so via non-fictional reportage – the left-wing publisher and writer Victor Gollancz, for example, who in 1942 had predicted the murder of six million Jews by the Nazis, or the social critic and film-maker Alexander Kluge.

Kluge's *Neue Geschichten* (*New Histories*), published in 1977, is a collection of several hundred tales, some of them only a page long. The stories are embedded in an easily accessible prose style, the text interspersed with "non-literary" documents, charts and images. In light of the way Max was to arrange his own later literary works – especially the visual content – it's clear to me that he took inspiration from Kluge. What Max admired above all was Kluge's ability to present material without a trace of sentimentality – his refusal to mythologise.

XII

I thought his memory was like the other memories
of the dead that accumulate in every man's life – a vague
impress on the brain of shadows that had fallen on it in
their swift and final passage ...

Joseph Conrad, *Heart of Darkness*, 1902

Monday, 1 February 1982, Harberton

The sense of loss is keen. It's a fantasy, of course, but in this fantasy,
my father isn't dead – he's just taking a rest on his walk along the
Devon lanes ...

I made my way home via London – trying to restore a degree of "normality"
by doing what I had always done for solace: stay with friends, book a ticket
for the theatre and go to an art exhibition. There was a production of
Mozart's unfinished opera *Zaïde* at the Old Vic on Saturday evening; the
Japan Exhibition at the Royal Academy on Sunday morning, followed by
a reading at the Riverside Studios to be given by the poet Basil Bunting
that afternoon.

I got back to Norwich late at night, ready to fall into bed and be overtaken
by sleep for as long as may be. During the next few days, my job at the day
centre came to an end.

I faced up to the idea that recent events were bound to have had an
impact on my work; now, however, I found myself in a strange kind of limbo.

Saturday, 13 February 1982

The grief's working through and I experience everything in waves
– waves of grief, waves of anger; now and again, moments of clarity.
The overall sensation is one of bewilderment: I keep losing track,
forgetting what day it is. Last night, at 2am, it reached a pitch ... the
tears keep on welling up ...

How often with my patients I had enlarged on the effects of grief! It was
now a case of "physician, heal thyself".

During that week, there were times when I thought I might be losing
it altogether. No one had told me that grief had the power to make one
feel ill.

Sunday, 21 February 1982

Went to bed early to try and catch up on sleep. In a half-awake state,
I found myself thinking of Max and just then, he phoned ... He's not a
happy man – I could tell from his voice.

We were both in grief – both, I imagined at the time, for the loss of fathers.
Max's burden had surely been the heavier. Whilst his father had not yet died
– that didn't happen until much later, in June 1999 – on his return from the
war, Georg Sebald had disabused his son as to what a father should be. In a
sense, Max had also lost his mother: she hadn't been able to protect him from
the consequences of her husband's inner turmoil.

Sunday, 28 February 1982

Felt in a better mood today. Cleaned my bike, cooked an ox-tongue
and put it to press. Then, after a gin and lime, got out my cello. Tuned
the A and D strings but, in my enthusiasm, over-tuned the G string (!)
and it snapped ...

Another week had gone by with no word from Max – I guessed that, like me, he needed time to reflect. Then, on 3 March, came another phone call:

> ... he sounded diffident at first, then suddenly quite desperate ... said
> he absolutely had to talk ...

Oddly, it felt as though we'd been working things through in tandem and were now ready to pick up from where we'd left off. We agreed to meet the following week. Max finished the conversation by suggesting we didn't stay in – said he'd give some thought as to where we might go.

XIII

'... We come out of the dark and go into the dark again,
and in between lie the experiences of our life. But the beginning
and the end, birth and death, we do not experience; they have no
subjective character, they fall entirely in the category of
objective events, and that's that.'

Which was the Hofrat's way of administering
consolation ...

Thomas Mann, *The Magic Mountain* [*Der Zauberberg*], 1924[33]

I was conscious of needing to brace myself for the meeting with Max. I realised he had been waiting for an opportunity to unburden – for him, a rare undertaking – and thought I knew why he would want to do so in neutral surroundings.

I also thought I knew what was coming: the focus would be on him and, for the time being, my family concerns must be put on the back burner. My job, like that of Hofrat Behrens, director of the sanatorium in *The Magic Mountain*, was to adopt a sensible, clinical stance and "administer consolation". In the event – and in a way I least expected – Friday, 12 March turned out to be a remarkable evening.

Whether or not Max had given the matter of the venue further thought, the place we ended up in was unspeakably desolate: a big, modern hotel down by the station, tastelessly furnished, poorly lit, with vast, empty reception rooms: the epitome of soullessness. It felt like the East Anglian equivalent of an Edward Hopper interior.

We sat in a corner of the hotel lounge and ordered a drink, both of us on edge and unsure how to begin. Hesitantly at first, Max recounted the quandary he was in: he felt bitterly let down, he said – a strong sense of betrayal. For a man whose life was dedicated to words, it struck me he was finding it very hard to express himself.

Even as I write, I feel what I felt then: a dilemma. As a psychotherapist, you stay mum; as an ordinary person and friend, you want to react spontaneously. On top of that, as a memoirist, surely you're obliged to be truthful.

I listened – all I could do was listen and take note. At one point, to my astonishment, Max removed his glasses to wipe away the tears. It seemed we'd become companions-in-pain, each a mirror for the other, each unable to assuage the other's grief. As friends, the most natural thing to have done would be to put our arms round one another. But that was against our code – his and mine.

Next day, still very preoccupied with what had passed, I went to Bury St Edmund's to see Elisaveta and, from there, to Exeter for another funeral – this time, my grandmother's. It rained; it was cold; and my mother was distant.

On the train back to Norwich, I realised I was developing symptoms of flu. Nothing for it but retire to bed and get a proper rest – have time and space to process what had happened. No doubt the best place to do so was not in Norwich – or even in the UK – but on the Continent.

Over the following fortnight I felt useless, not up to doing anything constructive – except for this, a letter to Max.

Sunday, 21 March 1982

It seems like years since Friday the week before last. I've only just realised that the shock and distress of the past few months proved more than I could bear with equanimity; finally I just gave in. The fever's beginning to go down now but I'm physically and emotionally exhausted.

I still hope to go to Paris and Berlin in April but I'll have to be careful how I play it because I haven't yet confronted my employers with regard to the job situation. However, it's looking as though they'll get round the difficulties by making staff redundant and closing down the day centre altogether...

After our conversation, I was left with various ideas going round in my head that strike me as important. This is how I remember the main points you made: affection as the initial basis of a good relationship; the sense one can have of being repulsive to someone and the self-doubt this causes (where is self-esteem?); the feeling that you've been generous but not rewarded for being so; resentment as a natural consequence of that; the (to me, very surprising) announcement that you don't need anybody to admire.

I would question that last point: it raises the related idea that you yourself don't require admiration. And yet, from what I know of you, you take pride in what you do and who you are – justifiably so, in my opinion! On the other hand, I'm aware that we were talking about two different things – and there is a distinction: admiration and, just as importantly, affection. All in all, it seems to be about acceptance of oneself and others, doesn't it? I won't go into more ramifications. I simply wanted to record some of my thoughts – at the moment, having thoughts is healing, whereas feelings are dreadfully painful.

Zu welchem Zweck, dieser Abriß? In der Hoffnung, natürlich, daß er Deinerseits Resonanz findet. Wie es Beim Dialog üblich ist. *[What's the purpose of this summary? one might ask. Naturally, in the hope that it'll resonate with you. As is often the case with dialogue.]*

Re-reading the letter, it's clear to me now that Max had continued to be exercised by what had gone wrong in his relationships from childhood onwards.

* * * * *

Later that week, I learnt from the day centre committee that they'd decided to make me redundant. In fact, the news came as a relief, providing me with more energy to finalise plans for my European trip. A couple of days later, I heard from Max, who, as it happened, was going to be in Berlin at the same time as me: he had been invited to present a paper on Herbert Achternbusch.

Recently, there had been some alarming items in the national and international news: trouble was brewing in the South Atlantic. It was in Paris, on the evening of 3 April, shortly after leaving the Bouffes du Nord (where I'd had the good fortune to witness Peter Brook's "pared-down" production of *Carmen*) that I got wind of war having broken out in the Falklands.

Four days later, I continued on my way to Berlin to see old friends – one of them in particular, Irene Leverenz. I had met Irene in 1974 during my first year studying Psychology and she, Ethnology; we had been attending the same seminar and the subject, I remember, was human motivation.

Irene and I took an instant liking to each other. By chance, it turned out we were both looking for accommodation, and ended up finding apartments in the same street in Charlottenburg, either side of Savignyplatz. For the next thirty-two years, until her death from cancer in 2006, Irene was to remain one of my most stalwart friends. This included the years after I had moved back to the UK, during which time she had been engaged in lengthy periods of field study in the Sudan and Upper Egypt.

Besides being a true scholar – she wore her learning with enviable lightness – Irene enjoyed the good things of life: amongst her many talents, she was a brilliant conversationalist and an audacious cook. We also shared a passion for books and reading – friends would tease her about her vast home library. Sadly, she never met Max – and it was entirely my fault that she didn't. Nevertheless, when *Austerlitz* first appeared in German, it was Irene who sent me a copy.

That Easter, we celebrated with a splendid feast in the flat at No. 12 Knesebeckstrasse – with Irene's husband Konrad and a small circle of friends. Max was due to arrive at Berlin Tegel Airport late the following evening.

MINETTI	MINETTI
Du glaubst es nicht	You don't believe it
Ich bin berühmt	I am famous
ich war berühmt	I was famous
Minetti	Minetti
der sich der klassischen	who drew the line at the
Literatur verweigert hat	literary classics
Ich spielte den Lear in Lübeck	I played Lear in Lübeck
Shakespeare	Shakespeare
die Schauspielkunst	the art of acting
ist eine hinterhältige Kunst	is a devious art, my
mein Kind ...	child ...

Thomas Bernhard, *Minetti*, 1976 [34]

Tuesday, 13 April 1982, Berlin

Now I'm here, I still have that feeling I'm more at home in a foreign country, speaking another language ... What was it Max said the other day? He thought I should be doing some writing, using the insights I've gained from my experiences at home and abroad ...

    Went to a screening of *Der Zauberberg* [35] at Cinema Paris this evening – it brought back memories of times past, the journey over the mountains all those years ago and the encounter with Katia in her

long black dress, Aunt Erika hovering in the background ... I wonder
how Christine is ...

When she was twenty-one, my friend Christine became engaged to
Thomas Mann's grandson, Fridolin. Christine's mother, Frau Elisabeth
Heisenberg, who herself came from a distinguished family, had strong
notions of protocol and what constituted good behaviour; and shortly
before the official announcement of the engagement, she had asked me to
accompany the young couple to Zurich, acting as chaperone.

Before I set off from Munich with Christine and Frido, Frau Elisabeth
had left me in no doubt as to my duties: I was to ensure that, whilst
they might hold hands in public, there was to be no other close physical
contact, and strictly "no kissing around bedtime"! And this was 1965...

It had been a beautiful late summer when we made our way south,
stopping off for the night at the alpine retreat belonging to Frido's
uncle, the historian Golo Mann. As for sleeping arrangements, despite
the fact that Golo wasn't in residence at the time, there were only two
proper bedrooms – it went without saying, one for Christine and one for
Frido. To my delight, that meant I could have Golo's study, surrounded
by books. By the time I got to bed, however, I had been so exercised by
Frau Elisabeth's orders – to watch out for and intercept any surreptitious
exchanges of affection between the other two – that no matter how hard
I tried, I couldn't sleep. The solution was to select a volume from the
shelves and read. This was my first encounter with the poetry of Friedrich
Hölderlin.

Next day, after breakfast, we took advantage of the weather and went
for a short hike along the mountain path. There weren't any other walkers
– until, all of a sudden, coming towards us from the opposite direction was a
middle-aged man with an earnest look about him. He and Frido exchanged
polite greetings and, as soon as the walker was out of earshot, I asked Frido
whether this was someone he knew. "Friedrich Dürrenmatt!" he replied in
a hoarse whisper. Much later, I realised what drama had been lurking in this

chance encounter: Christine, daughter of Werner Heisenberg, on the cusp of her introduction to the family of Mann, bumping into the playwright Dürrenmatt taking his morning constitutional – the person who, just a few years earlier, had written his satirical play *Die Physiker* (*The Physicists*).

We continued on our journey to the Mann family home in the Alte Landstraße in Kilchberg – where Christine was to be vetted by her prospective grandmother-in-law, Katia, who had been a widow for the past ten years and still wore black in the afternoon.

All this had been a very long time ago. Now it was 1982 and here I was, back in Berlin, looking forward to a literary event of a rather different kind. In the afternoon of Wednesday, 14 April, Max delivered his paper at the Wissenschaftskolleg on Wallotstrasse. I had mentioned the occasion to various people, several of whom had been at a conference in Paris and who, like me, had just returned to Berlin: Uli Raulff was there, along with his friends Claus Rath and Uli Giersch. How many of the audience were Achternbusch aficionados, I'm not sure; the important thing was, though, that Max's paper went down well.

I was aware that Achternbusch, especially his idiosyncratic use of language, had always captivated Max. But I think there was another reason for his empathic understanding of this particular writer: they had grown up in the same region of Southern Germany, surrounded by the same Bavarian landscape with its mountains and dense forests. For both of them, the forest represented nature of a distinctive kind, nature that is indifferent to and unaffected by human affairs.

In this paper, "Die weiße Adlerfeder am Kopf: Versuch über den Indianer Herbert Achternbusch" ("The White Eagle's Feather on His Head: Herbert Achternbusch the Red Indian"),[36] Max likens Achternbusch to a shaman – the shaman who, in a state of ecstasy, goes on a journey towards death and beyond, returning home again in order to tell extraordinary tales "over a mug of beer". The white feather of the title, worn as a headdress, had special significance for Max: wings and plumage enable the shaman to access another dimension. To become a bird, or be guided by one, represents the ability to travel beyond familiar existence – and to return to it. I detect a similar train of thought in the lines written by Max that were later to serve as his epitaph:

Er wird Dich	*He will cover*
bedecken mit	*you with*
seinem Gefieder	*his plumage*
&	*&*
unter seinem	*under his*
Flügel dann	*wing then*
ruhest Du aus	*you will rest* [37]

A recurring theme in Achternbusch's scripts is memory and remembrance; and importantly, the difference between the two. Whereas memory is concerned with recollection of the past in present time, an act of remembrance makes present the past – as with the rites associated with mourning. This trope preoccupied Max throughout our conversations and is everywhere to be found in his writing: from his reflections on Sir Thomas Browne to his descriptions of walking in Corsica.

Another thread running through Max's life and writing was his interest in theatre – and not only from a literary point of view. As a student, he told me, he'd greatly enjoyed acting and had taken a number of small parts in university productions, including, in 1964, that of Snug the Joiner in Shakespeare's *A Midsummer Night's Dream*. Having myself once been chosen for the role of Helena (being tall, I met the requirements for a "painted maypole"), I knew the play well; it was therefore easy to imagine Max as Snug the Joiner – especially in the final act when Snug plays Lion:

Lion *You, ladies, you, whose gentle hearts do fear*
   The smallest monstrous mouse that creeps on floor,
   May now, perchance, both quake and tremble here,
   When lion rough in wildest rage doth roar.

Then know that I as Snug the joiner am
A lion fell, nor else no lion's dam;
For, if I should as lion come in strife
Into this place, 'twere pity on my life.[38]

In 1965, Max had gone on to direct a play: a German production of J.P. Donleavy's *Fairy Tales of New York*. And three years later, having moved to the UK, he directed *Leonce und Lena* by Georg Büchner.

Never a person to brag about his achievements, it was only much later that I discovered he had actually been offered a job in the Drama Department at the University of Bangor. The remit was to teach nineteenth and twentieth-century German and French drama via English translations and he had turned it down on the grounds that this would have made him feel even more like an exile. My view is that it was not the teaching of drama Max looked for so much as, literally, the doing of it. In the longer term, however, it seems to me this was an aspect of himself he tended to suppress – thereby not allowing himself to give further expression to his theatrical talents.

That being said, I wasn't surprised when he suggested that, after delivering his paper at the Wissenschaftskolleg, we spend the evening at the Freie Volksbühne for a performance of Klaus Michael Grüber's adaptation of *Faust*.

This production had been designed to coincide with the 150th anniversary of Goethe's death, and Grüber was one of Europe's most influential theatre directors. Sure enough, what Max and I witnessed that evening was a groundbreaking piece of theatre: a radically cut text, a minimal set and just four actors, dominated by Bernhard Minetti, then seventy-seven and still a towering force of the German stage; alongside a young amateur actress, Nina Dittbrenner, playing Gretchen. In this version of the play, the emphasis was on the story of the love between an old, old man and an innocent young girl. It was extremely moving. Grüber and Minetti had worked together before, notably on a production of Samuel Beckett's *Krapp's Last Tape*, which I had seen in Bremen in 1973; on that occasion, the collaboration proved equally memorable.

Six years later, in his introduction to *A Radical Stage: Theatre in Germany in the 1970s and 1980s*, Max was to cite Gruber's *Faust* as an example of the way

> ... *theatrical practice (had) redefined itself as a critical encounter with received precepts and materials ... pitch and balance of visual and verbal intensity in this production were such that all discussions concerning the legitimacy of theatre in our time were rendered superfluous ...*[39]

Perhaps another reason for Max's particular interest was the fact that in 1976, Thomas Bernhard had written a play specially for Minetti. In this piece, Minetti plays himself: as an ageing, clapped-out actor who has fetched up in Ostend, awaiting the arrival of a theatre director in the lounge of an old hotel that has seen better days. He rails and rages against nature and humankind alike, harking back to the only role with which he has ever really been able to identify, Shakespeare's Lear. Max revered the writing of Thomas Bernhard; and of Shakespeare's plays, it was *King Lear* that touched him above all.

The intimacy of this production of *Faust* continued to absorb us as we left the theatre and walked out into the evening air. I sensed a hiatus, something to do with finding ourselves in Berlin together – both, simultaneously, at home and away from home. We made our way back towards the Ku'damm and into the Knesebeckstraße – my old stamping ground, full of memories. Max's hotel was further along to the east. We arrived at the huge entrance door to Irene's block of apartments. What now? I was tempted to invite him in to meet her – but hesitated: I'd failed to mention to her that I was going to the theatre – or at least that I was going *with* someone.

There was an awkward silence, which was broken by Max, saying he was tired and would therefore go back to his hotel. The parting was rather formal – not even a farewell peck. "No kissing around bedtime" ...

Following my return to Norwich, something peculiar happened. The stress had caught up with me and manifested in what I can only describe as a kind of paralysis, strangely similar to the words put in the mouth of Max

Ferber in *The Emigrants*: "pain of a kind I had never experienced before".[40] The staff at the Norfolk and Norwich Hospital took it to be a slipped disc, told me to rest and sent me home by ambulance. For the next week or so, all I could do was lie on my back and wait for the pain to subside.

During this time, between May and July, Max and I were out of touch.

XV

The lyf so short, the craft so longe to lerne,
Th'assay so hard, so sharp the conquerynge ...

Geoffrey Chaucer, *The Parliament of Fowls*, 1382

As soon as I was able to walk without discomfort, I started making brief excursions into Norwich. One day at the start of July, I was in town doing some shopping when, outside The Body Shop, I bumped into Max.

April and Berlin seemed light years away. Even so, the gap was swiftly bridged. With a knowing smile, he told me he'd just got back from Deauville. "On holiday?" I enquired. "Not exactly, no. I needed to do some research – for an idea I've got." I was intrigued by the combination of "Deauville" and "research". "Why Deauville? What sort of research?" I ventured. "The casino!" came the cryptic reply; then, before I'd had time to ask more questions, "What about you these days? Are you doing any writing?" Yes, I was thinking about it, I told him – but rather than go into detail standing in the street, perhaps we could meet again soon, somewhere a bit less public. Max promised to get in touch towards the end of the week.

Saturday, 10 July 1982

Max has just phoned to explain why he didn't come and see me yesterday as intended. He hadn't been able to because on Thursday, he'd had a car accident. Whilst not injured, he's badly shaken – reluctantly, he admitted he'd escaped with his life by a matter of seconds ...

No, Max, not you! I can't bear the idea of him dying, not now, not like that ... He has so much still to do, so much writing ...

Mercifully, in Max's case, it hadn't come to this. But it took another week for his news to sink in. Whilst it's hard to judge whether the accident had had anything to do with the vehicle's left-hand steerage, I do remember him telling me that he was in the habit of going over to Germany to buy his cars because it tended to work out cheaper.

There was, however, another aspect. Many years later, it came back to me that Max had developed a reputation for being averse to technology – and when at the wheel, his mind was quite likely to have been on other things.

Whatever the case, when I'd met him in town the previous week, there was no doubt Max had been very preoccupied with the outcome of his trip to Deauville. And having renewed contact, I had no wish to lose touch again. On 17 July, I wrote to him in German:

I was shattered by what you told me: about the accident. Perhaps I tend to be oversensitive in that regard because of what happened eighteen years ago. One of my closest friends at university lost her life in a car accident – and although I realise it's completely irrational, that's why I've never been keen to learn to drive ...

Another thing: I wanted to say how much I'd like to carry on with our conversations about "post-Freudian" mourning and melancholia. You should definitely write something on the subject.

Now that I have time to myself, I'm actually starting to enjoy being jobless – though there's no knowing how long that's going to last. In any case, the building work has started and should be finished by the middle of August.

Earlier today, George and Sue (who also live in Ampthill Street) asked me if I'd like to join them in renting a house in the Dordogne sometime

around the end of August/beginning of September. Tempting! As the day's
gone on, it occurred to me you too could do with a quiet break, have time
for writing ...

No other news at the moment. Things will just take their course.
Do hope you're feeling better – let me know, won't you!

Two days later, he turned up. He struck me as more than usually distant,
which I put down to the accident and delayed shock. It may also have been to
do with the fact that an old friend of mine had just arrived from Berlin. This
meant we couldn't have a one-to-one and that Max, polite and circumspect
as ever, felt unable to talk freely.

Monday, 9 August 1982

Thinking over my friendship with Max, I'm aware that, since
the spring, he seems to have beaten a retreat ... as he readily
acknowledges, he's prone to melancholy – is by nature reclusive and
solitary. Even so...

Three weeks later, I bumped into him again in town, outside the Hungate
Bookshop (at that time, in Princes' Street). As it happened, he was in rather
a hurry, so we didn't stop long to talk.

Saturday, 4 September 1982

Max has been round ... so this is what it's all been leading up to!
He asked if I'd be willing to "take him on", as he put it – in other
words, offer him therapy! I'm not sure whether he envisages this
as a way of dealing with current difficulties or as something more
far-reaching, e.g. to arrive at a better understanding of what
makes him tick ...

Naturally, I was flattered by Max's request; at the same time, I was taken
aback. Apart from the fact that in terms of therapeutic skills, I wasn't sure I

was up to it, other issues came into play – the most obvious having to do with the nature of our relationship up to that point.

As a professional therapist – even one who was currently unemployed! – I was obliged to adhere to a code of ethics in which psychotherapy between friends is deemed strictly "not in order". This was my dilemma: were I to go along with the request, change tack and become his therapist, I would be duty bound to forego the personal friendship (but still liable to break the rules). On the other hand, were I to turn him down as a patient, it might not sit easily with Max – indeed, I ran the risk of losing sight of him altogether.

Whilst Max appeared to sense that I'd been put on the spot, he remained curiously insistent. Even at the best of times, he didn't put much trust in other people, he said; but now he needed help and had complete faith that I was the person to provide it. Aware of the danger of complying with his wishes – alongside the temptation to do just that – I resorted to a delaying tactic: I told him I wanted time to think about it.

A week later, I was due to attend a job interview entailing a trip via London. Whilst I'd come to feel fairly despondent about the whole business of job-hunting, the prospect of a weekend away was another matter.

I took full advantage of the break. On Saturday morning, I went to the Tate to see the de Chirico Exhibition and then joined my friends Wolfgang Koethe and Rita Pokorny. At this time, Rita was working for the BBC Overseas Service at Bush House and, over supper, she mentioned that her department was always on the lookout for interesting contributions. Would I consider submitting a piece for their current series *Letter from* ..., a fifteen-minute slot that involved the description of a city? In this case, the city might be Norwich and the script would need to be in German. No guarantee of acceptance, but even so. Buoyed up by the idea – and the challenge – of getting started on the writing, I told her I'd try and put something together.

Whatever the outcome of Friday's job interview, Max's suggestion – that I follow my literary star – suddenly seemed by far the more attractive option.

XVI

No idea is so outlandish that it should not be considered
with a searching, but at the same time, a steady eye.

Winston Churchill,
from *A Speech Delivered to the House of Commons*, 4 June 1940

On Sunday afternoon, revived by the weekend if not by the experience of
Friday's interview, I caught the train home. As always, the journey provided
me with thinking time. By the time the train drew into Norwich at Thorpe
Station, I'd made up my mind to keep going with the job search. Which
was why, on Monday morning, I went along to the City Library to scan
the newspapers. There on the Situations Vacant page of *The Guardian*,
something unusual caught my attention:

Churchill College, Cambridge
seeks to appoint a
Chaplain/Counsellor

The idea of myself as a potential priestess was so preposterous that I decided
to concoct an application.

Monday, 4 October 1982

No word from Max – what's going on with him, I wonder? Am still
preoccupied by that request for psychotherapy ... to be sure, he has

emotional conflicts. But alongside those, I sense that he's deeply afraid of his physicality ... despite the care and attention he pays to his outward appearance, I can't help feeling he's somehow at war with his body ...

Monday, 18 October 1982

... I was just contemplating the plant Max had given me, realising how well it would go in the new bathroom, when he knocked at the door. We hadn't seen each other for six weeks, but the old warmth returned immediately. It's a delight to see him again – the familiar mixture of delicacy and perceptiveness. On top of which, he seems incredibly pleased about the way my house is progressing, enthuses about it almost as though it were his own! His eyes positively lit up as he went round the rooms. Whatever is he thinking?

Basically, 28 Ampthill Street was a late Georgian/early Victorian terrace house consisting of "two up, two down" with an additional cellar and loft-space, plus a tiny upstairs dressing room that I had converted into a study. The recent alterations included an extension of the kitchen, long and narrow like a ship's galley; and a complete overhaul of the bathroom. I had had the idea of "sinking" the bathtub below floor-level, repositioning it under the eaves. This – and the arrangement of the study to accommodate the books – appealed to Max no end.

Tuesday, 19 October 1982

Three hundred years ago to the day Sir Thomas Browne had died – Sir Thomas, whose preoccupations included order and harmony. I've commemorated him by beginning to write my piece for the BBC. It took all afternoon, a lot of coffee – plus a break with the latest copy of *Vogue* – to complete two sides; I still need to do a third. Don't think I'd appreciated the effort involved in original, imaginative composition before now – writing for a readership is obviously not the same as keeping a private diary! In order to do it well, it seems all the more necessary to read as well as write; listen to music; absorb stimuli actively rather than coincidentally ...

Sunday, 24 October 1982

At last I can relax; have overcome resistance and managed to complete my piece for the BBC. Feel OK about it except that I've just caught a cold and seem to have lost my voice. Even so, I've made a recording of it and, allowing for traces of English accent, it doesn't sound too bad – the general effect is quite lyrical ...

Monday, 25 October 1982

It's just occurred to me that writing out of past personal experience, the material can always be expanded in retrospect. The disadvantage is that memory's so unreliable ... the actual process of writing feels a bit like a therapy session – work with and on oneself ...

The current spur comes from various sources, not least the conversations with Max; very discreetly, he's been prompting me to do something with my literary skills. On second thoughts, perhaps there's something else going on, i.e. he's giving himself a prompt to apply his *own* literary skills ...

As a media novice, I suppose I had half-expected what was to become of my *Letter from Norwich*: the BBC already had enough material to fill that particular slot. But this didn't dent my enthusiasm – maybe, with a bit of judicious editing, the piece could be adapted, used in another way. Since Max had been instrumental in getting me started, I decided to send him a copy of the cassette recording. I trusted him to be both critical and kind.

No way had I bargained for what happened next. A few days later, I received a letter from the Senior Tutor of Churchill College, Cambridge. Dr Colin Campbell wrote to inform me that I'd been shortlisted for the advertised post and was inviting me to attend for interview. He explained that this would involve an overnight stay – offering candidates a chance to meet representatives from all sections of the College community: academic and administrative.

I had continued to wonder about the significance of that slash between the words "Chaplain" and "Counsellor" but now took steps to find out by phoning a friend of mine, Nicholas Garthwaite, who had been an undergraduate at Churchill during the 1970s. He confirmed that some years before, there had indeed been a terrific rumpus over the siting and building of the College Chapel, bringing about the resignation of the molecular biologist Francis Crick. Nicholas suggested I would do well to take Crick and Watson's *The Double Helix* to read on the train.

In 1961, Crick, an avowed agnostic, had submitted his resignation to the founder of the College, Sir Winston Churchill, on the grounds that as a forward-thinking academic institution with an emphasis on the natural sciences and engineering, the existence of a college chapel – even an "all-purpose", multi-faith chapel – was wholly inappropriate. The ensuing debate, within the College and beyond, proved lengthy and divisive. The controversy went on for another six years until eventually, in October 1967, a chapel was completed – sited as far away as possible from the main body of the College on the western boundary, way out across the playing fields.

There were seven candidates for the post. We were given a very warm welcome; and over the following two days, mercilessly grilled. By the time I left Cambridge on Friday, in addition to the formal interview, I counted up having had sixteen informal ones with every conceivable "special member" of the College: from the Master to the Head Porter, the President of the Senior Common Room to the Housekeeper. All in all, a bizarre experience.

I had imagined that because Churchill was one of the newer colleges – and certainly its architecture reflected the taste of the 1960s – there would be less observance of Oxbridge tradition. Besides its strong academic record, it prided itself on having a more relaxed outlook; all the same, the old hierarchies were just as much in evidence.

Sunday, 21 November 1982

I spent all day yesterday thinking it through and finally convinced myself I haven't a hope in hell ... then this morning came a call from Colin Campbell asking me if I'd mind returning on Tuesday to meet members of the College Council. Well, of course I wouldn't mind!

I went back to Cambridge to find that the panel had whittled down the shortlist to three candidates. By the end of the day, still no decision had been reached. Under the circumstances, it was just as well I had other things to think about: I hadn't forgotten about the cassette recording – had Max liked it? I wondered. Also, my mother was coming to stay.

Thursday, 25 November 1982

It's a beautiful morning. Ma's arrival has done much to contribute to the general mood of cheerfulness. As has a visit from Max ...

Over the previous year and a half, Max had been in the habit of turning up without warning. On the few occasions when someone else was in evidence – my friend from Berlin, for example, and now my mother – the atmosphere changed completely. I noticed how, in company, Max assumed an altogether different persona; and whilst he never failed to make himself amenable, there were certain things that could not be talked about – notably, himself.

This occasion was no exception. The three of us spent a pleasant afternoon chatting about this and that; and then Max asked for an account of my Churchill experience. It was a good excuse to weigh up the situation. I launched in, telling how, initially, looking at the list of names in the

Porter's Lodge, I had assumed I was the only female candidate. It had then emerged that out of the seven of us, four were "reverends", one of them a woman. Being neither a priest nor a man, neither an Oxbridge graduate nor from a student counselling background, I hadn't fitted into any common category.

There had been a lot to take in in a relatively short time. I remembered odd details such as the signs on the loo doors along the main walkway into the building: "Men" and "Ladies". Once again, this made me consider the knotty issue of the gender ratio; also – more immediately – what sort of image I should project at High Table on the first evening. Before going along for preprandial drinks, I had had a decision to make: whether or not to apply nail varnish; and, if so, coloured or clear (in the end, I had settled for clear). The token female postgraduate selected to quiz me over dinner had informed me she was researching the harmful effects of intestinal worms. On my other side was a student intent on engaging me in earnest conversation; this required delicate handling – he had a calamitous speech impediment...

I paused. Max was finding all this very much to his taste. "Ah, these Oxbridge eccentrics..." he began. Back in 1968, Max himself had had dealings with the University of Cambridge. Wishing to turn his attention to the study of Alfred Döblin, he had applied for a three-year Junior Research Fellowship at Sidney Sussex College. In support of his application, he requested a reference from the philosopher Theodor Adorno, with whom he had been in correspondence since April 1967. To Max's chagrin, the reference never materialised and the idea of pursuing his doctorate in Cambridge had had to be abandoned.

"In my view," he continued, "the College would do well to offer you the job." He had excelled himself in graciousness – not lost on my mother, who had clearly taken a shine to him. At the same time, I couldn't help thinking that were Churchill to accept me, it would be a struggle to maintain our friendship at its current level from a distance – there would be no more surprise visits and probably no more literary mentoring...

Friday, 3 December 1982

No news from Churchill – makes me nervous. In the end, I decided it wouldn't hurt to forget all this for a bit and go to London. Time to think on the coach – about Norwich and Cambridge – and what if...

Saturday, 4 December 1982

When I got back from London this afternoon, there was still no letter from Churchill. Felt fidgety and disconsolate so went and had a bath – was in it when the phone rang. It was Colin Campbell. He offered me the job ...

... which, stark naked and soaking wet, I accepted.

PART TWO

A LABYRINTH OF PATHS

He decided to follow a path that was well marked ... Unfortunately,
none of the numerous existing paths coincided with the theoretical
direction he had selected; he was therefore confined, from the start,
to one of two possible detours. Besides, every path looked winding
and discontinuous – separating, reuniting, constantly interlacing,
even stopping short in a briar patch. All of which obliged him to make
many false starts, hesitations, retreats, posed new problems at
every step, forbade any assurance as to the general
direction of the path he had chosen.

Alain Robbe-Grillet, *Le Voyeur*, 1955

I

Some of the lighter-coloured trees seemed to drift
like clouds above the parkland. Others were of a deep,
impenetrable green ... Yet the densest and greenest was for me
the Somerleyton yew maze, in the heart of the mysterious estate,
where I became so completely lost that I could not find the way
out again until I resorted to drawing a line with the heel of my
boot across the white sand of every hedged passage that had
proved to be a dead end.

W.G. Sebald, *The Rings of Saturn*
[*Die Ringe des Saturn*], 1995[41]

The day before setting off for Churchill, I had been to collect some things
from the dry cleaners when I ran into Max. We didn't talk long – long
enough, however, to prompt pangs of regret: I was about to move on and,
inevitably, my transfer to Cambridge was going to affect our relationship. Or
so I thought.

The first few weeks in the College were more disjointed than anticipated.
As people were eager to point out, my post represented a radical break with
tradition – up to then, Oxbridge colleges had always employed chaplains.
This was the first appointment of its kind; with no precedents and no job
description to serve as a guide, I would need to be inventive.

It took me a while to establish a proper work pattern. Therefore, to
clear my head, I realised I should make a point of returning to the house in

Norwich at regular intervals; 28 Ampthill Street was my bolthole and fuel station. One such weekend, I heard from Max.

Friday, 18 March 1983

... out of the blue, a phone call from Max. How did he know I was back in Norwich? I asked him. "Seventh sense!" came the reply. He'd like to come and see me, he said, but, being without the car, he'd have to find another way of getting here ...

Sunday, 20 March 1983

Max rang no less than three times! First, to say he wouldn't be able to get here, then to say he would; finally, to cancel again – until I suggested ordering a taxi ... Once here, he stayed more than seven hours, presenting a long catalogue of reasons as to why everything was (inevitably) going to go from bad to worse. I found myself becoming more and more confused – it was like being lost in a maze ...

As a last resort, I took the Socratic position, providing a consistent counterpoint to Max's train of thought; so, for example, instead of going along with his fear (that everything would turn out badly and "anyway, the prospect is grim"), I made it my business to stick to my guns: all change involves unpredictability, movement, dynamics. He took some convincing but in the end ...

... through dialogue, we established that Max has been working from the premise that the only steps into the future for which he could plan were those with a negative outcome – "the positives, thank God, will always come as a surprise," he put in – as though making the point that the energy needed for dealing with a positive turn of events had to take one unawares, burst in on one unexpectedly.

I offered him the view that, over time, he had become the prisoner of a mindset so inflexible that it was threatening to undo him. He took this on board and tried to deflect the gist of the conversation to more enjoyable matters.

> Briefly, the talk turned to gardens; then reverted to Max ... I needed to assure him that no, he wasn't "boring" me – rather the opposite, in fact: I was interested in what he was saying; also that, generally speaking, my interest in and curiosity about people had preceded my choice of profession. He responded by saying he only became interested in people for what they could give him, but that in the context of work he got very little feedback. This left me wondering whether he ever really did give of himself. All he wanted, he said in that lugubrious way he had, was peace. I thought he was being funny. But then he went on, " ... deep peace – something I did once find..."

His voice trailed away and he appeared to have gone into a reverie. I'd been tempted to persist, but then didn't: it was none of my business, this wasn't therapy and I wasn't his therapist.

> Max is very unclear. The trouble is, this caution of his is catching – and I'm dogged by it, too; can't bring myself to take the bull by the horns ... I find myself getting irritated by his indecisiveness even though the irritation is always tempered by affection.

II

Zwar die tägliche Scheußlichkeit
stört,
doch sie wundert uns wenig.

True, the daily horrors are
disturbing
but hardly surprise us.

Hans Magnus Enzensberger,
Der Untergang der Titanic – eine Komödie, 1978[42]

The apparent impasse brought about by my not entering into a formal therapy contract with Max was to have unforeseen consequences.

Back in 1981, about six weeks after we had first been introduced to each other, I had caught a bus out to Poringland and gone to see Max at home – the one and only occasion I visited him rather than he me. He showed me round the garden, talking animatedly as he did so. It became obvious that here was a place of refuge: tending his plants and devising schemes – how to conserve energy, harness solar power – were a good way of distancing himself from what he thought of as the increasingly maddening power politics of academia.

By 1983, he had begun to discover another antidote to the frustrations of university life. This was writing – writing of a different kind than that required for the production of academic papers. He told me he didn't wish anyone else to know what he was doing and, for the time being at least, would prefer the details of his literary activities to be kept between the two of us.

On 20 April, aware that Max was soon to go on sabbatical leave, I wrote to him from Cambridge:

I'm getting in touch on the strength of having just re-read your Achternbusch article (in the latest issue of Manuskripte) – *the paper you gave in Berlin last year. It's such a lovely, dense piece of writing and I wanted you to know how glad I am to have the text …*

The start of the summer term coincided with the weekend of the annual Cambridge Poetry Festival. Two poets of particular interest to me, James Fenton and Hans Magnus Enzensberger, had been billed to feature at the opening event.

In 1965, Enzensberger, together with Karl Markus Michel, had been responsible for setting up the cultural magazine *Kursbuch*, to which I had subscribed throughout my time in Berlin. Some years later, as editor of the book series *Die Andere Bibliothek*, it was he who was to play such a crucial role in the promotion of Max's literary work.[43]

The paths were crossing.

I had come back from the poetry reading and remembered that Max had mentioned some poems of his own he wanted me to see. My letter goes on:

The other impetus for getting in touch comes from having been to some of the events at the Cambridge Poetry Festival last weekend, where I met Hans Magnus Enzensberger: he's just done a magnificent English translation of his own most recent work … We had a short exchange and managed to establish several points about translation, poetry and parallels between poetic language and the language of psychotherapy.

And then I thought of you, because I seem to remember you telling me about your own recent poetry. Would it be presumptuous of me to ask if I might read it?

III

I hear those voices that will not be drowned …

Montagu Slater, *Peter Grimes*, 1945[44]

April was coming to an end and May was imminent. It would soon be Max's birthday and the 65th anniversary of my father's – the dates virtually coincided. Dates had always been important to me; and in my work, too, I had noticed how dates hold special meaning for people, were often associated with nostalgia or regret for the past; anxiety or hope for the future.

The near-coincidence of the two birthdays started me thinking about the very circumstances into which my father – and Max – had been born: about war and its aftermath. Whilst I was growing up, my mother had always become intensely irritated when my father began talking about his experiences as a soldier; if ever he tried, she would pounce on him, telling him to "shut up". This was nothing compared to the way the youth of Germany had been kept in the dark about the Nazi past; nevertheless, for the most part, I was also ignorant. In retrospect, I realise this had something in common with what Max said about the behaviour of his parents' generation.

Although I had never lived in Cambridge, the names of the streets and the location of the colleges were already familiar to me – the reason being that the city had been of key importance in the lives of both my parents.

My mother was sent to The Perse, a boarding school for girls, and had subsequently done her teacher training at Homerton College. Likewise, as a boy of eight, my father had been packed off from home to live with his uncle and aunt and attend King's College Choir School. From there, he moved to public school, Dover College in Kent; and in October 1936, back to Cambridge to read for the Modern Languages Tripos at Pembroke. No sooner had he graduated than war broke out. But before he left to join the fighting, hoping he would live to return, he and my mother became engaged.

It was 1940. My father had joined the 1st Essex Regiment serving in North Africa (Tobruk), and was later to become a member of Major General Orde Wingate's Chindits in Burma, an experience he would never forget. It was only during those sailing holidays alone with my father in the fifties that he had spoken to me in any detail about his time in the Far East – always emphasising "the good times", never referring to the level of physical and mental trauma he had sustained.

Peter, the youngest of five children, was born in Hutton, Essex during the night of 17 May 1918. According to my grandfather's account, this coincided with the start of the last German air raid over East Anglia – that is, the last raid of the First World War. Another report states that the raid took place two days later.[45] However the case may be, the point remains: my father had begun his life to the sound of one World War and, as a young man of twenty-two, had had to take leave of his fiancée to do his duty in the Second. Not unlike the young couple, Georg and Rosa Sebald.

For Max, too, both in life and in his writing, dates were important – often imbued with something like talismanic significance. Against the backdrop of memories recalled, the precise details of days and years stand out like punctuation marks. Similarly terrifying circumstances had prevailed around the time of his birth – more particularly, within two days of his conception.

The third part of *After Nature*, "Dark Night Sallies Forth", begins with a meditation on prehistory, then fast forwards to the twentieth century by means of images conjured up through photographs: his grandparents' wedding in 1907 (Grandmother dressed "in a black taffeta dress/with a bunch of paper flowers, Grandfather/in his uniform, brass-embellished/

helmet on his head"); the next generation, by a school photograph of 1917 that includes his father; and then a picture taken in a botanical garden in Bamberg one summer day in 1943. The photograph depicts a swan with its reflection on the black surface of the water – "the perfect emblem of peace"; trees and plants, their species carefully named – leaving "an impression/that is somehow un-German"; and two people, Max's parents. Mother displays "a lightness she was/later to lose"; and Father "too, it seems, with no cares".

It was on this day, 27 August 1943, that Georg and Rosa Sebald had taken leave of each other: Georg, a professional soldier, was about to depart for Dresden "of whose beauty his memory, as he/remarks when I question him,/retains no trace". The episode is recorded again in the poem *In Bamberg*, written and dated "May 1996, May 1997", i.e. within Max's fifty-second year:

Ein Stück	*A little way*
flußaufwärts	*further upstream*
droben im Hain	*up at the Hain*
spazieren der Schorsch	*Park Schorsch*
und die Rosa an einem	*and Rosa are taking*
Augustnachmittag	*a stroll one August*
des dreiundvierziger	*afternoon in '43*
Jahrs im leichten	*she in a light*
Staubmantel bzw.	*dust-cloak he*
die Trachtenjoppe	*with his traditional jacket*
über die Schulter	*slung over his*
gehängt. Beide	*shoulder. They*
scheinen mir	*both seem happy*
glücklich, sorglos	*to me, carefree*
zumindest und viel	*at least and a good*
jünger jedenfalls wie	*deal younger than*
ich es jetzt bin.	*I am now.*[46]

During the night of 28 August, there had been a massive air attack on Nuremberg. Rosa had planned to return to her parents' home in the Allgäu the next day, 29 August – as it happens, the very day, thirty-eight years later, that I first met Max. Her train got no further than Fürth, from where she could see Nuremberg, five miles away, in flames. She travelled on, reaching Bad Windsheim – the spa town in Franconia and birthplace of the botanist and zoologist Georg Wilhelm Steller. Here, Rosa had an acquaintance with whom to stay and wait until the worst was over. It was then that she realised she was pregnant with her second child.

Over the following eighteen months, there was no let-up in the scale and intensity of destruction, including the area around Wertach. The nearby town of Sonthofen was subject to two aerial bombing raids. Max was not yet one year old.

Allusions to the impact of the raids can be found throughout Max's writing. In *The Rings of Saturn* (1995), he focuses on the raids over Germany as imagined by an Englishman, William Hazel. Hazel, who now works as a gardener at Somerleyton Hall, tells the narrator how, as a youngster, he had watched the bomber squadrons heading out over Somerleyton and "night after night ... pictured in my mind's eye the German cities going up in flames, the firestorms setting the heavens alight, and the survivors rooting about in the ruins ..."[47]

By April 1945, the Allies were closing in and the German war effort was in a state of terminal collapse. In the course of his third Zurich lecture, Max recalls how he himself, as a boy of eight, saw the town of Sonthofen still bearing scars from the air raids and later, as a teenager, wondering whether these had been an act of God:

... when I moved with my parents and siblings from my birthplace of Wertach to Sonthofen, 19 kilometres away, nothing seemed as fascinating as the presence of areas of waste land here and there among the rows of houses ... few things were so clearly linked in my mind with the word "city" as mounds of rubble, cracked walls, and empty windows through which

you saw the empty air. On 22 February and 29 April 1945, bombs had been dropped on the totally insignificant little market town of Sonthofen, probably because the place contained two large barracks for the mountain troops and the artillery, as well as an establishment known as the Ordensburg, one of three training colleges set up for the formation of the new Fascist elite directly after the Nazis came to power. As for the air raids on Sonthofen, I remember when I was fourteen or fifteen asking the parson who taught religious education ... how we could reconcile our ideas of divine providence with the fact that neither the barracks nor the Ordensburg had been destroyed during this air raid, only, and as if in place of them, the parish church and the church of the hospital foundation, but I do not remember what he said in reply ...[48]

Parallels and coincidences. One such was that, living within seventy miles of each other at this stage of the war, were the two families: Sebald and Heisenberg. Due east of Sonthofen, at the northernmost tip of the Walchensee (Lake Walchen) in the Bavarian Alps, lies the village of Urfeld. Before the war, Werner Heisenberg had bought a property there. The house, which had previously belonged to the Impressionist painter Lovis Corinth and his wife Charlotte, is a substantial wooden chalet perched high up on the mountainside with a breathtaking view over the treetops and across the water.

Between late April and early May, Heisenberg, a fit forty-three-year-old and father of six, had taken his bike and toured the Allgäu, including the area around Sonthofen. As he recorded in his diary, air raids were taking place on a more or less daily basis.

On 20 April, he goes from Waldsee to Leutkirch, American fighter planes roaring overhead. From a sheltered spot near a little chapel, he watches as Memmingen, a town less than forty miles north of Wertach, is destroyed:

... Huge plumes of smoke and the sound of the blast; glad I didn't go via Memmingen. In Krugzell in the Iller Valley, about 9 km north of Kempten,

I find an inn and have a decent meal, followed by a long nap under the trees on a glaciofluvial hummock. From there one gets a panoramic view of the Allgäu Alps, including the mountains around Sonthofen, where I did my stint of training with the mountain brigade seven years ago. At 5, head off in the direction of Kaufbeuren. Cloudless sky. Having already done 50 km today, the uphill climb from the Iller Valley is hard going. Arrive in Kaufbeuren around 8 in the evening, fight for a glass of tea in the overcrowded station waiting room. Am hungry – beginning to feel the strain of the past few days. Catch the 10 o'clock train for Schongau where I have time to spare; from 1 to 5 in the morning, pace up and down in the waiting room. It's full of youngsters in SS uniform; from the Balkans, probably. Fearing for my bike and bags, I don't dare fall asleep ...[49]

A couple of days later, he's back in Urfeld. He paints the scene: it's a Sunday and his wife, Elisabeth, has baked a cake. The older children are out on the terrace, playing in the sun; the baby, Christine, is asleep indoors.[50] It's as in peacetime – no sound of low-flying aircraft. Even so, as Heisenberg writes, at the Fischer am See Hotel down by the lake, a regional officer training college has set up its headquarters. However it might seem, Urfeld is "a Nazi hotbed" and many of the locals are secretly making plans to escape.

The very next morning, as Heisenberg works on his vegetable patch, bomber squadrons fly over Urfeld, heading east. He bikes over to Sachenbach to fetch the milk. The ball bearings are defective, meaning that from now on, he'll have to use the other bicycle. He thinks about what else needs to be done to weather the situation and decides that his priority is to lay in enough food supplies. In the afternoon, he digs a hole in the garden where he'll be able to hide a crate of tinned food. On the radio, there's news of fighting in Ulm and Regensburg; also, Berlin has been surrounded – the Führer's in the city.

According to Max, 29 April is one of the dates that Sonthofen was bombed. In his 2001 essay "Moments musicaux", we hear how

Zobel, the music teacher ... was also organist of the parish church of St Michael, from which he barely escaped with his life on Sunday 29 April 1945 when the tower suffered a direct hit during High Mass. For an hour, I was told, the music master wandered around among the bombs still exploding everywhere in the lower part of town and the falling buildings, until just as the all-clear sounded he entered the sick-room where his wife had been lying for months. He was covered from head to foot with plaster dust and looked like the spectre of the catastrophe that had befallen S.[51]

For Werner and Elisabeth Heisenberg, that day had begun calmly. It was their wedding anniversary, which they had hoped to be able to celebrate in peace and quiet. But they need provisions and Werner knows that, despite its being Sunday, the store in Kochel – a town about two and a half miles away – will be open until mid-afternoon. When he gets to the shop, there's a long queue and he realises there will be several hours to wait. He phones Elisabeth who comes by bike to join him, bringing food so that they can take turns standing in the queue. The town is crawling with soldiers, SS officers and foreign labourers; and, at the station, he sees "a train full of prisoners from Dachau – they looked starving and terribly pale ..."

Whilst Elisabeth stands in line at the store, Werner goes off to the hill behind the station and lies in the sun. From there, he picks out the signs of the first grenade hits in the area, along the stretch between Murnau and Ohlstadt. Around midday, the couple go for a walk through Kochel and the next thing they know, they've run into First Lieutenant Schuster. Schuster describes how he's spent the previous night in Schongau with the rest of his unit and almost witnessed the occupation – information that earns him an invitation to Urfeld for the evening.

A little later, Heisenberg returns to the hill behind the station to try and picture the ongoing battle – judging by the plumes of smoke, it looks as though the offensive is taking place in the valley running between Weilheim, Murnau and Garmisch. Meantime, Elisabeth has found out that during the night, Colin Ross and his wife – also called Elisabeth – have shot themselves.

Colin Ross, a Nazi officer, had been popular with the locals and people are talking about the suicide in terms of his having done the decent thing: "The decent Nazis take the consequences, leaving behind the scoundrels," they are saying.

The Heisenbergs finally obtain their provisions at half past four. In the meantime, the way home along the old mountain road has been blocked off so they have to take the long route, pushing the bike up the hill. In Urfeld, they are greeted by the daughter of a neighbour who tells them they should waste no time in getting to the house of the Ross couple, who are about to be buried. The Heisenbergs go just as they are, Werner in his lederhosen, along with the rucksack full of provisions.

The bodies are laid out in the living room, shrouded in tarpaulins, with just the faces uncovered. Colin Ross's face looks very angular, Werner observes, though at peace – it makes a profound impression on him. "Nevertheless," he writes, "the times are so fraught with tension and events that even death doesn't move me much any more ... Elisabeth feels the same." The dead are carried by soldiers to graves dug a few metres above the house and Lieutenant Schneider reads out Ross's last letter: "He did not want to live to witness the downfall of Germany and the new idea. His wife, his companion on so many walks, wished to accompany him on this walk, too." The mourners give the Hitler salute "for the last time".

After supper, Schuster arrives and it's agreed he should come and live with the Heisenbergs so they can wait together for the occupation. According to the news bulletins, the advance is supposed to take place along the Murnau–Mittenwald–Innsbruck line, meaning they could be occupied from either the north or the south. At the same time, the ring is closing more and more tightly round Berlin; one of these days, the Führer will simply be no more... besides which, it's been rumoured that Himmler has offered to surrender to the Western Allies. The diary entry for 29 April closes with Heisenberg musing, "So now there's a race as to which of the four scenarios could bring us an end to this War. And what will this end look like in Urfeld?"

This was the world – the same corner of Europe – into which Max had been born. Even though the war was coming to an end, as he was to describe in the third part of *After Nature*, his early years continued to be dominated by a sense of impending catastrophe:

... bin ich,
dem anderwärts furchtbaren Zeitlauf
*   zum Trotz,*
am Nordrand der Alpen, wie mir heut
*   scheint,*
aufgewachsen ohne einen Begriff der
*   Zerstörung.*
Aber daß ich vielfach auf der Straße
*   gestürzt*
Und mit einbandagierten Händen oft
*   im Fenster*
Bei den Fuchsienstauden gesessen bin,
auf das Nachlassen der Schmerzen
*   gewartet*
und stundenlang nichts als
*   hinausgeschaut habe,*
brachte mich früh auf die Vorstellung
von einer lautlosen Katastrophe, die
*   sich*
ohne ein Aufhebens vor dem
*   Betrachter vollzieht.*

... I grew up,
despite the dreadful course
of events elsewhere, on the
*   northern*
edge of the Alps, so it seems
to me now, without any
idea of destruction. But the
*   habit*
of often falling down in the
*   street and*
often sitting with bandaged
*   hands*
by the open window between
*   the potted*
fuchsias, waiting for the
pain to subside and for hours
doing nothing but looking out,
early on induced me to imagine
a silent catastrophe that occurs
almost unperceived. [52]

IV

He jests and charms, and men and women trust him with their
laughter like a brother. He turns serious, and they find his anger
in their own hearts. It is a rare, heavenly gift, and like most of
those who have it, its display leaves him melancholy.

Neal Ascherson, *Stone Voices: The Search for Scotland*, 2002[53]

Towards the end of May, I had returned to Norwich for a break. I resolved
to phone Max to find out if he had received my letter – the one I'd sent him
in April. In the end, there had been so many things that needed doing in the
house, I didn't get round to it. On arrival back at Churchill, however...

> ... I picked up my post from the Porter's Lodge; it included a large
> manila envelope containing a letter (in a separate smaller envelope)
> along with eleven sheets of typescript.
>   The typeface is instantly recognisable as that of Max's crazy old
> typewriter – the one with the keys that keep getting stuck, making the
> lines go all wobbly ... I'm eager to read it and intrigued by the way it's
> been set out on the page. At first sight, it looks like prose, arranged in
> sections with the lines further divided by forward slashes ...

Except where he'd signed off and added a cryptic postscript about the
number of "C"s in my Churchill address – five of them! – the accompanying
letter was in German. Dated 31 May, it began with an apology for not having
tried to make contact earlier.

Since we'd last seen each other, he wrote, apart from one weekend abroad, he had spent all his time in Norwich. He went on to describe his plans for the immediate future: a trip that would take in Germany, Austria and Switzerland and for which, as he put it, he would be like "a door-to-door salesman touting his wares". He was aiming to visit Aachen, Freiburg, Zurich and Innsbruck; possibly Salzburg and Graz as well. And since he would be going on holiday in Switzerland at the end of July, wondered if I could send him dates for when I'd be back in Norwich before that. Surely, he joked, Churchill College would be granting me "release" some time soon – or were they intent on keeping me for themselves 365 days a year?

There was good news from Jan Franksen, Max's media contact in Berlin. It seemed that the TV station, Sender Freies Berlin, had contrived to secure a hefty sum for the "Kant Project" – one and a half million marks, he thought. And whilst the studio was proposing to start filming next year, Max remained sceptical: he'd believe it when he saw it ...

A digression is necessary at this point. It was at the cinema that we'd first met and, from then on, often made reference to films. With Max, however, this enthusiasm hadn't stopped at straightforward moviegoing; he had also tried his hand at scriptwriting. It was the first draft of his screenplay *Jetzund kömpt die Nacht herbey – Ansichten aus dem Leben und Sterben des Immanuel Kant* (*And Now the Night Descends – Scenes from the Life and Death of Immanuel Kant*) that he had brought me to read in September 1981.

For Max, approaching a subject "via side-entrances and backdoors" was more likely to open up an unusual perspective; and the use of images was the ideal way to represent the life and works of thinkers of the past. (The same held for his use of images in a book: instead of "instructing" the reader how or what to think, pictures spoke for themselves.)

Rather than trace Kant's development as a philosopher, or treat his metaphysics in any abstract sense, Max chose to introduce the reader/viewer to a human being of fragile constitution and marked eccentricity. His express intention, he claimed, was to describe Kant's "paranoid inner world".

Obsessed with notions of mortality, Kant is presented as a creature of habit putting to the test his idiosyncratic theories concerning breathing, walking and the importance of taking regular exercise in the open air; these routines are granted equal importance with his ideas about the planetary system. Not far into the script, we see the twenty-two-year-old Kant, barely able to suppress his feelings for the young lady of the household in which he's been taken on as *Hofmeister* and private tutor. He and Fräulein von Lossow share a passion for ornithology. And it is the *Pirol*, the golden oriole, *Oriolus oriolus*, that serves as the emblem of their affection.

In the introduction to the first draft, as an instruction to the film director, Max makes the following remark:

> *Women appear very little in the piece and for that very reason, are of central importance. Care should be taken to ensure that whenever they make their "appearance" in male company, they should have about them an almost tangible "aura".*[54]

Might this offer a clue, I wonder, to understanding an aspect of Max's own view of women? I believe this aura the women are to have when in the presence of men is in keeping with Walter Benjamin's definition of "the aura" in his 1936 essay "The Work of Art in the Age of Mechanical Reproduction".[55] In other words, like the cult object, the beloved should embody the idea of something inaccessible and elusive, highly valued yet forever out of reach. In this respect, maybe Fräulein von Lossow can be seen as a cousin of Charlotte Ives (in *The Rings of Saturn*) – and even of Marie de Verneuil (in *Austerlitz*). And perhaps Charlotte is ascribed just such an aura of goodness and purity by the Vicomte de Chateaubriand as is Marie by Austerlitz.

Some years after writing the Kant screenplay, Max started work on another one, this time a film about Ludwig Wittgenstein – in the form of a series of tableaux arranged in achronological sequence. For various reasons, neither project came to be fully realised. Nevertheless, it strikes me as no coincidence that Max had taken film as his medium of choice – a medium that would benefit from his keen sense of the visual and involve him in both "discursive" and "non-discursive" modes of expression.[56]

* * * * *

On the writing front, he went on to say in the letter, he'd been busy. In between "cobbling together" various papers for his forthcoming trip to the Continent, he said that "as always", he was continuing to "scribble away". He'd forgotten whether I already knew – which in fact I did – that he'd now finished his essay on colour – "Helle Bilder und dunkle – Zur Dialektik der Eschatologie bei Stifter und Handke" ("Nature and Eschatology in the Work of Stifter and Handke");[57] and that he'd "done something quite wicked" for the Freiburg Colloquium on Alfred Döblin entitled "Prussian Perversions".[58] He wondered if, this time, the paper would get him "thrown out"! On top of all this, Max explained, he needed to think up something about Kafka in English – an article that was scheduled to appear in the *Times Higher Educational Supplement* over the next couple of weeks.

Max was still writing poems, he told me – hence the enclosure of a piece he'd been working on "in fits and starts" over the past few weeks. He hoped his friend Jan Peter Tripp would contribute some illustrations but – at this point he seemed hesitant – wasn't sure whether Jan Peter would like the poem. At all events, he hoped I would and that we'd have an opportunity to talk it through some time soon.

The letter finished by saying there was nothing special to report from Norwich except that it was "bloody cold", and that though our mutual friend Walter Bachem was in town, they hadn't yet met up. Before signing off with greetings in English, he hoped I wasn't working too hard.

The tone of the letter was not just modest; it was tentative. The words "hope" and "hoping" occur throughout. I couldn't help feeling that the new venture, the writing in which Max had begun to immerse himself, was giving rise to a lot of anxiety; and that in seeking my opinion, he was also seeking reassurance.

At the same time, I was enormously flattered to have been sent the sample – the "*sehr ausführliche Affäre*" ("very detailed piece") he'd been engaged on during sabbatical leave. It was a draft of "Und blieb ich am äußersten Meer" ("And if I Remained by the Outermost Sea"), concerning the life of Georg Wilhelm Steller.

But for the reversal of the first two letters, Max's initials coincide with Steller's – the kind of detail Max always relished. Indeed, I think it might have been one reason why W.G. Sebald chose G.W. Steller as the subject for his poem.

This is how Max summarises Steller's legacy:

Manuskripte am Ende des Lebens,	*Manuscripts written at the end of*
geschrieben auf einer Insel im	*his life,*
Eismeer,	*on an island in the glacial sea,*
mit kratzendem Gänsekiel und	*with scratching goose-quill in*
galliger Tinte,	*bilious ink,*
Verzeichnisse von zweihundertelf	*lists of two hundred and eleven*
Verschiedenen Pflanzen,	*different plants, tales of white*
Geschichten von weißen Raben,	*ravens,*
seltsamen Kormoranen und	*unknown cormorants and sea-*
Seekühen,	*cows,*
eingebracht in den Staub	*gathered into the dust*
einer endlosen Registratur,	*of an endless inventory,*
sein zoologisches Meisterwerk,	*his zoological masterpiece,*
de bestiis marinis,	*De Bestiis Marinis,*
Reiseprogramm für die Jäger,	*travel chart for hunters,*
Leitfaden beim Zählen der Pelze,	*blueprint for the counting of pelts –*
nein, nicht hoch genug	*no, not steep enough*
war der Norden.	*was the North.*[59]

As well as the sea cow, *De Bestiis Marinis* contained descriptions of other creatures destined to bear its author's name, notably the "sea otter" and the "Steller (Northern) sea lion". Steller had ranged into the realm of the fabulous, laying claim to the first recorded sighting of a mysterious beast he called a "sea ape" – a "cryptid", in other words, a creature not recognised by science, whose existence is regarded as improbable.

In this context, it's worth noting that Steller's book had appeared within a century of the rise of the *Wunderkabinett* – the cabinet of curiosities, collections of exotic objects brought back by European explorers for the benefit of their patrons. The treasures, often purporting to be unique, were housed in a specially designed chamber, forming a kind of small private museum. In Max's works, the cabinet of curiosities constitutes an important link – between, say, Steller, Sir Thomas Browne (the Musæum Clausum) and Jorge Luis Borges (*The Book of Imaginary Beings*).[60]

One finds a reference to the background research for the Steller poem in a later work, the second story of *The Emigrants* (published in Germany in 1992). Here, the narrator describes coming across his former classmate, "Fritz Binswanger", years after they had last met:

> ... *one April morning in 1984, in the reading room of the British Museum, where I was researching the history of Bering's Alaska expedition and Fritz was studying eighteenth-century French cookbooks. By chance we were sitting just one aisle apart, and when we both happened to look up from our work at the same moment we immediately recognised each other despite the quarter century that had passed. In the cafeteria we told each other the stories of our lives...*[61]

Whilst this represents another instance of chance meetings and "paths that cross", what I find particularly noteworthy is the date the narrator gives of his encounter with "Binswanger": April 1984. Since Max had been in a position to send me the draft of his poem in May 1983, he had clearly completed his preparatory research at least eleven months previously!

This is surely a good example of Max's "creative distortions", the insertion of material to suit his literary purpose. In this case, he has used – and altered – dates for the sake of the story, in exact accordance with the details of its timeline. In my view, the device also serves to highlight the theme of memory and the passage of time.

It was to take a while longer before "And if I Remained ..." appeared in print: a year and a half later, in October 1984, in *Manuskripte*; and then, as the second part of *After Nature*, first published in Germany in 1988, thereby launching Max's literary career.

My subsequent reading of all three parts of *After Nature* brought to light many allusions to Max's own life and personality, some so subtle as to be easily missed. In this respect, as well as in terms of diction and content, it seemed to me that the poem bore comparison with Eliot's *The Waste Land*.

* * * * *

On 24 June, realising Max would shortly be back from his European tour, I sent him a postcard from Cambridge. I said I hoped everything had gone well, adding that I'd read what he had sent me and looked forward to sharing my thoughts. I also mentioned that, thanks to his encouragement to "do more writing" myself, I was planning to spend the summer vacation working on an essay. It was to be about gardens – more specifically, the concept of the *genius loci*.

The following month would be my birthday and I had decided to spend it in Norwich – invite a few friends to help celebrate. Given what I knew about Max's wariness of social gatherings and doubting anything would come of it, I nevertheless asked him if he'd care to come along.

By the time the guests started arriving, I had only just managed to get the table ready: since the Berlin days, most of the china and glass was still stowed away in tea chests and had had to be dug out at the last minute.

Mike drove over from Colchester, George and Sue came from across the road. Vanessa brought an enormous bunch of flowers, Julia an upbeat gift of lipstick and matching nail varnish – Charles of the Ritz "Radiant Red" with glittery bits – not my usual colours but then, why not try a different look for the start of a new year? ... Last of all, and, greatly to my surprise, there was Max.

As had been the case the previous November, when my mother came to stay, he showed no sign of awkwardness. On the contrary, here was a consummate entertainer. He made us smile, he made us laugh – some of us till the tears ran down our cheeks. Truly!

No doubt the birthday cocktail, a large punch bowl of *sangria*, helped things along. In the lulls, however, I noticed that Max became unusually subdued and abstracted. Whatever it was he had on his mind, I didn't find out for a long time. It was to be another nine months before I heard from him again.

V

I began to set out the oval garden at Sayes Court,
which was before a rude orchard, and all the rest one entire field
of 100 acres, without any hedge, except the hither holly-hedge
joining to the bank of the mount walk. This was the beginning of
all the succeeding gardens, walks, groves, enclosures,
and plantations there.

The Diary of John Evelyn, 17 January 1653[62]

From the time he first set foot in Manchester in 1966, Max had never understood himself to be anything other than a "guest" in England. For all that, he had always taken pleasure in immersing himself in all things English; and gone a long way to adopt an English way of life at the Old Rectory in Poringland.

Looking back, it seems likely that it was my very "Englishness" – roots and family connections, no matter how remote – that formed the cornerstone of his interest in me.

Ever since he had first shown me round his garden in 1981, the subject of horticulture had continued to find its way into our conversation.

On one such occasion, it had led to another reading from my grandfather's *History of the Comber Family* – specifically, a passage relating to the diarist John Evelyn, whose maternal grandmother had been a Miss Comber:

Thomas Comber of Allington, the eldest son of John Rivers Comber, was born in 1530 and had two sons and three daughters, the youngest of whom was Eleanor. Eleanor married John Stansfield of Cliffe and they had one child, also named Eleanor. She married Richard Evelyn and bore him five children, Eliza, Jane, George, John and Richard ...

John, the second son, was born at the family estate at Wotton, Surrey on 31 October 1620. In the *Diary*, he was to describe the Comber connection in the most touching terms. At Max's request, I went and fetched my Everyman edition and proceeded to read the opening pages:

My mother's name was Eleanor, sole daughter and heiress of John Stansfield, Esq., of an ancient and honourable family (though now extinct) in Shropshire, by his wife Eleanor Comber, of a good and well-known house in Sussex. She was of proper personage; of a brown complexion; her eyes and hair of a lovely black; of constitution more inclined to a religious melancholy, or pious sadness; of a rare memory, and most exemplary life; for economy and prudence, esteemed one of the most conspicuous in her country ...

There's a painting of Evelyn by Robert Walker, which now hangs in the National Portrait Gallery in London.[63] Having seen reproductions of both this portrait of John and another of Eleanor, I could vouch for their striking family resemblance: the same long nose, the same sad, dark eyes. Yet despite the strength of John's attachment to his mother, he was to see very little of her during his childhood and adolescence. And, to his lasting dismay, not long before his fifteenth birthday, she became seriously ill and died.

At the age of five, John had been sent to live in Lewes with his maternal grandfather, John Stansfield, who, following the death of his first wife, also named Eleanor, had married again. Referring to her as "my too indulgent grandmother" (although in fact she was his step-grandmother), young John held this lady in the highest regard. Whilst overseeing his primary education, it seems she had allowed him all the freedom necessary to enable him to follow his star. So much so that, just before his twelfth birthday, when it had been his father's intention that he continue his schooling at Eton, John was "so terrified with the report of the severe discipline there" that he managed to persuade his father to let him to stay on in Lewes until the age of seventeen – in other words, the year he went to university.

Max was quick to pick up on the idea that growing up in a household so free of restriction would be bound to have a positive impact on the child's subsequent development. Indeed, on the evidence of even a few random excerpts from the *Diary*, it had become clear that John Evelyn was very much his own man.

At heart a Royalist, he spent much of the Civil War abroad; and then, on returning to England, established himself at Sayes Court, Deptford where he remained for the next fifty years. It was here that he had set about planting his famous garden – making it into a showcase for any number of exotic plants and ornamental trees.

As an accomplished linguist, Evelyn had made translations – for example, of a work in French on the management of kitchen gardens. His 1664 treatise *Sylva, A Discourse of Forest Trees*, the first publication to be officially sponsored by the Royal Society, remained a standard work for more than a century.

It was for the *Diary*, however, that he became best known in later centuries – most of all on account of his lively portraits of contemporaries and the quality of detail of his observations. Here, for instance, was his entry for 19 February 1653:

I planted the orchard at Sayes Court; new moon, wind west ...

Somewhere or other I had read that gardening calendars of the early 1600s frequently made reference to the phase of the moon – roughly speaking, sowing and planting were done when the moon was waxing; picking and pruning when it was waning – and the idea of caring for plants in sympathy with planetary factors appealed greatly to Max.

Leafing through the pages in the second volume, I suddenly caught sight of a reference to Norfolk. In 1660, Evelyn had been amongst those who founded the Royal Society and in 1671, as one of the Society's most active Fellows, he had accepted the office of Secretary. In his entry for 17 October of that year, he wrote that "having a desire to see that famous scholar and physician, Dr. T. Browne ... now lately knighted", he had travelled to Norwich ...

> ... to see Sir Thomas Browne (with whom I had some time corresponded by letter, though I had never seen him before); his whole house and garden being a paradise and cabinet of rarities, and that of the best collection, especially medals, books, plants and natural things. Amongst other curiosities, Sir Thomas had a collection of the eggs of all the fowl and birds he could procure, that country (especially the promontory of Norfolk) being frequented, as he said, by several kinds which seldom or never go farther into the land, as cranes, storks, eagles, and variety of water-fowl. He led me to see all the remarkable places of this ancient city, being one of the largest, and certainly, after London, one of the noblest of England, for its venerable cathedral, number of stately churches, cleanness of the streets, and buildings of flint so exquisitely headed and squared, as I was much astonished at; but he told me they had lost the art of squaring the flints, in which they so much excelled, and of which the churches, best houses, and walls, are built ... The suburbs are large, the prospects sweet, with other amenities, not omitting the flower-gardens, in which all the inhabitants excel. The fabric of stuffs brings a vast trade to this populous town ...

... clear evidence that Evelyn had been on very much the same wavelength as his host.

Like Browne, Evelyn was an ardent bibliophile, a polymath whose diversity of interests was reflected in his writing: not only on the subject of horticulture and forestry, but also numismatics, chemistry, air pollution, refrigeration, architecture, the ordering of libraries and – of particular interest to Max, whose close friend, the artist Jan Peter Tripp, specialised in making engravings – the history and art of copper engraving.

Over and above the wealth of information contained in the *Diary* excerpts, it was the chance remarks and pleasing turns of phrase that we liked so much. Another example: having been to inspect the Oxford Physic Garden, Evelyn comments that whilst he had found bamboo, olive trees and rhubarb, there had been "no extraordinary curiosities". To top it all, what delighted Max was the discovery that this man had been a connoisseur of fruit trees – indeed, that he had had an apple named after him.

On a more sombre note – and in the light of Max's preoccupation with the theme of catastrophe, both natural and man-made – I decided to finish off by looking up the entry for 2 September 1666 concerning the outbreak of the Great Fire of London.

Oh, the miserable and calamitous spectacle! Such as haply the world had not seen since the foundation of it, nor can be outdone till the universal conflagration thereof. All the sky was of a fiery aspect, like the top of a burning oven, and the light seen above forty miles round-about for many nights. God grant mine eyes may never behold the like, who now saw above 10,000 houses all in one flame! The noise and cracking and thunder of the impetuous flames, the shrieking of women and children, the hurry of people, the fall of towers, houses, and churches, was like a hideous storm; and the air all about so hot and inflamed, that at the last one was not able to approach it, so that they were forced to stand still, and let the flames burn on, which they did, for near two miles in length and one in breadth. The clouds also of smoke were dismal, and reached, upon computation, near fifty miles in length. Thus, I left it this afternoon burning, a resemblance of Sodom, or the last day. It forcibly called to my mind that passage – non enim hic habemus stabilem civitatem: the ruins resembling the picture of Troy. London was, but is no more! Thus I returned ...

Max listened intently – it had moved him deeply.

Thirty years on – as I write, it is September 2011 – it's tempting to speculate whether it was the reading of just this passage that had inspired Max's decision to cite Samuel Pepys, the other great diarist of the age, in the final pages of *Vertigo* (as well as in Part II of his poem "Day Return").[64] Max introduces this account of the Great Fire, describing how he had "idly ... turned the pages of an India paper edition of Samuel Pepys's diary, Everyman's Library, 1913" that he had "purchased that afternoon ..."[65]

Incidentally, it's worth mentioning that the Everyman edition he had picked up in London was likely to have been that of *1912*, not 1913[66]. In my view, Max deliberately wrote "1913" since this was a year of great significance to him personally, most of all as it relates to earlier passages in *Vertigo*. (For example, at the beginning of Part III, we read that it was on Saturday, 6 September 1913 that Dr K. went to Vienna in his capacity as Deputy Secretary of the Prague Workers' Insurance Company "*to attend a congress*" – appropriately enough, in the context of urban disaster – "*on rescue services and hygiene*" (my italics).

The way in which Max integrated details of Pepys's account within his own narrative is masterful. Whilst Pepys's record doesn't fail to capture a sense of awe and terror, it tends to be couched in a homely idiom – as one might expect of a diarist who originally set out to write for his eyes only: " ... we were in great trouble and disturbance at this fire, not knowing what to think of it. However, we had an extraordinary good dinner ..."

With his knack for finding and lifting the most arresting word or phrase from another writer's text, Max elevates the tone, thereby imbuing the end of his book with a truly apocalyptic, visionary quality – a quality found in both the original German and in Michael Hulse's English translation. Naturally, I'm biased but "[t]he glare around us everywhere, and yonder, before the darkened skies, in one great arc the jagged wall of fire ..." culminating in " ... a silent rain of ashes, westward, as far as Windsor Park" strikes me now as closer in style to John Evelyn than Pepys.

In *Schwindel. Gefühle* (though not in *Vertigo*, the (published) English translation) that final sentence is followed by:

– 2013 –
Ende

I take this to carry a double meaning. On one hand, it signifies the end of the book, as in the customary insertion of "The End" or "Finis" once a tale (or film) has been brought to a close; on the other, it provides an answer to the rhetorical question on the penultimate page, "Is this the end of time?" In the mind of the author, the year 2013, one century on from the date of publication of his Everyman edition of Pepys's *Diary*, represents the ultimate end.

It also contains autobiographical significance. Had Max, born in 1944, lived to 18 May 2013, he would have entered his seventieth year. According to the Psalmist:

> ... *the days of our years are threescore years and ten; and if by reason of strength they be fourscore years, yet is their strength labour and sorrow; for it is soon cut off, and we fly away ...*[67]

In biblical terms, 2013 represented the end of his lifespan.

VI

And since even in Paradise itself, the tree of knowledge
was placed in the middle of the Garden, whatever was the
ambient figure, there wanted not a centre and rule of decussation.
Whether the groves and sacred Plantations of Antiquity were
not thus orderly placed ... may favourably be doubted. For since
they were so methodical in the constitution of their temples, as
to observe the due situation, aspect, manner, form, and order in
Architectonical relations, whether they were not as distinct in
their groves and Plantations about them, in form and
species respectively unto their Deities, is not
without probability of conjecture.

Sir Thomas Browne, *The Garden of Cyrus*, 1658

In the course of the first six months of 1983, the novelty of having a
resident psychotherapist within Churchill College had begun to wear
off – most people, at least amongst the students, now accepted me as
part of the furniture. At the same time, the set of rooms I'd been offered
at the outset didn't allow for a satisfactory distinction between work
space and private space – I needed an extra study, somewhere I could
retreat to during the daytime or simply be "unavailable". Having discussed
the issue with Colin Campbell and the Bursar, it was agreed that during
the long vacation I would move to a larger set on a staircase reserved
for Fellows.

The new rooms afforded much greater freedom of movement and overlooked a courtyard on either side. One of these provided the setting for a black mulberry tree – a *Morus nigra* – that had been planted by Sir Winston at the founding of the College in 1959. Over the months – and through the changing seasons – I was to discover more about the nature of mulberry trees. By now, the branches had had time to reach down to the ground in such a way that they formed a kind of secret inner chamber – reminiscent of a weeping willow. And when the tree bore fruit, it was hard to pass by without getting spritzed with juice – leaving purple stains on skin and clothes. It made me think of Max's love of trees and I made a note to myself to tell him about it when we next saw each other.

As summer drew on, college life came to a virtual standstill. Max and I had agreed it was always a good idea to have a second string to one's bow in the shape of writing and I had mentioned to him my plan for the summer vacation. With fewer demands on me professionally and access to an unlimited numbers of books in the University Library, I looked forward to a return to academic life by proxy.

Earlier in the year, I had been invited to make a presentation at a conference in Vienna. It was due to take place in September meaning that, if I put my mind to it, I would still have just enough time to prepare for it. Whilst not yet sure of the shape the paper was going to take, I did have an idea of my aim. The background research would involve looking at the representation of gardens in historical accounts and works of literature; from which I wanted to trace how the topology of a garden both encapsulated the zeitgeist and reflected the sensibility of its creator – be that a landscape designer or a writer.

By way of initial preparations, I had read Andrew Marvell's *The Garden*. In the stanza before the one with the line that gets quoted most often, "... a green Thought in a green Shade", there was this to spur me on:

> *Stumbling on Melons, as I pass,*
> *Insnar'd with Flow'rs, I fall on Grass.* [68]

A glorious thought, the idea of stumbling on melons and being ensnared with flowers. And later on, that phrase "curious peach" – curious, I think, in the sense of "full of care" or of "possessing healing powers". The English love their lawns. Gardens and the soul: the soul is man's "nature"; gardens are man's attempt to master, tame, impose order on nature, perhaps "reinvent" it ...

I had noted in my diary.

On 8 September, armed with the completed essay and a sheaf of extra notes, I flew to Milan and from there by train to Linz, the city on the Danube. My thoughts returned to Max who had once shown me a poem he'd written about journeys not unlike this one – a poem containing the idea that as the train speeds on its way and you gaze out of the window trying to take in the landscape, the landscape is watching you:

Schwer zu verstehen	*For how hard it is*
ist nämlich die Landschaft	*to understand the landscape*
wenn du im D-Zug von dahin	*as you pass in a train*
nach dorthin vorbeifährst,	*from here to there*
während sie stumm	*and mutely it*
dein Verschwinden betrachtet.	*watches you vanish.*[69]

In Linz, I had arranged to meet up with Eva Meyer, a friend who had come from Berlin to take part in an arts festival currently being held in the Brucknerhaus. From here, we managed to secure a lift with two others who would be driving back via Vienna. One of these was Elfriede Jelinek.

Like Max, Elfriede had been a regular contributor to *Manuskripte*; also like him, she had gone on to receive a string of literary prizes (for her, this included, in 2004, the Nobel Prize in Literature).

The overall theme of the Vienna Conference was concepts of the soul – specifically, the idea that in contemporary West European culture, "the soul" had all but disappeared. There was much talk of the soul as "anima", the breath of life – a noun that in German, as in Latin, takes the feminine gender. Looking around at the assembled presenters – thirty or so of us – I was struck by the thought that here, at any rate, the feminine principle was seriously under-represented: only three women.

My paper, *The Garden as a Reflection of Sensibility: An Attempt to Find the Genius Loci*, had been billed for the second day, 22 September.[70] Whilst realising I would be presenting to a largely German-speaking audience, I decided to deliver it in English – in homage to the writers from whom I had drawn inspiration. I was nervous to start with. However, by inhaling deeply and reading very slowly – especially the passage from Sir Thomas Browne's *The Garden of Cyrus* – I calmed down and found a rhythm. When I reached the end, there was a long silence, followed by what I dared think of as enthusiastic applause.

VII

As you enter into the heart of that city, you cannot tell
what you will see next or indeed who will see you the very next
moment. Scarcely has someone made an appearance than he has
quit the stage again by another exit. These brief exhibitions are of
an almost theatrical obscenity and at the same time have an air
of conspiracy about them, into which one is drawn
against one's will.

W.G. Sebald, *Vertigo* [*Schwindel. Gefühle*], 1990[71]

Vienna had been a boost to morale. Following my return, I sent Max a copy of the essay along with a letter, in which I reminded him about the idea he'd put forward several months before: that whilst I was away in Cambridge, he could use my house as somewhere quiet to work. I hadn't heard back and assumed that either he didn't want to pursue the plan or had too many other things to deal with.

I also had a lot to think about. In particular, I'd become increasingly concerned for my godmother and had taken to visiting her more frequently. On one such occasion, with uncharacteristic hesitancy, she said she had something to tell me – something she didn't want anyone else to know. The cancer could no longer be held in check, her condition was rapidly deteriorating and she'd like to discuss "arrangements".

It seemed that all of a sudden, the tables were turning: Elisaveta, the person who had always been my most trusted confidante, was now confiding in me and, whilst "not wishing to burden me", talking about the details of her will and "the end" – her end. She continued to take as much care as ever over her appearance – indeed, she looked remarkably well. At the same time, I couldn't help wondering how long she'd be able to keep secret what was happening to her.

Her courage never failed to astonish me – not least in the middle of October, when she phoned to announce that, come what may, she was determined to celebrate her seventieth birthday. She wanted me to be there, she said; and she hadn't forgotten about "that interesting German friend of yours" whose visit she had had to put off the previous year... except that, much though she would have liked to be introduced to Max, she feared the challenge of meeting new people was now too much for her.

On 13 November, slipping a copy of the garden essay into my bag, I caught an Eastern Counties bus – one of those much favoured by Max on his peregrinations through Suffolk – and made my way to Bury St Edmunds. The other guest was Michael, the son of a lady Elisaveta had met whilst on holiday in Italy. We were welcomed in style, with glasses of champagne. Raising his glass, Michael wished Elisaveta "many happy returns"; to which she responded with a gracious smile. My heart missed a beat.

A couple of months later, there were further celebrations to mark Russian Christmas. Michael and I were invited again – this time, along with Michael's mother, Claudine. As before, Elisaveta pulled out all the stops, preparing a sumptuous feast with home-made *pirozhki*, caviar from Harrods, pork loin flavoured with truffles and more bottles of champagne.

Despite the pleasure of the event – due in large part to Elisaveta's natural sense of occasion – there was no doubt that the planning of it all, including the trips to London to buy ingredients, had taken its toll. On the bus home, I was much preoccupied with the thought of losing her.

It was typical of Elisaveta that, even though she was coping with the advanced stages of cancer, she was anxious for my welfare. She insisted that I needed a holiday and suggested Venice – a city that had always appealed to her. And why not take my mother, whose 65th birthday was coming up in March? A good idea – or so it seemed.

When it came to the point, I had very mixed feelings. Given the state of Elisaveta's health, it didn't seem right to be leaving the country, even for a short time; on the other hand, to a certain extent, I would be doing so on her behalf.

It wasn't my first visit to Venice, but this time was different. The mood fluctuated between tearful and tetchy. There were aspects of the city I now found curiously disturbing: the vast number of ratty little feral cats, the water-hearses – and a vague notion that, once off the beaten track, one was being watched. Even so, there were also moments of glorious surprise, displays of exuberance – of *sprezzatura* – such as the nun encircled by her charges, a group of children, dancing in the precincts of Santa Maria della Salute; and the flasher on a balcony overlooking the Grand Canal, disporting himself for all he was worth.

The day before we left, having treated ourselves to morning coffee at Florian's, I persuaded the waiter to sell me an espresso-sized cup and saucer decorated with the café's famous logo, as a gift for Elisaveta.

She received it graciously. But the look in her eyes told me she had had enough of the world – she was preparing to move on.

VIII

... today I know why I felt obliged to turn away when anyone
came too close to me, I know that I thought this turning away
made me safe, and that at the same time I saw myself transformed
into a frightful and hideous creature, a man beyond the pale.

W.G. Sebald, *Austerlitz*, 2001[72]

Back in Cambridge, the Easter Term had begun and, for the undergraduates,
a frenzy of last-minute revision, exam nerves and sleepless nights. For me, it
meant working at full stretch with no prospect of a breathing space much
before July. And then, at the start of May, I got a surprise letter from Max,
again in German but this time handwritten.

It opened with an apology for not having been in touch sooner. The
phrase Max used to describe himself – or rather, how he imagined I would
have come to regard him – was "*der ungehobelste Mensch*", "the most boorish
creature". *Ungehobelt* also translates as "uncivilised" or "uncouth"; in terms
of etiquette, the opposite of refined or gracious. It's striking because this was
the same phrase as the one he'd used at the start of a letter he'd sent eleven
months before. Of course, I could choose to see it as simply a manner of
speaking, slightly tongue-in-cheek, self-deprecating – all of which fitted with
Max's public persona. However, in the context of the letters having been
addressed to me, to whom he had let down his guard, I offer an alternative
reading – one with much darker connotations: Max really had come to think
of himself as personally and socially wanting – even, at times, repellent. Such

notions – notions of self, learnt from others and internalised as "true" – have their origins way back in childhood.

In the letter, he'd gone on to say how much he liked my essay – " ... the things you know!!" he wrote, " ... many a professional *Literat* [*littérateur,* "man of letters"] would do well to take note ..." – and was wondering why, if I wasn't already doing so, I didn't write <u>more</u> – the "more" was underlined.

The reason I hadn't heard from him, he explained, was that over the past few weeks everything seemed to have gone wrong: "a great long list of things ... a succession of calamities". He had had so much on his hands, he hadn't known where to turn: "piles of post, including urgent correspondence, all untouched" plus "the rubbish from last term and preparations for next term yet to be dealt with". On top of which, the garden needed doing...

Max had been all set to get in touch over Easter, he wrote, but had then had to go to London for a week to attend a colloquium on Karl Kraus; after which he'd been busy writing an essay on Stifter for a collection to be published by Residenz Verlag. This essay, he thought, would be of special interest to me: it was "all about clothes, fashion, fetishism – that kind of thing".

Were anyone in any doubt as to the real-life identity of the narrator in *Vertigo*, Max's letter provides an interesting clue. On the opening page of the second part of the book, "All'estero", we read:

> *In Vienna ... I found that the days proved inordinately long, now that they were not taken up by my customary routine of writing and gardening tasks, and I literally did not know where to turn ...*

In the letter to me, his "customary routine" having been disrupted, Max laments that he doesn't know where to turn. The sentence in German reads: "*Resultat: ich wußte die letzten Wochen wirklich nicht, wohin ich mich zuerst wenden soll ...*"; I compare this with " ... *erwies es sich aber ... daß ich nicht mehr wußte, wohin mich wenden ...*" from *Schwindel. Gefühle* (*Vertigo*), written six years later: the same predicament expressed in the same phrases!

In the closing lines of the letter, Max went on to say he had tried phoning

Ampthill Street several times over the Easter weekend; and also, "in passing, knocked on the door ..." followed by a note of exasperation, slight yet unmistakeable, " ... but you obviously weren't there!" When I was next back in Norwich, he hoped, maybe something could be arranged. He signed off with a "micro-poem":

Jedenfalls	*Anyhow*
Einstweilen	*In the meantime*
Grüße	*Greetings*
Herzliche : Max	*Heartfelt ones : Max*

To my mind, the letter represents vintage Sebald: generous with his praise and encouragement; and containing news in the form of a catalogue of doom and gloom, to be taken with a large pinch of salt.

From the outset, Max struck me as someone possessed of a natural gift for self-irony; he was now proving to be a specialist – a specialist in the art of the Jeremiad. The net result is that the bleaker he paints the world around him, the more entertaining he becomes; and, in story-telling mode, he is at his funniest when at his most "miserable".

A number of people, including colleagues at the University of East Anglia, have vouched for Max's particular brand of humour. On returning to Norfolk from Europe, he would put on a great performance, regaling his listeners with tales of woe that never failed to draw a positive response. Accounts of personal misadventure, delivered in a deeply sonorous voice, reduced people to helpless laughter. One might say that whenever Max went on his travels, he could be relied upon to bring back a report in which everything that could go wrong had done.

I believe this was something he actively cultivated. By nature repressed, the adoption of a persona – a mask – allowed Max a safe means of expression in public; it was only in the intimacy of the one-to-one situation that he had given rein to his vulnerability.

* * * * *

It had been nine months since we had last seen each other and a lot had happened during that time that Max hadn't known about – most particularly, the situation with Elisaveta. It had left me at sixes and sevens; and, although I hadn't lost interest in writing, I had lost my nerve.

Monday, 7 May 1984

> ... What seems to be holding me back from doing more writing is that I'm plagued by the thought that my experience isn't rich enough ... As long as I'm dealing with academic, clinical or research-type stuff, I don't have a problem; if it's a personal letter, that's OK as well. But the purely imaginative is a different matter. There, I feel hampered – a bit like having all these dressmaking fabrics and patterns and, even though I could actually do with some new clothes, being hesitant about turning the fabrics into things to wear ...

It strikes me now that, whilst Max hadn't known what had been going on in my life, the question he'd put to me – "Why aren't you doing <u>more</u> writing?" – was the very question he was asking himself. At one level, the recounting of the "succession of calamities" can be regarded as a skilled performance – of the kind Max put on to entertain his colleagues. Yet behind the mask, there's a sense of his mounting frustration: too many obligations were preventing him from getting on with what meant most to him – his writing.

IX

It was much more and much less than pity ... where could you
find pity or any comprehensible association of human ideas if on
some other evening I find under a nut tree a half-full watering can
that a gardener's boy has forgotten there, and this watering can
and the water in it, dark from the shadow of the tree, and a water
beetle sculling on the surface of the water from one dark shore
to the other, this confluence of trivialities shoots through me
from the roots of my hair to the marrow of my toes with such a
presence of the infinite that I want to bring out words,
knowing that any words I found would vanquish
those cherubim in which I do not believe?

Hugo von Hofmannsthal, *A Letter*, 1902[73]

By now it's probably clear that a key element of the conversations with
Max – the one that provided the yeast, so to speak – was our mutual love of
language and words. Nonetheless, we had also come up against the counter
to this, the sobering realisation that there were times when words proved
inadequate.

The written text presented another aspect of the problem. Since
sending Max the cassette recording of my *Letter from Norwich* and in turn
receiving the draft of his Steller poem, it was as if we'd been feeling our
way towards the idea of finding a form of writing – and a language – that,
whilst it might reflect a scholarly approach, embraced the subjective. On

more than one occasion, Max had expressed extreme irritation with the convention adopted by many twentieth-century writers of academic research papers: the use of the third person singular, presumably intended to imbue the material with a more objective, "scientific" tone. What Max favoured – indeed, what we both favoured – was the unashamed inclusion of the "self" in the form of the first person.

By this stage of his career, Max had no need to supply further evidence of his *academic* credentials; and now, against all the odds – of other demands, domestic and professional – his focus was shifting towards a different genre.

My attention was shifting, too; for the time being, literary pursuits would have to be put on hold. With every passing day, Elisaveta had become more and more bed-bound, less and less able to tolerate solid food. By the third week of August, the cancer had reached her brain and her condition was such that the doctor could do no more. He advised me that the time had come for her be moved to the hospice in Cambridge. It was here, early in the morning of Saturday, 25 August, that she died.

Having been to pay my last respects, I returned to Norwich to catch up on sleep and prepare for the funeral. That same evening, who should turn up but Max. He didn't shy away but listened attentively – palpably moved by what I told him about the weeks and hours leading up to Elisaveta's death. How, towards the end, she'd found solace in dabbing herself with Eau Sauvage de Dior; and sipping tiny amounts of champagne from a lead crystal tumbler, holding it to her lips with difficulty. And later, as she was being carried downstairs by the ambulance men, how she'd reverted to the Russian of her childhood, saying repeatedly, "*Ya poslooshnya! Ya poslooshnya!*" ("I'm a good girl! I'm a good girl!"). "Ah, these Russians," remarked Max, "like Chekhov..."

Twelve years later, in June 1996, Max was to publish a poem about the death of Chekhov:

Wie der Morgen graut,　　　*As dawn breaks*
legt ihm der Arzt　　　　　*the doctor, placing*
Eis auf das Herz,　　　　　*ice on his heart,*
gibt ihm Morphium　　　　*prescribes morphine*
und ein Glas Champagner.　*and a glass of champagne.*
Ans Heimreisen dachte er ...　*He was thinking of returning*
　　　　　　　　　　　　home ...[74]

Monday, 3 September 1984

Friends have rallied, been very kind – it's times like these I realise how much I need them but also how little people really know about each other during their lifetimes ... it occurs to me that nobody had ever known much about Elisaveta – she'd never allowed them to – except in fragments ...

Not unlike Max. During this time, and over the next six weeks, whenever I was back in Norwich, he continued to keep in touch, dropping in to see how I was doing. We talked more about the way the year had gone – about Elisaveta and the impact upon her of life-long exile; about bereavement and loss. He observed that what Elisaveta meant to me, his grandfather Egelhofer meant to him; the dead – in this case, those we loved – would always be with us.

We also spoke about Venice and the trip with my mother. What was it about this city that I had found so unsettling? he wondered. Had it been to do with the time of year or the light? Or the thought of all that water and what went on beneath its surface? Maybe it was the sights my mother and I had chosen to visit: the Piombi, for example – the prison cells within the Doge's Palace from where Giacomo Casanova had planned his escape for the last day of October in 1756. And the fact that we'd kept on getting lost, especially towards evening. I couldn't put my finger on it. Max said he thought he understood the feeling and, after a pause, mentioned an essay he'd been working on.

The essay "Venezianisches Kryptogramm" ("Venetian Cryptogram")[75] concerns Hofmannsthal's novella, *Andreas*. Hofmannsthal had begun work on *Andreas* as he was approaching forty, which – as Max comments – he regarded as the *annus mirabilis*, the year in which, like the gambler in the story, a man reaches the most precarious point in his life, the time when he has nothing more to gain and everything to lose. For Max, the figure of the Maltese, the Knight Hospitaller, represents the embodiment of Hofmannsthal's own panic, "the complete breakdown of the man of forty". At the time of preparing his essay, it had been a matter of months since Max himself had turned forty; neither would he have forgotten that it was at the age of forty that Kafka had died.[76]

It seems to me that whilst the novella – which remained an unfinished fragment – would fit the format of the *Bildungsroman* (a novel concerned with the intellectual or spiritual *development* of the main character), for Max, it is the opposite: a study of the *fragmentation* of personality – the protagonist serving to illustrate the aetiology of a pathological condition.

Clinically speaking, Andreas is subject to episodes of dissociation – he goes in and out of dream states, many of which have the quality of hallucinations. But the fear of disintegration does not lie within him alone; it permeates the whole tale. Characters emerge and just as quickly dissolve or split into two; the general atmosphere is both sexually charged and sexually ambiguous. For these reasons, Venice, a decaying city, represented the ideal backdrop.

For Max – Max the person, as much as Sebald the scholar – I believe the writing of "Venetian Cryptogram" had served more than one purpose: it was an academically "respectable" way of confronting his demons.

X

**The empire of women is much too extensive in France;
the empire of woman much too restricted.**

Stendhal, *On Love* [*De l'amour*], 1822[77]

During the autumn of 1984, I spent much of my spare time clearing Elisaveta's house prior to putting it up for sale. Amongst her books was a collection that had been of special importance to my godmother: the works of Stendhal in the primrose-coloured Classiques Garnier edition, to which she had added her notes in pencil – many of them to do with the subject of textiles, clothes and fashion.

After her death, I had also taken to wearing a ring she had left me – a gold wedding band of Scandinavian design that I'd had made smaller to fit my finger.

On the last day of October – All Hallows Eve – I had a visitor.

Saturday, 3 November 1984

Last Wednesday evening Max was here ... there's no doubting we have a lot in common – for one thing, we both keep getting told we're just "too serious" and, worse, "so old-fashioned". But what the hell, that's exactly why we like each other – and why I value the friendship ...

Whilst we talked, I caught him glancing at my ring. I explained that it had belonged to Elisaveta. It looked well on me, he thought – it suited my hand.

This led us on to the topic of my godmother's books, amongst which were the works of Stendhal including, as it happened, the essay *De l'amour*. I asked Max if he'd like to have them as a gift. His eyes lit up – he said he'd be honoured to accept.

Sadly, nothing came of it. From this point on, the gaps between sightings of Max began to lengthen. But Stendhal hadn't been forgotten, as the following goes to show.

Two years after the original publication of *Schwindel. Gefühle* (*Vertigo*), Max gave an interview, which started off with him saying – perhaps somewhat tongue-in-cheek:

> *I am not a* littérateur *in the true sense of the word ... For decades ... I stuck to academic work. But I've always kept small notebooks in which I used to make very chaotic notes.* Vertigo *came about by chance. I bought Stendhal's* De l'amour *in a bookshop in Lausanne ...*

This detail suggests to me that he had tracked down a copy of the book whilst on a visit to Lausanne in May 1985. He goes on:

> *... [De l'amour] resonated with a great many things that were on my mind because it contained many Italian place names which were familiar to me from the trips I'd made to Italy as a child. I knew Kafka's works well, but not Stendhal's, and yet I was immediately struck by a remarkable convergence ... So then I wrote two literary-biographical essays on the two authors whom I wanted to bring closer together ...*[78]

"A remarkable convergence" – and not the only one. The first part of *Vertigo* – thirty-seven pages in the German original – is entitled "Beyle, or Love is a Madness Most Discreet", an account of how Marie-Henri Beyle, later to be known as Stendhal, had attempted to confront his traumatic memories of past events – revisiting the sites of battles in which he'd fought; going over in his mind the liaisons he'd had with a whole series of women.

Having contracted syphilis at the age of seventeen-and-a-half, Beyle's life continued to be plagued by disease and the effects of treatment – self-administered, highly toxic substances. In the face of desolation, he determined on writing an essay. As Max has it:

> ... *it was in the autumn* [of 1801] *that he resolved to become the greatest writer of all time. He did not, however, take any decisive steps towards the fulfilment of that ambition until Napoleon's empire began to crumble, nor did he make a first real advance into the world of literature until in the spring of 1820 he wrote* De l'amour, *a kind of resumé of the hopeful yet disconcerting years that had gone before* ...[79]

When it came to his choice of mistresses, matters had gone disastrously wrong – a case in point being his relationship with Métilde Dembowski Viscontini, "a woman of great, melancholy beauty". Beyle managed to spoil his chances via a breach of etiquette: believing he would be able to win Métilde by following her incognito, he dressed up in clothes acquired specially for the purpose. The plan failed to work – in fact, she rejected him. So as to console himself, he wrote *De l'amour* and, as a kind of *aide-mémoire*, kept on his writing desk ...

> ... *a memento of Métilde ... a plaster cast of her left hand which he had contrived to obtain shortly before the debacle – providentially, as he often reflected while writing ... the slight crookedness of the ring finger occasioned in him emotions of a vehemence he had not hitherto experienced* ...[80]

Max includes a photograph of the plaster cast: the impact of the disembodied, chalky white hand against a black background is macabre.

In the subsequent narrative, Beyle is described as keeping " ... a minute record of the fluctuating state of his health and in due course noted ... his sleeplessness, his giddiness, the roaring in his ears, his palpitating pulse ..." – amongst other symptoms, those of vertigo.

Finally, "on the evening of the 22nd of March, 1842, with the approach of spring already in the air", Beyle "fell to the pavement in the rue Neuve-des-

Capucines (in Paris) in an apoplectic fit." From there, "he was taken to his apartments in what is now rue Danielle-Casanova" where "in the early hours of the following morning, without regaining consciousness, he died."

The name Casanova had great significance for Max. In an interview of March 2001, he was asked about the importance of coincidence in his writing and used this as an example:

> *The first section of* Vertigo *is about Stendhal, and ... finishes with Stendhal's death in a certain street in Paris, which is now called the rue Danielle-Casanova. I didn't know who Danielle Casanova was, except that Casanova meant something to me in the same context of that book* [i.e. Giacomo Casanova], *but not* Danielle *Casanova. The following summer I went to Corsica, walking through the mountains ... and I came to the coastal village of Piana, and there was a little house with a plaque on it ... a memorial plaque for Danielle Casanova, who had been murdered by my compatriots in Auschwitz. She'd been a dentist and a communist and was in the French Resistance. And I went past the house three or four times and it always seemed closed. Then on one occasion I went round the back and there was her sister. And then, you know, I talked to her for a week ... These things do happen. I have all her papers now, and I don't know what I shall do with them, but ... it's a sort of connection ... If that sort of thing happens to us, then we think, perhaps, that not everything is quite futile. It gives one a sort of passing sense of consolation ...*[81]

In one of the folders relating to Corsica housed in the German Literature Archive in Marbach, there's evidence to suggest that Max had wanted to pursue the story of Danielle Casanova – possibly envisaging her as the subject of a full-length work. It's tempting to speculate that Danielle might have been the precursor of Jacques Austerlitz.

* * * * *

Two weeks after Max had visited me in Ampthill Street, I was myself in Paris, having been invited to a wedding. Elisaveta's nephew, Alexis de Wrangell, was at last getting married to Cathérine Colonna d'Istria – the girlfriend he'd been courting with unstinting devotion for years. The ceremony was to take place in the Russian Orthodox church, and be followed by a reception at Les Salons de la Maison des Polytechniciens in the seventh arrondissement.

It promised to be a lavish occasion. It turned out to be a test of stamina – a tale I looked forward to telling Max when next I saw him.

XI

There is no empty space. Kleist is in the direct line from Berkeley to Ernst Mach. Relativity is a problem only to the intellect, eager for analysis. In nature it is not a problem but a fact. But the human intellect busily produces absolutes, categories, obstacles to check the disturbing flow and hold it for analysis. Kleist too is human; he wants to know. But is it possible to know, when every observation is coloured by subjective thought?

Idris Parry, "Kleist on Puppets", 1981[82]

That opportunity didn't arise; indeed, it was to be over three years before I saw Max again. Considering the importance to us both of the friendship, this strikes me as astonishing – until I begin to piece things together and put them in context. Doing so involves another detour – one that nevertheless leads back to Max in a surprising way.

At the start of 1985, I was approached by Tim Cribb, Director of Studies in English at Churchill, telling me that the Senior Tutor had invited someone to the College whom he was sure I'd want to meet: an actor from the Isle of Mull, off the west coast of Scotland.

Whereas the idea of having a resident counsellor was still regarded with scepticism by some of the Fellows, it had become an accepted part of my role that I welcome visitors to the College, especially those from overseas. In this case, the description "overseas" hardly applied – at least not in the usual sense. But then, as I was shortly to find out, there was never anything usual about Barrie Hesketh. I wrote a polite note, explaining who I was and suggesting that, once he'd had time to settle in, he get in touch.

Within twenty minutes of taking the note to the Porter's Lodge for delivery and walking back to my rooms, the phone went. It was Barrie – saying he'd received my invitation and wondered if we could make arrangements to meet. When would it suit him? I asked. How about now! came the instant reply.

The first thing I noticed about Barrie was his eyes – dark, alert and expressive. Having come in and sat down, he wasted no time in telling me why he was here. He had visited Churchill once before, as a guest of the College, together with his wife, Marianne. They were professional actors who, over the past two decades, had built and run a tiny theatre on Mull, putting on plays and poetry readings for the entertainment of the holidaymakers in summer; and the rest of the year, taking the shows on tour throughout the length and breadth of Britain.

Latterly, they had ventured into mainland Europe, including Germany – where they offered a double bill consisting of George Bernard Shaw's *Village Wooing* and Marianne's own half-hour adaptation of Oscar Wilde's *The Importance of Being Earnest*. Their final destination had been the Scharfrichterhaus in Passau on the Danube. Since 1977, the Scharfrichterhaus – the historic executioner's house – had been developed as a venue for small-scale arts events, jazz and political cabaret in particular. It was here, in November 1983, that Marianne, by then gravely ill with cancer, had given her last performance. She died five months later.

On hearing of Marianne's death, Colin Campbell had contacted Barrie: on behalf of the College, he invited him back to spend a term at Churchill. Barrie would not have to *do* anything unless he felt like it. "Just be," said Colin, "and maybe get some respite."

So here was Barrie – here we both were: two people recently bereaved and needing to talk about it. It didn't take long for us to establish a regular pattern of afternoon chats in which we continued to compare notes, offer each other moral support and let our minds range over all manner of subjects, including the similarities between our professions.

As a professional actor, Barrie was in the business of giving expression to emotion, making the personal public; whereas I was employed to help people explore and make sense of emotions, an activity conducted mainly behind closed doors. All very well, said Barrie, but given the myths and fantasies around psychotherapy, how were people – especially young people – to know what it involved and, being assured as to its benefits, take advantage of my services?

It was at this point we started talking about projection – projection in the consulting room as well as in the theatre. In classical psychoanalysis, projection is understood as the process whereby one's own traits, emotions or dispositions are ascribed to another person. It's conceived of as being preceded by denial, e.g. a person denies that he or she feels a particular emotion; or has a wish but asserts that it's the wish of someone else.

Barrie and I were feeling our way towards common ground, eventually arriving at the idea that, whilst therapists made conscious use of projection to help bring about change in their clients, it was also a phenomenon that habitually occurred in the theatre, between actors and their audience: the audience willingly suspended its disbelief and shared the experience of the ongoing performance by reading emotions into the character being portrayed by the actor. (It also happened in the cinema, we remembered: strong men had been known to weep at the death of Bambi's mother.) It was this element of trickery – the actor's ability to stimulate projection – that was later to strike a chord with Max.

My interest in theatre went back a long way – at one point, after leaving university, I'd even considered applying for a place at drama school. This might explain why, having met a professional actor all these years later, I jumped at the idea of embarking on a venture that drew on more than one set of skills.

Mind the Drama, Mr Rops! was to be an improvised therapy session in which Barrie, dressed in black and wearing a gold Venetian mask, worked a puppet; and I played a version of myself as therapist. The client was Mr Rops – to give him his full title, Monsieur Félicien Rops.

Created by Barrie using odds and ends from Oxfam, Mr Rops was a disreputable character who, whilst seeking treatment, was a therapist's nightmare. He presented with every symptom in the book: several types of personality disorder, multiple manifestations of psychosomatic illness, hysterical paralysis, dyspraxia, dyslexia and aphasia, along with a marked resistance to being helped. He was disinhibited, behaved outrageously and transgressed all codes of common decency. By the end of the "session", however, it was important that Barrie and Mr Rops reverted to what they properly were: a man with a puppet.

As an experiment in projection, it worked: Barrie had "disappeared" behind a mask, freeing the audience to project their thoughts and feelings on to what went on between the "client" and the therapist. Following the event, the general response from the audience was that it had been enlightening – for a few, "chilling".

As a means of raising my profile in college, *Mind the Drama, Mr Rops* also proved effective; for Barrie, too, it helped release a fresh bout of creative energy. Yet there was another, altogether unexpected outcome: Mr Rops was a matchmaker, something neither of us had reckoned with.

Over the months that followed, despite geographical distance, our relationship flourished. Having returned to Mull, it wasn't long before Barrie began to take stock and realised that continuing to run the theatre as a single-handed operation wasn't feasible; neither was it doing him any favours living on his own in a draughty old manse in the middle of nowhere with only the sheep and the feral cats for company. Eventually, after a good deal of soul-searching, he wound down the theatre, sold the house and moved to East Anglia.

Dividing his time between the University Library in Cambridge and the house in Ampthill Street in Norwich, Barrie began immersing himself in further projects. One in particular, a commission to write and perform a dramatic monologue, was to have special significance with regard to Max.

XII

What manner of theatre is it, in which we are at once playwright,
actor, stage manager, scene painter and audience?

W.G. Sebald, *The Rings of Saturn* [*Die Ringe des Saturn*], 1995[83]

By July of 1988, my contract with Churchill had run out, meaning it was time
to pack up my belongings and return to Norwich and join Barrie in Ampthill
Street. Though once again living in Norfolk, the jobs I now had were taking
me further afield. Over the next three years, much of my time was spent on
the road, commuting between Norwich and Colchester, Colchester and
London, resulting in a rather fragmented lifestyle. I feared friendships would
suffer – and that my friendship with Max would be no exception. Then, one
evening in October, there was a tap at the door...

This was the first time Max met Barrie. Introductions made, we caught up
with recent events. That summer, he told us, the three parts of *After Nature*
had been published as a single volume; he was especially pleased with the
look of the book: it had been bound in green cloth with two double-page
black-and-white photographs by Thomas Becker forming the endpapers. He
promised to bring me a copy next time he was round.

"There's some other news," Max went on. "For my sins, UEA have seen fit
to promote me." He claimed he wasn't looking forward to what this would
entail: as Professor of European Literature, he'd "be expected to attend ever
more of these endless committee meetings, get landed with piles of useless
admin ... all very well but what's going to happen to the garden?" he groaned.

The lament gathered pace. "And the writing? When will I get time for *that*?" Max was clearly on form – as if there had been no gap at all since last I'd seen him.

Whilst very caught up in university life, he continued to drop in for chats whenever he could. There was much to share, with Barrie, too – not least, memories of Manchester and the North West. Barrie had grown up in Buxton, in Derbyshire – a fact not lost on Max, who clearly knew the place. Here's a passage from *The Emigrants*:

> ... *after basic training at Catterick, in a God-forsaken part of north Yorkshire, he* [*Ferber*] *volunteered for a paratroop regiment, hoping that that way he would still see action before the end of the war, which was clearly not far off. Instead, he fell ill with jaundice, and was transferred to the convalescent home in the Palace Hotel at Buxton, and so his hopes were dashed. Ferber was compelled to spend more than six months at the idyllic Derbyshire spa town, recovering his health and consumed with rage ...*[84]

Barrie went on to tell Max how in 1940, as a boy of ten – from his bedroom window – he had watched the glow rising above Manchester twenty-eight miles away: the bombing of the city.

It was the story of Barrie's experience on Mull, however, that most captured Max's imagination – the everyday business of living on the island. However, they always returned to the subject of theatre: the technicalities of putting on a show; how an actor goes about "inhabiting" his or her character; or why it was that the plays of August Strindberg resonated so strongly with the Highland psyche. Of particular interest to Max was the question of how one coped with the phenomenon of audience projection – especially when, as in this case, it concerned an audience so physically close to the stage, there were times when the actors had a job not to step on the feet of people sitting in the front row.

It was the practicalities of acting and staging as much as the text of plays that absorbed Max – and had done since his student days. This seems to be reflected in his choice of speakers at the colloquium he'd convened at the end of March/beginning of April the previous year. At *A Radical Stage: Theatre in Germany in the 1970s and 1980s*, discussion of the work of the new generation of German-language playwrights was given equal billing with that of recent experiments in staging – including the groundbreaking work of Peter Stein and his ensemble at the Schaubühne am Halleschen Ufer.

I had witnessed a good deal of Peter Stein's work in Berlin during the 1970s – indeed, it was one of the aspects of life in the city I missed most. Trying to describe what it had been like to Max and Barrie gave me an excellent chance to share my enthusiasm. There had been two unforgettable productions in 1974, I recalled: Euripides' *The Bacchae*, staged from start to finish in blinding white light, emphasising the savagery of the piece; and Gorky's *Summerfolk*. I could still picture the stage and the opening scene: how, with studied languor, the *datshniki* amused themselves amongst the birch trees – real birch trees, these ones, transported by lorry from the surrounding Brandenburg countryside. Then in 1976, there had been *Shakespeare's Memory*, an extraordinary evocation of Elizabethan England performed as a series of tableaux in a vast, disused film unit in Spandau. Members of the audience were invited to engage with the actors, question them about what they were doing and how and why they were doing it – anything from dramatic technique to sixteenth-century politics.

"Total immersion, then?" asked Max. "Yes, and the show didn't stop there, either!" I explained how, as soon as the play was over, there used to be a rush for the door and everybody – audience and actors alike – would make their way to one or other of the nearby restaurants or bars. Here, we would continue talking – often, long into the night. One of our favourite haunts had been Café Einstein – organised along the lines of a Viennese coffee house. And then there was Exil, the restaurant at Paul-Lincke-Ufer 44A, known to Berliners as "the artists' living room".

The brainchild of Oswald Wiener, this establishment had first opened in 1972. Ossi Wiener came from Vienna, where he had been a member of the Wiener Gruppe, a group of avant-garde artists and writers that included Gerhard Rühm and Konrad Bayer. This last name meant a lot to Max: Konrad Bayer, a gifted young Austrian noted for his pessimistic view of things, had committed suicide in 1964 at the age of thirty-two. His experimental prose work, *The Head of Vitus Bering*, was amongst the books that had interested Max when he was preparing "And if I Remained by the Outermost Sea".[85]

It was in the context of discussions such as these that Barrie began talking about his own recent project: a dramatic monologue entitled *The New Prometheus*. Having had a taste of Max's wry sense of humour and interest in psychopathology, he gave him a copy, suggesting Max treat it as "light entertainment" between university committee meetings.

XIII

My sleep depends totally on the celestial constellations;
as soon as God withdraws too far away ... sleep becomes
entirely impossible. If I then stay awake, the senseless rumbling
of the voices in my head produces intolerable mental agony
compounded on and off by fits of bellowing ...
which have lasted for more than a year ...

Daniel Paul Schreber, *Memoirs of My Nervous Illness*, 1903[86]

Despite our new-found happiness, there continued to be days when, like me, Barrie caught himself succumbing to waves of grief. On one such occasion, I happened to be scanning my bookshelves and came across a paperback I had first read in 1978. "This'll take your mind off things!" I told him, handing him the book. The cover alone was enough to stop one in one's tracks: it depicted a naked, robotic child, its limbs and torso held together by a series of leather straps attached to a metal frame. Whether Barrie was more startled by the sight of the cover or my sudden gesture is hard to say. Either way, his response was to crack out laughing and begin to read. He was unable to put the book down.

Morton Schatzman's *Soul Murder: Persecution in the Family* is a study of Daniel Paul Schreber, the eminent nineteenth-century German judge who, at the height of his career, suffered a series of floridly psychotic episodes that led to his being admitted to Sonnenstein Asylum near Dresden.

Schreber wrote about his experiences in *Memoirs of My Nervous Illness* – a remarkable work that reflects both the extent of his erudition and his highly complex, delusional belief system. The central feature of this system was the belief that he had a mission to redeem the world, to restore mankind to its lost state of bliss by giving birth to a new race. This was to involve his physical transformation from a man into a woman – a process that would take a very long time.

The *Memoirs* were published in 1903. In 1911, the very year of Schreber's death, Sigmund Freud published his classic monograph "Psycho-Analytic Notes on an Autobiographical Account of a Case of Paranoia" – the work that was to immortalise Schreber in the world of analytic and psychiatric literature.

Schatzman takes a different approach from Freud. Basing his argument on what is known about the history of the Schreber family, he traces the connection between Daniel Paul's experience and the methods of childrearing practised by his father, Daniel Gottlob Moritz Schreber, a leading orthopaedic physician, prolific author and well-known educational reformer.

Schreber senior was a man of strong views, particularly as regards the moral climate of the age, which he thought of as degenerate. This had moved him to write a series of books on health, "indoor gymnastics" and methods of childrearing, advocating a rigorous – not to say, repressive – system to which he had subjected his own children. He urged parents to exercise extreme vigilance at all times; and to help them raise truly healthy offspring, he recommended various devices made to his own specifications for the correction of posture and the prevention of "bad habits", masturbation in particular. More benignly, from the viewpoint of a later age, Dr Schreber had also initiated and given his name to the *Schrebergärten* movement in Germany – the cultivation of allotment gardens.

The more Barrie read Schatzman, the more it struck him that here was material for a play or a television docudrama. He began researching the subject, and out of this came *The New Prometheus*.

It was then that I had introduced him to a friend of mine, the psychotherapist Brett Kahr, who suggested Barrie perform his play at a forthcoming convention on "Psychoanalysis, Trauma and Child Abuse" to be held at New York University in Brooklyn. The event was being organised to honour the work of the psychoanalyst William G. Niederland, an acknowledged authority on the effects of trauma, who had also written about the Schreber case.

So it came about that on 24 April 1987 – as it happened, three weeks after Max had convened his colloquium *A Radical Stage* in Norwich – Barrie gave his first performance, dedicating it to Niederland. The event was afforded great poignancy by the fact that, shortly before Barrie was due to go on stage, the death was announced of the writer and Holocaust survivor Primo Levi.

The following January, Barrie gave another performance, this time in Berlin. It was memorable for having taken place in an apartment belonging to a friend – Hanna Blösser – overlooking the courtyard of the Memorial to the German Resistance, close to the spot where, following their abortive attempt to assassinate Hitler, Stauffenberg and others had been executed in July 1944.

It turned out that Max was already familiar with the Schreber case – it hadn't been long since he had written an essay in which he focused on Canetti's interpretation of Schreber's paranoia.[87] He was also aware of the writings of W.G. Niederland, in particular his pioneering work on Holocaust survivors and his concept of "the survivor syndrome"[88]. A few years later, in the early 1990s, Max had planned to invite Niederland to Norwich to take part in a series of seminars at the University of East Anglia on "Writing in the Shadow of the Shoah".

Whilst he hadn't witnessed Barrie in performance, from his reading of the script, Max was curious to hear how he had dealt with the portrayal of a character at the mercy of paranoid delusions. Of course it hadn't been easy, Barrie explained; in order to preserve his own sanity, he'd had to find ways of protecting himself on stage. This he had achieved with the help of various theatrical devices, one of which was the "head harness".

Recognising the risk of having to learn such emotionally highly-charged lines, Barrie had thought up a means of prompting himself, using an audio recording of the text. The cassette, with an on/off switch to be operated between finger and thumb, he kept in his pocket. The wires led to earphones that fitted inside his headgear, a helmet made of leather straps similar to the contraption invented by Schreber's father as part of the regime to ensure "correct" posture in children, his own included.

Although the play was in the form of a monologue to be performed by one actor, it contained three separate characters – Schreber the father; Schreber the son as a child; and Schreber the son as an adult. In order to achieve this "three-in-one" effect, Barrie had used a small black rug. Thus, when Daniel Paul was engaged in memories of his childhood, in dialogue with his father, he stepped on to the black rug (representing the past) and taken both parts.

It occurs to me that this kind of "multi-layering" has something in common with a device used by Max in his books – the interweaving of narrative voices. What Max appreciated in Barrie was his skill as a "shape-shifter"; what I came to detect in Max's writing was his tendency to disappear, and then re-emerge in another persona. Further, where Barrie was both the actor and the creator of the three characters – two of whom engaged in dialogue with each other – Max was both the author of the story (as W.G. Sebald) and the first-person narrator.

Besides being the creator of all the characters who speak to/listen to each other, including those based on real-life people, there is, of course, a further layer, discernible to anyone who knew Max personally: he shared traits with many of his characters, notably Jacques Austerlitz.

In March 2001, following the publication of *Austerlitz* in Germany, he gave an interview to the weekly news magazine *Der Spiegel*, in the course of which he was asked about this issue:

Interviewer: The first-person narrator in your book, who emerges as Austerlitz's interlocutor, clearly bears your traits. Does it bother you if one equates him with Sebald?

WGS: The everyday person is somewhat different from the writer. The writer is somewhat different from the narrator. And the narrator is in turn somewhat different from the characters he describes.

Interviewer: But the data and details are those of your biography?

WGS: As a general rule, that's pretty much the case.[89]

Typical Max! He wouldn't tell a lie; but neither was he going to give much away.

XIV

It was May 1976 ... Tripp gave me a present of one of his
engravings, showing the mentally-ill senatorial president Daniel
Paul Schreber with a spider in his skull – what can there be more
terrible than the ideas always scurrying around our minds? – and
much of what I have written later derives from this engraving,
even in my method of procedure: in adhering to an exact
historical perspective, in patiently engraving and linking together
apparently disparate things in the manner of a still life ... I have
kept asking myself since then what the invisible connections that
determine our lives are, and how the threads run ...

W.G. Sebald, "An Attempt at Restitution"
["Ein Versuch der Restitution"], November 2001[90]

Not all the conversations between Max and Barrie were about matters to do
with the theatre.

There came a point when, in addition to his university responsibilities,
Max had stretched himself beyond the limit. Towards the end of *The
Emigrants* in the story of "Max Ferber", the narrator alludes to his sense of
mounting despair as a writer:

> *During the winter of 1990/91, in the little free time I had (in other words,
> mostly at the so-called weekend and at night), I was working on the
> account of Max Ferber ... It was an arduous task. Often I could not get*

on for hours or days at a time, and not infrequently I unravelled what I had done, continuously tormented by scruples that were taking tighter hold and steadily paralysing me. These scruples concerned not only the subject of my narrative, which I felt I could not do justice to, no matter what approach I tried, but also the entire questionable business of writing. I had covered hundreds of pages with my scribble, in pencil and ballpoint. By far the greater part had been crossed out, discarded, or obliterated by additions. Even what I ultimately salvaged as a "final" version seemed to me a thing of shreds and patches, utterly botched...[91]

To Barrie and me, it had become increasingly evident that Max was carrying an emotional burden he needed to share, the nature of which we could only guess at. On one occasion, he had phoned in a state of extreme distress, expecting to find me at home. In my absence, Barrie asked him if there was any way he could help – whether there was anything Max felt able to say to him. In tears, Max had responded with: "I don't know – I don't know what to do; I can't find the words."

This was by no means the first time Max had hit rock bottom. There's another passage, this time in *Austerlitz*, in which, so I believe, he uses his character to give voice to that existential terror, his own:

... now I found writing such hard going that it often took me a whole day to compose a single sentence, and no sooner had I thought such a sentence out, with the greatest effort, and written it down, than I saw the awkward falsity of my constructions and the inadequacy of all the words I had employed ... like a tightrope walker who has forgotten how to put one foot in front of the other, all I felt was the swaying of the precarious structure on which I stood, stricken with terror at the realization that the ends of the balancing pole gleaming far out on the edges of my field of vision were no longer my guiding lights, as before, but malignant enticements to me to cast myself into the depths ... in this dreadful state of mind I sat for hours, for days on end with my face to the wall, tormenting myself

and gradually discovering the horror of finding that even the smallest task or duty, for instance arranging assorted objects in a drawer, can be beyond one's power. It was as if an illness that had been latent in me for a long time were now threatening to erupt, as if some soul-destroying and inexorable force had fastened upon me and would gradually paralyse my entire system. I already felt in my head the dreadful torpor that heralds disintegration of the personality ... that all my life had been a constant process of obliteration, a turning away from myself and the world.[92]

Barrie experienced grave concern; indeed, as he told me later, he feared for Max's safety. "All I could do," he explained, "was listen – and wait." Barrie asked no questions; he felt it would be inappropriate to pry. All the same, the impression remained: here was a person in pain to whom something deeply traumatic had happened. And whilst Barrie couldn't take away that pain, he realised that, temporarily at least, he had been a source of consolation. For this, Max was later to express his gratitude, not through words but through the gift of a picture.

* * * * *

In 1994, two close colleagues of Max's had died: Michael Parkinson in April and Janine Dakyns in August, of cancer. On 10 September, a month after Janine's death, Max came to see us and stayed to dinner, bringing with him a pair of engravings that he had framed himself.

These engravings, done by his friend Jan Peter Tripp, and which Tripp had given Max in May 1976, depict two versions of Schreber, arranged side by side. The one on the left shows a three-quarter-length portrait of Schreber senior, positioned "above" the head of his son; the other is a bust of Daniel Paul with his head split across the top and a spider coming out of his skull.

Here, I would like to make a tentative suggestion. The two heads that feature in both engravings might be understood as a representation of two kinds of male authority in the lives of both Daniel Paul Schreber and Max

Sebald: the good and the bad. In the case of Daniel Paul, at various stages of his illness, he had endowed his two physicians with just those qualities: Dr Weber was "good", Dr Flechsig "bad". Max was constantly at loggerheads with his father Georg and regarded him as a force for the bad; his grandfather Josef Egelhofer, on the other hand, had always been a force for the good.

Max had added a handwritten inscription in French – an example of *ekphrasis*:

Daniel Paul Schreber
Le père, le fils et le saint esprit

Ekphrasis is a rhetorical device whereby one medium relates to another in a work of art. In this case, Max's words – in a language not his mother tongue – offer a clue as to the essence of Tripp's engravings. The textual element (the discursive mode) establishes a point of view, adding another narrative layer to the image (the non-discursive mode) without seeking to interpret it. Here again, we encounter a kind of "layering".

Max was always generous and the fact that he had made a present of this particular engraving was his way of acknowledging Barrie both as an artist and as a friend. It seems to me now that what Max had valued above all was Barrie's understanding of Schreber's state of mind – the disintegration of personality (as dramatized in *The New Prometheus*); and by extension, of him, Max Sebald, and his fear of going mad.

What makes the gesture doubly poignant is the significance the engraving continued to hold for Max – right up to the time less than a month before his death. In his speech at the opening of the Literaturhaus (House of Literature) in Stuttgart on 17 November 2001, it was to this same engraving that he referred – in terms of it having been one of the most important keys to his writing.

XV

Language is a labyrinth of paths. You approach from one
side and know your way about; you approach the same place
from another side and no longer know your way about.

Ludwig Wittgenstein, *Philosophical Investigations*, 1958[93]

The essays of the 1970s and early 1980s had helped establish Max's reputation
in academic circles. True, he had courted controversy in the process – as
with his dissertations on Carl Sternheim and Alfred Döblin. When it came
to literary criticism, Max was uncompromising; he didn't flinch from stating
what he thought.

There's a good example dating from 1985, by which time he had become
an acknowledged champion of Austrian literature. As part of the twenty-
fifth anniversary celebrations of the magazine *Manuskripte*, he was invited
to contribute to the autumn issue with a "Statement". Max approached the
subject with characteristic aplomb:

> *As a passionate reader, I was recently reminded of how badly I'd fare
> without the literature of Austria. I was on the train between Munich and
> Frankfurt, so bored that for want of anything better to do, I read an excerpt
> from the latest novel in a series by a well-known West German author
> which had just appeared in the* Frankfurter Allgemeine Zeitung. *It
> made me feel so unwell that I was obliged to go to the restaurant car and
> knock back a brandy.*[94]

As the decade came to a close, his gloom-laden predictions regarding his role as a professor of literature at a British university proved unfounded. On the contrary, it seemed to have opened the way to an ever more fruitful working life. From then on, alongside new responsibilities and initiatives – such as the setting up of the British Centre for Literary Translation in 1989 – Max remained loyal to his mission, finding time to produce a steady stream of literary work.

Admittedly, visits from Max had become quite rare. Nevertheless, it was always a pleasure when he did drop by; or when he'd included us in an invitation to events at the University. One such occasion was in December 1992. Under the auspices of the British Centre for Literary Translation, with funding from the Arts Council, Max had organised an evening on the theme "The Possibility of a European Culture", for which Hans Magnus Enzensberger had been asked to give the opening reading.

Shortly before the proceedings were due to begin, Barrie and I were walking side by side along the corridor when we noticed Max coming towards us. He stopped short, looked at us attentively, smiled and commented: "Well, now I get it – it's obvious why you two belong together! It's the eyes – you have the same eyes!"

The memory of this encounter puts me in mind of the start of *Austerlitz*. What strikes the narrator about the animals in the Nocturama in Antwerp is that ...

> ... *several of them had strikingly large eyes, and the fixed, inquiring gaze found in certain painters and philosophers who seek to penetrate the darkness which surrounds us purely by means of looking and thinking.*[95]

Eyes, for Max the most vulnerable part of a person or an animal, had always preoccupied him. In his writing, they feature as crucially in the opening section of *After Nature* as later in *Austerlitz* and *Unrecounted*. To my way of thinking, it's rendered all the more poignant by the fact that, for as long as I had known him, Max had been anxious about his vision. He confessed to being horrified at the thought of ever requiring surgery on his eyes, and feared losing his sight. On this last point, however, he felt ambivalent. Were he to go blind, he said, it would prevent him from reading; at the same time, it would relieve him of the "necessity" of having to write.

By the summer of 1993, my own health had become precarious, requiring surgery. I hesitated to tell my friends, but decided it was only fair to alert the closest amongst them, including Max. In mid-November, shortly before leaving for my appointment at the Elizabeth Garrett Anderson Hospital in London, I received a parcel: two hardbacks, first editions of *Schwindel. Gefühle* (*Vertigo*) and *Die Ausgewanderten* (*The Emigrants*). Inside *The Emigrants* was a postcard reproduction of Frans Post's *View of Itamaracá*.[96] After the greeting, he had written "17.xi.93" – so typical of Max, and especially touching, that he had remembered the precise date of the operation.

There are several entries in my appointments diary for the following January that read "Max phoning". I remember he had got in touch to ask how things were going. He explained that the University had granted him study leave to continue his research into post-war and contemporary German literature but that, actually, he was using it to prepare his next book.

In view of the fact that I was on extended sick leave and had time to spare, he went on to ask whether I'd like to think about doing some literary translation. This didn't come as a surprise – the subject of translation had often been part of our conversations in the past. In this instance, however, what Max was referring to was the idea that I translate *him*, specifically, an English version of *After Nature*. He'd been on the lookout for someone suitable and thought he had spotted "one or two possible candidates"; all the same, he said, he had great faith in my abilities – a feel for the language and idiom of the work – and would be happy for me to give it a try.

Unfortunately, it was not to be. For various reasons, including that I was still rather fragile, I felt unable to take up his suggestion. Eventually, it was Max's friend, the poet and translator Michael Hamburger, who met the challenge; but another eight years before the UK edition appeared in print – in August 2002.

* * * * *

From the start of my time at Churchill, I had been aware that amongst the most illustrious members of the Senior Common Room was the polymath and cultural analyst Professor George Steiner. On Tuesday, 26 April 1994, Max invited Barrie and me to attend the inaugural St. Jerome Lecture, to be delivered by George in the Sainsbury Centre at the University of East Anglia. As expected, it was a fireworks display of rhetoric and erudition – at the same time, deeply personal. For all his scholarly glosses, George never fought shy of using simple, complex words like "love" – to startling effect:

> *Translation is an exact art. Exactitude and art are often exacting. They press exaction on the translator, to the point ... of self-suppression, of near-derangement. The reader also should be under some pressure. At their best, the rewards are those of a radiant, ever-renewed dissatisfaction. They are, quite simply, those of love.*[97]

As the months wore on, Max's books were attracting more and more public acclaim in Europe – most particularly, in Germany (English translations had yet to appear). Yet the trappings of fame never sat comfortably with him, neither at this point nor in the years that followed. This can be illustrated by something Max told us later that summer.

He came round and gave a jaw-dropping account of how things had gone in Berlin in June, where he'd been to receive the Johannes Bobrowski Medal for *The Emigrants*. "An outrageous lump of metal," he fumed, "which I had no intention of bringing home with me..." After the award ceremony, he'd taken the "lump", made his way to the Kleiner Wannsee – down to the eastern shore of the lake – and hurled the medal into the water, where it sank without trace.

As so often with Max's stories, the comedy of the situation was bitter-sweet: it was on this precise spot that on 21 November 1811, the thirty-four-year-old Heinrich von Kleist, having entered a suicide pact with the terminally-ill Henriette Vogel, had first shot his friend and then turned the pistol on himself.

XVI

It's not easy to be a saint; not only do you have the whole world and your own self against you, but the Church too.

Claudio Magris, *Microcosms* [*Microcosmi*], 1997[98]

Having completed *The Rings of Saturn* and submitted the corrected proofs to the publishers, Max embarked on a new literary venture, one conceived along similar lines to his "English Pilgrimage" – this time, to Corsica. In September 1995, he set out on the first of two research trips.

It was in January 2005 that I first came across "The Alps in the Sea", one of the essays that formed part of the Corsican project. Here Max describes how he ...

... began to read Flaubert's version of the legend of St Julian ... that strange tale in which an insatiable passion for hunting and a vocation for sainthood do battle in the same heart. I was both fascinated and disturbed by the story ...[99]

This brought back memories of when I myself had first read Flaubert's *Trois Contes* (*Three Tales*): I was seventeen and steeped in notions of doing one's Christian duty and what happens if one doesn't. I remembered the story of St Julian as having been extraordinarily rich in detail – like a medieval tapestry; also, as extremely bloody. Julian's love of hunting becomes an obsession that leads to indulging in orgies of killing; and, ultimately, the murder of his parents. Full of remorse, he determines on a life of poverty.

One day, he encounters a leper to whom he offers everything he has: food, drink and shelter. The leper is still not satisfied; he is cold, he says – will accept nothing less than for Julian to lie with him and warm him "with his whole body". In the embrace, Julian is released from his torment and, finally, in a state of ecstasy, is taken up to heaven.

Having finished "The Alps in the Sea", I was moved to read Flaubert's legend again. It was then that it came back to me: the memory of a conversation – maybe it'd been a series of conversations – I'd had with Max back in 1982. What I remember clearly is that all this took place shortly after his essay on Ernst Herbeck appeared in *Manuskripte*.

We had been talking about the lives and writings of those who, in Max's view, had been unjustly sidelined: Herbeck, certainly; but Herbert Achternbusch and Robert Walser as well. In his reading of other authors, too, Max seems to have been drawn to works featuring characters who have been marginalised: Peter Handke's Kaspar Hauser, for instance; and, as in this case, Flaubert's St Julian. Whether real or fictionalised, what all these lives have in common is the experience of mental suffering. Furthermore, for Max, questions of psychopathology in literature were always key.

From the outset, he'd wanted to know what it was that had motivated me to embark on a career as a psychologist. Following my return to Britain, I'd been extremely reluctant to expand on the subject; but with Max it was different – his was no idle curiosity. My real reason for switching to psychology, I told him, was a wish to understand what made me as well as the rest of my family tick.

Whilst my parents – and particularly my mother – had found it wholly unacceptable to have such things pointed out to them, I believed there was evidence of mental instability reaching back at least three generations. One thing had come home to me: the difficulty of distinguishing between "dottiness" and "pottiness" – "potty" had always been a favourite word with Max. What counts for eccentricity (often amusing and relatively harmless) and what for mental disturbance (at times florid, if not actually dangerous) is a grey area. It occurred to me that my uncle John was a case in point.

Round about this time, in 1982, my mother had happened to ask me if, wearing my "editorial-literary" hat, I would write an appraisal of a book about her younger brother. *Strange Vagabond of God: The Story of John Bradburne* was due to be published the following year and the author, John Thurston Dove, a Jesuit priest and close friend of John's, had been in touch requesting feedback regarding his latest draft.[100]

It was a daunting task. The tone of the book was fulsome, at times so personal that to be reading it at all felt uncomfortably voyeuristic – an intrusion on private grief. The text, moreover, was interspersed with copious quotes from John's poems – poems couched in a language that was, to say the least, idiosyncratic; and which I found rather embarrassing. From what I knew of my uncle, the poems hadn't been written for public consumption. I faced a dilemma: how to remain objective and offer a fair critique whilst voicing my reservations in a constructive way. I decided to share my misgivings with Max and began by putting him in the picture as to John's story and what had happened a couple of years before.

During my childhood, we had received occasional visits from John and, as I grew older, began to suspect that "Johnny Hornbeam" – as he came to be known by us children – was not merely eccentric; there was something distinctly odd about him. He would turn up in canvas plimsolls whatever the weather; and, apart from a recorder, appeared to have very few possessions – certainly never any money. On the other hand, what he *did* have was the most beautiful voice; and when the mood took him, he would burst into song, often in Latin – Gregorian plainchant – or play tunes on his recorder.

John was born in Skirwith, in Cumbria, in 1921 – a year later than Ernst Herbeck – the third of five children. When he was twelve, the family moved to Norfolk, where my grandfather, an Anglican clergyman, had been appointed rector of St Agnes, Cawston, with responsibility for its sister church at Salle. My grandmother, a great teller of family stories, would often include the ones about John: as a boy, he'd always been up to something or other, as often as not making a nuisance of himself. On one occasion, he'd climbed up on to the roof of Cawston Church and, flinging wide his arms, called down that he was going to see what it'd be like to fly. My mother, whose job it was to keep an eye on him, managed to persuade him not to jump – but only just. The wish to fly was something that stayed with him all his life.

At the mention of Salle, the roofs of churches and the urge to fly, I noticed Max smiling – he knew all about East Anglian churches.[101] He encouraged me to go on.

When war broke out in 1939, John joined the army, serving in Malaya. The Japanese invaded, Singapore fell, and John and his men were told to pair off and try to avoid being captured. He went off into the jungle, where he spent the next few weeks foraging, living off roots and fruit. This proved decisive: it was here he underwent a mystical experience – something akin to an epiphany – that would change his life.

His first attempt at escape resulted in shipwreck; with the second attempt, he was in luck. Having managed to board the last British destroyer to leave Sumatra, he reached Burma. By this time, he was in very poor shape, suffering from heat stroke and malaria. No sooner had he recovered, however, than he rejoined the fighting, this time as one of Orde Wingate's Chindits. It was then that he met Thurston Dove, with whom he became firm friends.

For John, the last stage of the war proved the most traumatic. There was one incident in particular that affected him so deeply, he was unable to speak about it, even to Thurston. There had been veiled references to this within the family and it was my belief, as I told Max, that it had involved a more than usually brutal killing perpetrated by John. When I think about it now, it strikes me as the first link with the legend of St Julian.

After his return to England, John had been unable to settle. He took on a series of jobs, none of which lasted long; in any case, by this time it had become clear to him that by far his greatest need was to search for God. To that end, in 1947, he converted to Roman Catholicism. It was at this time, too, that he began writing poetry. He tried becoming a monk but was turned down by both the Benedictines and the Carthusians – on the grounds that he was not cut out for life in a closed community and adherence to rules. Undeterred – and trusting entirely to providence – he went on his way and made a pilgrimage to Jerusalem, via Rome, Naples, Athens and Cyprus. When not abroad, he led the life of a wandering minstrel, playing his recorder and often, quite literally, singing for his supper.

In 1961, John wrote to Thurston, who was now working at a Jesuit mission in Rhodesia (Zimbabwe). "Do you know of a cave in Africa where I can pray?" John asked. The response was positive. The following year, he left England and established himself at the mission on the outskirts of Salisbury (Harare). By this time, he had been accepted as a member of the Third Order of St Francis – laymen who undertake to say certain prayers each day and help the poor.

It wasn't until 1969, however, that John discovered his true vocation: on a visit to the remote region of Mtoko, he was taken to a leper settlement at Mtemwa (which in the Shona language means, "You are cut off"). Horrified by the living conditions of the lepers – the hunger, the lack of hygiene and the rat-infested buildings in which they were housed, he made up his mind on the spot: this was where he would stay. From then on – and for the rest of his life – he dedicated himself to the care of the lepers, feeding them, washing them, dressing their wounds, treating each one as a special individual, with dignity. Beyond the day-to-day duties, he would pray with them, sing to them and write each one a personal poem.

There was, however, a problem: whilst capable of inspiring deep affection, John was also stubborn, and insisted on doing things on his own terms. This was certainly true of his relations with the mission authorities, with whom he'd engaged in a running battle for as long as he'd known them. He was criticised for being extravagant – for example, in trying to ensure that each leper was provided with one loaf of bread a week. And he infuriated the Rhodesian Leprosy Association by his refusal to go along with the idea of hanging numbers round the necks of the lepers, insisting that they were human beings, not cattle. As a result, he was given the sack as warden of the settlement.

John's response was typical: he took his blanket and went and camped on nearby Mount Chigona, from where he still had a view of the settlement. Aware that a leopard was known to prowl about the mountain at night, a local farmer took pity and provided John with a tin hut just outside the perimeter fence. It was here that he spent the next six years, living the life of an ascetic, wearing his Franciscan habit and allowing his hair and beard to grow very long. His only source of bathing water was a rock pool on Chigona; he ate next to nothing. As in the past, John continued to have an extraordinary affinity with creatures – birds, beasts and insects; his special allies were eagles and bees. (I suppose this could be seen as a kind of inversion of the case with Julian, whose passion is for hunting and killing wild animals.)

John still had access to the chapel, where he sang and played the harmonium; and, under cover of darkness, he would steal into the settlement to minister to the sick and the dying. None of this made him popular with the locals, who had come to regard him with increasing suspicion and hostility. It seems to have been this antagonism that fuelled a plot to abduct him and hand him over to the Patriotic Front guerrillas.

At the outset of the civil war, John had refused to heed government warnings and leave the country. By the end of the 1970s, Mtemwa was in the conflict zone; but, even now, John's friends could not persuade him to move. On the night of 2 September, shortly before midnight, a group of *mujibhas* – bandits, mostly teenagers – came to his hut, kidnapped him and marched him off to a remote cave, a guerrilla outpost where he was subjected to a mock trial and accused of being an informer for the Rhodesian security forces.

The guerrillas were in an uncomfortable position. Their commander was an admirer of John's work and angry at the *mujibhas* for having taken him prisoner. Realising the charges were false, the commander ordered John's release. However, his security officer argued that John had seen too much and proposed instead that he leave the lepers and take his services elsewhere. John would have none of it.

In the early hours of 5 September, the guerrillas set off with John, making for the main Mtoko road. Just before they reached it, the security officer ordered him to walk a few paces ahead. He obeyed, fell on his knees and began to pray, showing no sign of fear. As he rose to his feet, the officer shot him dead.

At his requiem mass in Salisbury Cathedral a further event occurred that ensured the fulfilment of his "third wish" (the first had been to care for leprosy patients; the second, to die a martyr). A friend had placed three white flowers on the coffin in memory of John's devotion to the Trinity and, shortly after, eyewitnesses saw three drops of blood fall from the coffin, forming a single pool – according to the undertaker, this was fresh blood, bright and crimson, unlike that from a dead body. When the coffin was reopened, no traces of blood were found; at the same time, it was noticed that his body had been dressed in a shirt. It was replaced by the Franciscan habit John had wished for.

What was Max making of this? I wondered. He'd never denied having been brought up a Catholic; at the same time, I knew that when he was seventeen, he had taken the bold step of leaving the Church.

Pre-empting what I was about to tell him, he said: "So your uncle will be made a saint..." This put me on the spot. Whilst my experience in Berlin had thrown everything into question, including ideas about the High Anglican tradition in which I'd been raised, I still felt ambivalent. And now, with regard to John...

Nevertheless, I had to admit that Max was probably right. From my mother, I'd gathered that people all over the world were claiming to have had their prayers answered by invoking John's name; and, on the strength of events following his death and subsequent reports of "miracles", the Archbishop of Harare had been petitioned to advance the cause for his canonisation.

XVII

If you look for things that are like the things that you have looked
for before, then, obviously, they'll connect up. But they'll only
connect up in an obvious sort of way, which actually isn't,
in terms of writing something new, very productive.

W.G. Sebald, Interview with Joseph Cuomo, 13 March 2001[102]

Having told him the story of John, what I wanted from Max was advice on
what to do about the appraisal of Thurston Dove's book. Whilst I no longer
recall his exact words, I remember him as having been reassuring, telling
me not to worry – just write what I honestly thought and send it off. As for
John's poems, he was sure someone would be interested.

He was right again. That "someone" was Professor David Crystal, an
acknowledged authority on language and linguistics. In the mid-1990s, he
took it upon himself to collect and edit the poems, estimating that during
the last ten years of his life, John had achieved a prodigious output – no
less than six thousand poems – many of which had been marked with the
exact hour and date of writing. This showed that at times he had composed
as many as a dozen in a day, filling every inch of space on the paper and
without corrections.

Typically, the poems are the expression of a highly personal belief system,
bearing witness to a delight in sound, rhyme and rhythm, often involving
exuberant wordplay and inventive use of imagery. There's nothing obvious
about the way John made connections: the ordinary is juxtaposed with the

startling. And although the quality of the poems I've read – admittedly, only a fraction of the total output – is very uneven, ranging from the lyrical to the quirky, sometimes descending into bathos and doggerel, I have to remind myself that John's motivation for writing, like Ernst Herbeck's, didn't lie in a desire for public acclaim.

* * * * *

Curiously, another thread links Max and John. At the start of *By Hook or by Crook*, David Crystal writes that the inspiration for this book came from reading *The Rings of Saturn*. In 2005, his literary editor had suggested he try writing a linguistic travel book and, handing him a much-thumbed copy of *The Rings of Saturn*, wondered if David could use it as a model. This was how he described his response:

> *This was a first encounter with Sebald. When I first saw his book I was appalled by his long paragraphs, and thought I would hate it, but I went with his flow and found it enthralling. What I took out of it mainly was that sense of flow, and also of the ambiguity in his account – did these things happen or not? Was I reading fact or fiction? The distinction didn't seem to matter.* By Hook *blurs that boundary too ...*[103]

Amongst the journeys taken by David on behalf of *By Hook or by Crook* – in which he explores aspects of the English language and how it is spoken in various parts of the world – he met my sister Celia.. As secretary of the John Bradburne Memorial Society, she and David had agreed to discuss the idea of developing a website for John's poetry, the Internet having struck them as the most appropriate means of publishing such a vast oeuvre. Finding his way to her house, however, proved less than straightforward: Celia lives somewhat off the beaten track and David certainly won't have been the first to get lost. Having searched out a replacement copy of *The Rings of Saturn* in Hay-on-Wye and crammed it into the already-full boot of his car, he proceeded down the country lanes:

The trouble with country lanes is that if you start thinking of poetry, you can easily miss your turning ... a signpost suggested that I had turned left instead of right. A second signpost confirmed it. I was approaching a long dark wood. If I didn't do something about it soon, I was going to renew my linguistic love-affair with Leominster.

I reversed into a gap into a field. Bradburne was right. There is always a marsh by a long dark wood. The wheels of my car found it. And, thanks to the bootload of Hay books, the wheels looked very comfortable, settling down in the welcoming Herefordshire mud.

The field was full of ravens, looking for an evening meal ... they eyed me suspiciously, or perhaps it was hungrily ...

I opened my boot. Perhaps if I took the books out? They were in the carrier bags, so they wouldn't be harmed on the ground. But one of the bags, thanks to the lately acquired Sebald, had too many books crammed into it. And that bag didn't like the experience of being hustled out of its nice warm boot. There was a tearing sound.

And that was how the farmhand found me. Crouched in a marsh, scraping mud off a copy of The Rings of Saturn, *and glaring at the ravens. Sebald would probably have approved.*[104]

XVIII

Begeistert von dem wahrhaftig
grenzenlosen Wachstum
der Industrie hat der Staatsmann
Disraeli Manchester die
    wundervollste
Stadt der Neuzeit genannt,
ein himmlisches Jerusalem,
dessen Bedeutung allein die
    Philosophie
zu ermessen vermöge. Ein halbes
Leben ist es nun her, daß ich,
nach meinem Aufbruch aus der
    Provinz,
dort ankam und Wohnung bezog
zwischen den Ruinen aus dem
    letzten
Jahrhundert ...

In his excitement about the truly
boundless growth
of industry, the statesman
Disraeli called Manchester
the most wonderful city of
    modern times,
a celestial Jerusalem
whose significance only
    philosophy
could gauge. Half a life ago now
it is that, after leaving my remote
    home,
I arrived there and took lodgings
among the previous century's
    ruins ...

W.G. Sebald, *After Nature*, [*Nach der Natur*], 1988[105]

In December 1996, following his second visit to Corsica, Max had opted to abandon that particular writing project. At around the same time, Barrie and I were faced with a challenge of a different kind. I had applied for a post in Aberdeen and been successful at interview. Whilst the job represented promotion and a significant pay rise, the prospect of leaving Norwich and going so far north was daunting. The decision having been made, however, we sold the house in Ampthill Street and made our way up the east coast.

To my lasting regret, I possess neither record nor memory of having been in touch with Max over the remaining years of the decade. Relocating to the northeast of Scotland had the effect of putting up a big geographical barrier; it also meant we were out of touch with Max. But then, two and a half years later, we moved again – this time, to Manchester.

Manchester was a city I didn't know – except virtually, through my reading of Friedrich Engels' *The Condition of the Working Class in England in 1844* all those years ago when living in Berlin; and through having listened to – and read – what Max had to say about it.

For Barrie, Manchester represented a kind of homecoming; it was here that he'd set out on his career as a professional actor. For Max, it represented the start of his life in England. In March 1998, he wrote his introduction to a new collection of essays, *Logis in einem Landhaus (A Place in the Country)*. On the opening page, he described how, over thirty years before, in the early autumn of 1966, he had arrived in Manchester with three books in his luggage: Gottfried Keller's *Der grüne Heinrich* [Green Henry], Johann Peter Hebel's *Schatzkästlein des rheinischen Hausfreunds* and a well-worn copy of Robert Walser's *Jakob von Gunten*. This journey to England was Max's first long trip abroad; so perhaps the inclusion of the books was a means of taking his language and culture with him; and of providing comfort in a foreign land if the going got tough.

The essays that follow, he went on to explain, were written as a way of honouring those whose work had always meant most to him – of paying homage "*eh es vielleicht zu spät wird*", which might be translated as "before it is perhaps too late". I find this phrase poignant in its ambivalence. It could be interpreted as meaning "before more time goes by and these writers will perhaps have been forgotten"; alternatively, as though Max is indicating his own mortality – in other words, "before I die and can no longer pay homage to those with whom I feel an affinity". There is no single way to read it.[106]

However that may be, by this time, Max had begun work on another project, arguably his most ambitious yet. Related to the questions of memory and recollection first raised in *The Emigrants*, *Austerlitz* was to absorb his attention for the next three years.

XIX

In May, it's warm enough to fetch the garden chairs,
arrange them in the shade beneath the apple tree.
I think of ways to animate the years
since last we touched: how touch again?
Look in thy heart and write.

I sent the birthday letter – and you phoned:
how could we know this was to be our last exchange?
In December, when I heard the news,
it seemed my heart had stopped.
The heart that stopped was yours.

In snowy spring, the apple tree is white,
is bare. I go to find your grave. I weep.
Words had never failed us while we talked.
They wither now. *Look in thy heart!* I write.

Philippa Comber, 2006[107]

It was a warm Sunday afternoon in the middle of May and my thoughts turned to Max. His birthday was coming up and having been out of touch for such a long time, I wanted to bridge the gap. Taking a chair and going out into the garden, I wrote him a letter; doubtless it would amuse him to hear that Barrie and I were now living in Altrincham, on the outskirts of Manchester.

14 May 2000

Dear Max,

Somewhere in distant memory I seem to recall that you have a birthday approaching, so have seated myself in my new garden under the apple tree to wish you many happy returns.

This struck me as a good opportunity, too, to let you know about this somewhat surprising change of circumstances: a year ago (and in fact less) we had no idea of our good fortune. Aberdeen proved to be about the most anti-social of all my job-related moves, being cold [and] dark ... friends virtually refused to visit us even in "high summer" (when the central heating was likely to be turned on) and apart from the advantage of being helpful for my career, it was a mercy to see an advertisement for the job I now have.

Some things don't change: I'm still in the psychology business and I'm still working for the NHS. However, I'm now heading up the service for Community-based Psychological Services for Manchester. That sounds grand and important: important it is but grand it ain't!

We couldn't believe our luck when we looked for somewhere to live. It happened within two weeks of arrival (October last year) and by Christmas the deal was done. This is another way of saying that if you ever had reason to come back to Manchester (to promote a book or just for the hell of it), please let me know; we'd be delighted to see you. I still remember ... how you spoke of your own experience of Manchester. What a city – with huge contrasts and surprises! Although the new house is in Cheshire (officially), you may be quite certain that I shall not be assuming the role of a "Cheshire lady" – I will remain, for preference, a Cheshire cat: and when I disappear, it'll be into the garden, which is small but has a lot of potential.

Anyhow, that's more than enough about me. I have often wondered how things are with you – also UEA ... also [your] literary plans. I read with great interest the reviews of the [English] translation[s][108] *and one*

aspect really came over strongly: you present an enigma, even to the most
perceptive. That is exactly the quality I always relished and cherished –
and it's not something the English like at all: I can say that now, now that
I'm back in England!

I hope this finds you well and only slightly discontented! It would be
very good to hear from you, in due course.

Best wishes and birthday greetings,
Yours affectionately,

Philippa C.

The following weekend, I was in Liverpool to attend a psychology conference.

On my return home, the first thing Barrie told me was that Max had phoned, and that he would phone again. Sure enough, he did, early that evening.

His voice was instantly recognisable – the same resonant tones. He'd been delighted to get my letter, he said... And how was he? I ventured. "I'm OK," came the reply, followed by a pause. Then, "You know me – I've never been much good at making decisions. It's taken a long time, but I think at last I've got better at it..."

The conversation proceeded on a different tack and we talked about Manchester. He had fond memories of the place and had last been to visit a couple of years ago, in 1998. He still knew people there – one person in particular, his former landlord, Peter Jordan. Peter was an architect and Jewish émigré in whose property in Didsbury Max had once rented a ground floor flat. We ended the conversation with promises to stay in touch. One of these days, he said, he'd like to come and visit us.

Not long after this, he wrote an essay entitled "*Scomber scombrus* oder die gemeine Makrele – zu Bildern von Jan Peter Tripp" ("*Scomber scombrus*, or the Common Mackerel – on pictures by Jan Peter Tripp").[109] For Max, names and initials, his own included, were charged with linguistic potential – a rich source of language games. Years before, in 1981, he'd asked me about the origin of my surname – Comber – and whether it had a particular meaning. "Who knows," I had replied, "possibly it's a fish – or perhaps 'one who dwells in a combe'!"

Whilst there may be no connection between Max's writing of the essay and the fact that we had recently resumed contact, I like to think there is. If so, whilst I'm not too happy about being associated with the common mackerel – especially the French variety with its less than salubrious connotations – I feel bound to forgive him!

* * * * *

Another year and a half went by. And then, one Sunday morning in December, Barrie went out to buy the papers as usual. I was having a lie-in and still dozing when he came upstairs. "Sorry, but this is very, very sad ..." he said. There on the front page of *The Independent on Sunday* was the news that Max had been killed in a car accident two days before, Friday, 14 December. Andrew Motion, at that time a colleague of Max's at the University of East Anglia, had written an obituary.

In retrospect, I am shocked at my initial response. Not disbelief; rather, a sense of horrified inevitability: "So he's done it this time!" Without knowing any details other than what was in the newspaper report, I found myself telling Barrie how, years before, Max had been involved in another car crash and had a narrow escape. That time, too, he had been at the wheel.

* * * * *

Ten years on, I still have a clear memory of where I was and what I was doing on the day Max died. I had taken myself off to the small library at Dalton Ellis Hall, part of the University of Manchester, for a quiet lunch-break – away from the other participants attending a psychotherapy training day.

After eating my sandwiches, I had run my eye along the shelves and found a slim volume – an ancient Penguin – about Sir Walter Raleigh. Taking note of the details, I later managed to track down a copy in a second-hand bookshop to give Barrie as a Christmas present (he was busy working on Raleigh at the time). There was also a book by Lily B. Campbell, *Shakespeare's Tragic Heroes*, which looked interesting. I homed in on Chapter Two "The Value of Imitation in Teaching Drama as Teaching by Imitation". I felt very much at peace in this sunlit, rather dusty room, full of an odd assortment of books arranged in no particular order on the shelves.

It wasn't until some forty-four hours later that I found out Max had died at the wheel on the A146 Norwich to Lowestoft road. Clive Scott, whom I had phoned in Norwich, thought it had been a heart attack. Adam Czerniawski, another friend of Max's with whom Clive put me in touch, asked what I thought had happened. I said I thought Clive was right.

On Monday, 7 January and still in shock, I tried dealing with matters by writing in my notebook:

> All these years, the relationship has been safeguarded – not secretively, but privately. And now he's dead. The common denominator was our sense of exile – from the perspective of the person in exile. And the accompanying emotion? *Schwindel. Gefühle.* (Dizziness. Feelings.) ...
>
> It's no wonder to me that it was to Max I turned first, twenty years ago, in January 1982, having received the news that my father had died – also of a heart attack. My father, a man seeking solace but finding himself in a state of conflict ...
>
> Now, in the light of Max's own death, I've found myself reviewing why it was he'd declined to come round that night, why he had seemed to respond so coolly ... It must have been obvious from the way I spoke on the phone that I was strangely elated; all my usual defences were down and I was in the grip of an erotic charge, which I'd be only too ready to transfer on to the first man I saw. Being the

kind of person he was, Max had got round it in a very dignified, almost English way. "I'm afraid I have to take the dog out," he'd said.

Proof perhaps – if proof were needed – that caught off their guard, psychotherapists are no different from anyone else; and that, in difficult situations, they can rely on their "non-psychotherapist" friends to know where to draw the line.

And the dog? Max had always been very attached to his dog, the fellow creature that had brought him both respite and inspiration. As he once observed, citing Walter Benjamin, the dog is the age-old symbol of *Schwermut* (melancholia) in a man's soul.[110] His first dog, Jodok, was vegetarian (never before had I come across canine vegetarianism); and Jodok's successor – a black dog – was called Maurice (or Moritz, making this a case of *Max und Moritz*, as in the title of Wilhelm Busch's verse tale for children). I heard later that it was Maurice who had led the small funeral procession to the site of Max's grave on 3 January 2002; and, shortly afterwards, had also died.

* * * * *

Since the early 1990s, I'd had an important family commitment. This concerned my aunt, Margaret, the last surviving member of her generation of Combers. Since the death of her sister in the 1980s, she had been living in London on her own but had then begun to develop symptoms of dementia, making her increasingly vulnerable. Margaret had always been extremely devout and it was clear to me that in terms of her future care, in addition to her physical needs, spiritual ones would have to be taken into consideration.

Friends in Norwich had made me aware of the existence of a nursing home in Bungay, Adele House, run under the aegis of the Anglican convent at Ditchingham. Having established that this would be the one most likely to suit Margaret, she moved there in September 1995, a week before her ninetieth birthday.

Whilst still living in Norfolk, it was easy enough for me to make regular visits. From 1997 onwards, after Barrie and I had left Norwich, it involved longer-distance travel – from Aberdeen and Manchester. Despite the gaps, however, when I did see her, I always found Margaret very philosophical about her lot. Gazing into the middle-distance, she would calmly repeat her mantra: "But really, dear, it's high time for me to go..."

Her wish came true. On 10 February 2002, I received a phone call from the matron at Adele House to tell me that Margaret was fading fast and would I come as quickly as possible. Next day, just as I was about to set off, the phone rang again: Margaret had died.

Rail links in that part of the world were a rarity. There was nothing for it now but get in the car and drive across the country as fast as I dared. It was freezing – and, by the time I reached Suffolk, very late indeed.

I awoke next morning, St Valentine's Day, to find frost on the windowpane and a thick blanket of fog enveloping the landscape. After a couple of hours, the fog began to lift, giving way to pale sunlight. My first port of call was at the undertakers to pay my respects to Margaret. I came away from the viewing in a reflective mood. Noticing the florist's next door, I went in, chose some flowers and returned to the car.

Getting out of Bungay is not straightforward – indeed, it's very easy to get lost. Over the years, however, my regular visits to the nursing home meant the route was clearly imprinted on my memory. Even in my present state of mind, I would rely on instinct: leaving the town, head out on the Norwich road, pass Ditchingham Hall on my right, through to Hedenham, then Brooke, eventually reach Poringland... though I had no notion of how to get to St Andrew's Church in Framingham Earl.

It didn't seem to matter – I had a sensation of knowing exactly which turning to take and, once in the churchyard, where I'd find Max. The stillness was palpable. Laying the red carnations on his grave, I stood there a while. So this was journey's end – *il ritorno in patria.*

XX

As the mountains slowly drew nearer, a new world opened before
me ... the road climbs to the Kochelsee and then still higher into
the mountains until it reaches the Walchensee. There I saw my
first snow-capped peaks, and when I expressed my surprise
at being already so close to the snow line, I was told that only
yesterday there had been a thunderstorm followed by snow ...
I reached Walchensee at half past four, having met with
a pleasant adventure an hour or so before ...

Johann Wolfgang von Goethe, *Italian Journey,* **7 September 1786**[111]

For some time, Max's colleagues at the University of East Anglia had wanted
to organise a conference in his honour. As soon as news of a definite date
was announced – 5–7 September 2008 – I booked myself a place. Initially,
I had considered submitting a contribution but then, imagining that most
of the presenters were likely to be scholars attached to places of learning –
something I could not claim to be – I thought better of it, opting instead to
be a fly on the wall.

That year, there was another plan that looked as if it were going to come
to fruition. My friend Christine and I had discussed the idea of spending a
week's holiday in Urfeld, at the family chalet overlooking the Walchensee
in Bavaria. For me, the last time I had been there was as a teenager, with
Christine and her parents in 1963. Forty-five years ago: there were going to
be memories.

To make this more of a proper "sentimental journey", I decided to travel by rail. It was not an auspicious start: the train from Manchester to London turned out to have been cancelled because the power lines were down, meaning I missed my connections on both the Eurostar and the overnight sleeper from Paris to Munich. I re-booked and went back home, hoping for better luck the following day.

What kept me engrossed – more or less oblivious to discomfort and frustration en route – was what I had brought with me as reading material: by way of preparation for the conference in September, three of Max's books.

By the time the train drew in to Kochel on Sunday afternoon, the weather was apocalyptic: everything was awash and the rain so blindingly torrential I nearly missed Christine on the station platform. The road from Kochel to Urfeld was only just negotiable – and, after leaving the car in the parking area halfway up the mountain, it was debatable whether we'd make it the rest of the way on foot to the chalet. Christine insisted that if we simply take it slowly with the bags of shopping and luggage, we'd be rewarded at the top – cups of tea laced with something stronger. No such luck. On arrival, we heard an insistent gushing noise coming from the back of the house. One of the gutters had collapsed and the branch of a tree had fallen on to the roof of the outhouse. Fetching a ladder and an axe, Christine set to work with repairs; all I could do was stand there oafishly, holding the ladder steady and shouting words of encouragement.

The next morning, there was little let-up in the weather. "What shall we do? Is there anywhere you'd like to go?" Christine asked. Neither of us fancied staying indoors, gazing out at the rain. Somewhat hesitantly, I said there was a place I was keen to visit but didn't know whether it could be done within the day, especially given the state of the roads: Wertach-im-Allgäu. On the map, Wertach lay eighty miles to the west. We agreed to give it a go.

For the first part of the journey, the skies were clear. By the time we reached Garmisch, however, and from then on, we drove through a steady downpour. The great thing about Christine – something that hadn't changed in all the years I'd known her – was that once she'd set her heart on a plan, she persisted. As on this occasion: we were virtually the only car on the road.

Turning off into Wertach, there was a sense of unreality about the whole venture. Wertach is a small Alpine village. Advertising itself as a holiday resort, the approach is along a thoroughfare with a sprinkling of summer chalets on either side, forlorn and miserable in the driving rain.

By now, lunch was a priority – and then Christine remembered that, this being Monday, everything was bound to be closed. Winding our way through the town centre, which was almost wholly deserted, we finally spotted a hotel with a restaurant. Much to our relief, the door was open and meals were still being served. The dining area was vast and there wasn't a single other guest. No matter; like the keen young women we had been all those years before, we ordered the most appetising item on the menu – venison goulash – and tucked in.

When the young waiter came with the bill, I asked him if he could help us; we were looking for the house where "the writer W.G. Sebald" had been born. He looked blank; all he could suggest was that I enquire at the desk – except that, just then, there was nobody available.

We collected our brollies from the lobby and left; it was still wet, though not quite as wet as before. Christine and I looked at each other, unsure what to do next. Might as well try the church and graveyard for names and if we met anyone on the way, ask, I suggested. Nothing doing. We were on the point of giving up and driving away when Christine said that whatever else, she must have chocolate to sustain her on the journey home. In the local Spar shop, she had just bought her favourite brand, Ritter Sport, when I overheard her talking to the woman at the checkout. "Yes," the woman was saying, "it's not far... you could try the tourist information office as well; they'll have details of the Sebald-Weg..."

We didn't have far to go to find the house. There it was on the far side of a courtyard, set back from the Grüntenseestraße. On the façade was a simple memorial plaque, complete with a quill, the writers' emblem. This caught me out. Lines from *The Emigrants* came to mind:

> *A shock of recognition shot through me at the grave of Maier Stern, who died on the 18th of May, my own birthday; and I was touched, in a way I knew I could never quite fathom, by the symbol of the writer's quill on the stone of Friederike Halbleib, who departed this life on the 28th of March 1912. I imagined her pen in hand, all by herself, bent with bated breath over her work; and now, as I write these lines, it feels as if I had lost her, and as if I could not get over the loss ...* [112]

The rain had stopped and the cloud was showing signs of lifting. Christine was game for a walk and at the tourist office we were given directions for the Sebald-Weg: the trail was eleven kilometres long and could be reached from either end. Though we knew we wouldn't have time to make the whole distance, we decided it'd be worth seeing how far we could reach – allowing for getting there and back – before the light gave up on us. We drove to the Oberjoch, within a stone's throw of the Austrian border, and left the car.

The Sebald-Weg is a marked path tracing the route taken by the narrator in the final part of *Vertigo*, "*Il ritorno in patria*". The townsfolk of Wertach, judging this to be the most appropriate way of honouring Max's memory, had inaugurated the path in November 2005. It features six wayside steles, engraved with relevant excerpts from *Vertigo*, and takes the walker through a landscape that, in true Romantic tradition, is in turn idyllic and dramatic: past waterfalls and, now in July, through flower-filled meadows.

Christine and I were fortunate: for two hours and more, the rain held off.

We were reluctant to turn back but by way of compensation decided to drive home via a different route. In the Tirol, the clouds began to gather again; it suddenly became so dark that we needed to turn on the headlights. Within minutes, we were in the middle of a storm – everything the elements could throw at us: thunder, lightning, hail and gale-force winds. Water cascaded down the rock-face; branches whipped and cracked before our eyes. It was a spectacular display.

By the time we reached Urfeld, the fire engines were out – by all accounts, a rare event in these parts. There had been wholesale destruction, leaving trees uprooted and roads blocked. That included the way up to the chalet: a tree had fallen across the stream by the garden gate, diverting the flow of water, which was now rising at an alarming rate. Determined not to be outfaced by the elements, Christine managed to get across the stream, clamber up to the outhouse and fetch the pickaxe. It wasn't until two hours later that we stumbled in through the backdoor, exhausted yet exhilarated.

Nature had been playing tricks: next morning, we woke to brilliant sunshine. Over breakfast, Christine announced that she was all set to make good use of it. As early as at the planning stage of the holiday, she'd warned me of her ambition to climb the nearby Jochberg, a mountain of 1570 metres, something she'd last done with her father when she was sixteen.

We set off in good spirits. But halfway up, I began to notice that Christine kept lagging behind, showing signs of struggle – she was not on form. Fearing she was in danger of pushing herself beyond her limits, I persuaded her not to continue. We came down again and returned to the house and ate our picnic. She then went to rest on her bed and I took my book and sat on the terrace.

It was a glittering afternoon – through the trees, the Walchensee gleamed sapphire and emerald. By now I was coming to the end of the third part of *The Emigrants* – the story of Ambros Adelwarth – and completely absorbed. Up to this point, "the butterfly man" had put in more than one appearance.[113] And then ...

Yesterday I thought I saw a large dark hare, and a butterfly with gold-speckled wings ...

All of a sudden, I sensed a faint tickling on my wrist; absent-mindedly, I shook my arm and carried on reading.

Memory, he added in a postscript, often strikes me as a kind of numbness. It makes one's head heavy and giddy, as if one were not looking back down the receding perspective of time but rather down on the earth from a great height, from one of those towers whose tops are lost to view in the clouds.[114]

The tickling started again. It was a black butterfly. It settled first on my wrist, then on the book, where it refused to budge even when I moved my fingers on the page.

Then it came back to me – the memory of Kafka's Hunter Gracchus in his final metamorphosis:

> *"And have you no share in the world beyond?" asked the burgomaster wrinkling his brow.*
>
> *The hunter answered, "I am always on the immense staircase leading up to it. I roam around on this infinitely wide flight of steps, sometimes up, sometimes down, sometimes to the right, sometimes to the left, always in motion. From being a hunter I've become a butterfly. Don't laugh."*
>
> *"I'm not laughing," answered the burgomaster.*[115]

*   *   *   *   *

A couple of weeks later, I received a message from Frido Mann. Christine had suggested that he ask me to help with the translation of a libretto he'd been working on – a multi-media project entitled *Flood*, due to be performed the following year in Vilnius, Lithuania. Happy to accept, I spent the rest of the summer turning the text into "singable" English.

Pleased with the result, Frido proceeded to transfer payment but, due to bank charges, there had been a slight shortfall between the amount I received and the fee we'd agreed. I assured him that the easiest way to make up the difference would be for him to send me some books I particularly wanted – books I knew I wouldn't be able to get quickly enough in England. And this was how I came by my copy of *Über das Land und das Wasser:*

Ausgewählte Gedichte 1964–2001, the selection of Max's poems that had just been published in Germany.

I attended the Sebald Conference at the University of East Anglia and within a few days of getting back to Manchester, inspired by what I had seen and heard in Norwich, I knew what I had do next. Here was an opportunity to do as Max had suggested twenty years before: try my hand at translating his poetry. To my delight, amongst the poems contained in the new book, there were several he had given me himself.

I set to work, completing the first draft on the seventh anniversary of Max's death, Sunday, 14 December 2008.

PART THREE

ONE LEAVES BEHIND
ONE'S PORTRAIT

... O yes, if he were to walk in at this moment we should talk about
books and feelings and life and the rest of it as freely as we ever did,
and with the same sense, on both sides I think, of having
hoarded for this precise moment a great deal
peculiarly fit for the other.

Virginia Woolf, *Selected Diaries*,
entry for Wednesday, 22 January 1919

I

By the end of autumn 2009, I had started to turn my attention to another project: this book. A year and a half later, just when the end seemed in sight, it occurred to me there was still something missing. What it was, I couldn't be sure. Judging it wise to give matters a rest, I put aside what I'd written and tried catching up with the outside world.

Then I started having dreams – specifically, one recurrent dream – in which I was convinced of the existence of a book that provided the answers to all the questions that had arisen in the course of putting together *Ariadne's Thread*. What was more, it contained a feast of quotable lines – lines that lent themselves to being used as epigraphs – my love of epigraphs derived from noticing how Max had used them at the start of some of his essays. In the dream, the title of the book was on the tip of my tongue; but try as I might to recall the name, it always escaped me.

The realisation that my search had been merely virtual moved me to do something practical. In the spring of 2011, I got in touch with my friend Christine in Göttingen and we began discussing plans for a trip, similar to the one we had made with her mother in 1963 through South Germany, along stretches of the *Romantische Strasse*, the Romantic Road.

The journey, undertaken later that year, was a tribute to Max, taking us to places and works of art that had held special significance for him. At the same time, it gave me an opportunity to review the effect he'd had on me over the years since his death.

II

I had booked an afternoon flight to Hanover. Already, the days were growing shorter – by the time the plane touched down, the light had almost gone. Resetting my watch for an hour later, I caught a train to the Hauptbahnhof, and from there to Göttingen. This part of the journey was leisurely; it gave me time to dream. We stopped at places with names that, to my ear, contained the rhythm of a train approaching and then going over the points: Barnten and Banteln, Elze, Einbeck Salzderhelden, Nörten-Hardenberg. Max's poem came to mind, the one in which he refers to just such a station – Wolfenbüttel – where, one Sunday in the autumn of 1994, he had waited for the commuter train:

> *auf dem unbemannten*   *I am in the unmanned*
> *Bahnhof von Wolfenbüttel*   *station in Wolfenbüttel*
> *warte ich auf den Trieb*   *waiting for the railcar*
> *wagen von Göttingen nach*   *from Göttingen to*
> *Braunschweig.*   *Brunswick.*[116]

Christine was there on the platform. Before we'd given it another thought, we were back to exchanging family news, joshing each other in a mixture of germanised English and anglicised German – just as we'd done on Guernsey all those years ago.

Next morning, we took the car and drove into the country. We walked through the fields to the edge of a wood – the hot August sun had turned the crops to gold. We talked about music-making and the string quartet in which Christine played viola; about my ongoing projects and what I was reading:

Bunte Steine (*Coloured Stones*), a collection of short stories by Adalbert Stifter. The reason I'd brought it with me was Max's interest in Stifter – a taste shared by Christine's father, whose favourite novel of all time, she told me, had been Stifter's last book, *Witiko*.

After a late lunch in the garden, I continued sitting under the trees with my book. An hour or so passed whilst Christine rested, re-emerging to remind me of our discussion over breakfast. Before leaving tomorrow, we wanted to review our itinerary, look at maps and check on the Sebald website for references to works of art.

We started with Matthias Grünewald, which immediately brought back memories: one of the highlights of the trip with Christine's mother had been to stop off at the parish church in Stuppach to see Grünewald's *Madonna*. This time, we were setting our sights on his other masterpiece, the *Isenheim Altarpiece*, in Colmar.

The following day, with time to spare before leaving, I ran my eye over Christine's bookshelves and spotted a volume I'd last dipped into in Urfeld in 2008. This was Werner Heisenberg's letters to his parents, collected and edited by his eldest daughter, Maria Hirsch.

There were two passages of particular interest to me now. The first was a letter Heisenberg had written to his mother from Berlin on 19 May 1944 in which he describes a powerful air attack on the city. Whilst he had come out of it unscathed, it had left everyone feeling tired and nervous. The whole tenor of the letter was how best to offer comfort and reassurance to his mother and wife under these circumstances; first and foremost, his thoughts had always been for his family.

The second passage referred to the last days of April 1945. Shortly after the German surrender, American troops had come to Urfeld, taken Heisenberg prisoner and sent him to Britain where, along with a number of other German scientists, he was held under wartime laws in a former Intelligence safe house – Farm Hall in Cambridgeshire. It was another whole year before he had been allowed to rejoin his family in Germany. The British, keen to avoid the possibility of Heisenberg being snapped up by the Russians, had arranged for him to set up a laboratory in Göttingen; and it was here that he and his colleagues had gone about the fundamental reorganisation of the Institute of Physics. As Christine was later to tell me, her father had accepted the post on one condition: that the house that went with the job must have a garden – one large enough in which to grow things and where the children would have space to play.

III

We set off shortly after midday; this, the longest stretch of the journey, would take us to Colmar. As we drove over the border into France, I thought of the past: the times when, as a teenager, crossing borders had been exciting; and later, in divided Berlin, when the endless queuing at checkpoints and stamping of visas had made it such a hassle. Experiences like these, however, paled into insignificance compared with what others had had to put up with: the people who'd had no choice; or the ones who could count themselves lucky if they'd been supplied with a ticket at all. I remembered Max's poem:

Kalligraphisch	*Entered*
eingetragen von langer Hand	*well in advance*
der Paßvermerk	*the calligraphic endorsement*
ein analphabetisches Zeichen	*an analphabetic cipher*
gut zur einmaligen Reise	*valid for a single journey*[117]

By now we had come off the Autobahn and were driving through the Alsatian countryside. It was Christine's turn to talk about what she'd been reading. *Die Evolution des Geistigen* (*The Evolution of the Intellect*) is a huge, scholarly tome by Thomas and Brigitte Görnitz that she was using to back up her argument in the book she herself was writing – a book entitled *Denkvergnügen* (*The Pleasures of Thinking*). Over the past couple of years, whenever the word *Geist* – or its derivatives *geistig* and *geistreich* – had come up in conversation, we'd got sidetracked into a debate, at times quite heated, as to their meaning. Ultimately, we'd settled for the idea that *Geist* was untranslatable, a German invention that went way above the heads of us down-to-earth Britons –

an example of "the traditional aversion to the speculative and theoretical, inherent in the education and mind of the English" as Javier Marías has it.[118]

During the final few kilometres we were caught in a torrential downpour, bringing back memories of what had happened on our way to Wertach in July 2008. Nor was our arrival in Colmar helped by the traffic signs – any number of invitations to drive "*en toutes directions*" ("in all directions").

For an hour at least, we found ourselves going round and round the town centre before spotting what looked like a suitable place to spend the night. It was an Ibis hotel; we couldn't go far wrong with that, I remarked. Ibis was a chain that had served me well a few Christmases before when the plane destined for Berlin had apparently lost part of a wing, forcing us to make an emergency landing at Schiphol Airport – the airport and its globetrotting denizens that had featured in another of Max's poems:

In der Nacht auf	*On the Eve of*
Allerseelen neunzehn	*All Hallows*
hundertsiebenund	*nineteen hundred*
neunzig im Flughafen	*and ninety-seven*
von Schiphol zwischen	*at Schiphol Airport*
Weltreisenden aus Seoul	*among globetrotters*
& Saõ Paulo, Singapur	*from Seoul & Saõ Paulo*
& Seattle. Ganz in sich	*Singapore & Seattle.*
zusammengesunken	*There they sit*
mit neonblauen	*with neon-blue*
Gesichtern sitzen sie	*faces slumped*
auf den Bänken ...	*down on the benches ...*
Als die Geisterstunde	*the witching hour*
vorbei ist liegen	*past they lie*
sie alle in blaue	*stretched out under*
Decken gehüllt ...	*blue blankets ...*[119]

Like its sister establishment in Amsterdam, the Ibis was perfunctory, clean and moderately priced. The luxury element came later with our venture into town in search of supper. At the Winstub à la Ville de Paris, Christine ordered the local speciality, a *tarte flambée*, not unlike a pizza with a crisp base and topped with onion. For me, the *terrine de jarret de boeuf avec crudités* proved irresistible: pressed shin of beef interlaced with *foie gras*, and to go with it, a glass of local *Gewürztraminer*.

IV

Next day, Saturday, 6 August, according to the information at the hotel reception, was the Feast of the Transfiguration of St Octavian – an archdeacon in Carthage who, at the command of King Hunneric in AD 484, along with thousands of other Christians, had been executed by the Aryan Vandals. It seemed peculiarly appropriate to be put in mind of saints and martyrdom: we were about to make our way to the Musée d'Unterlinden to see Grünewald's altarpiece.

The work had been commissioned by Guido Guersi, the preceptor of the monastery at Isenheim, a village about fifteen miles south of Colmar and thought to have been painted between 1512 and 1516. Established around 1300, the monastery at Isenheim belonged to the Order of St Anthony, where the monks specialised in ministering to the sick, particularly victims of the plague and of ergotism – a disease otherwise known as St Anthony's Fire. Patients were cared for by being served good quality bread and made to drink *Saint Vinage*, a concoction made with wine, in which a special blend of herbs had been macerated first, then the relics of St Anthony.

The altarpiece consists of nine images arranged in three sets of panels, two of which have folding wings on either side. The central panel of the first set is a Crucifixion scene. It would have meant much to those afflicted with Saint Anthony's Fire: it was believed that contemplation of such an image – the crucified Christ, His body horribly twisted and mangled and pitted with plague-sores – would help them come to terms with their own suffering.

It had been a year or so since I had read Idris Parry's essay "Attitudes to Power" about Elias Canetti. It was here that I had come across the following:

Canetti talks in his autobiography about the spell cast on him in his student days in Vienna by Breughel's The Triumph of Death, *with its multitude of skeletons, crowds assembled beyond the grave. He says there is no better way to discover reality than through pictures. He stood for a whole day in front of the Isenheim altarpiece at Colmar, and when he was writing his novel he had reproductions of Grünewald pinned round the walls. The book* [Auto da Fé], *like that painter, is notable for the dispersal of illusion.*[120]

Knowing Max's regard for both Idris Parry and Canetti, it was easy to see why he'd chosen Matthias Grünewald as his protagonist in the first part of *After Nature*. "As the Snow on the Alps" concerns several of Grünewald's works – and the *Isenheim Altarpiece* in particular. This is how he describes the nature of the commission:

durch eine in den schönsten	*... to engage*
und schauerlichsten Farben	*the painter in a great therapeutic*
ausgeführte Vergegenwärtigung	*task through the representation,*
der Stunde der bleichen	*executed in beauteous and*
Eitergewässer und somit durch	*harrowing*
Die Krafft und die Würckung	*colours, of the hour of the pale*
Des Bildes eine zentrale therapeutische	*streams of pus ...*[121]
Aufgabe zufallen sollte ...	

The language is at once magnificent and lyrical, stark and tender. To my ear, at least, Michael Hamburger's translation doesn't always succeed in capturing the resonance and rhythm of the original or the poignancy of Max's intertextual "citations" in Old High German. Nevertheless, the message comes over clearly: the reader – the listener – is not spared any of the horror, including the horror of disease.

"As the Snow on the Alps" had first appeared in June 1986. Four years later, Max was to return to the impact on the viewer of Grünewald's altarpiece – this time in the person of the painter, Max Ferber/Aurach:

... I arrived in Colmar, where I spent a good night at the Hotel Terminus Bristol on the Place de la Gare and the next morning, without delay, went to the museum to look at the Grünewald paintings. The extreme vision of that strange man, which was lodged in every detail, distorted every limb, and infected the colours like an illness, was one I had always felt in tune with, and now I found my feeling confirmed by the direct encounter. The monstrosity of that suffering, which, emanating from the figures depicted, spread to cover the whole of Nature, only to flood back from the lifeless landscape to the humans marked by death, rose and ebbed within me like a tide. Looking at those gashed bodies, and at the witnesses of the execution, doubled up by grief like snapped reeds, I gradually understood that, beyond a certain point, pain blots out the one thing that is essential to its being experienced – consciousness – and so perhaps extinguishes itself; we know very little about this. What is certain, though, is that mental suffering is effectively without end. One may think one has reached the very limit, but there are always more torments to come. One plunges from one abyss into the next. When I was in Colmar, said Ferber, I beheld all of this in precise detail, how one thing had led to another and how it had been afterwards...[122]

Seeing the altarpiece for myself intensified my appreciation of both "As the Snow on the Alps" and "Max Ferber". The longer I looked, the more I recognised how selective Max had been; in the interests of both the poem and the story, he had focused on certain panels – privileging, as it were, "the dark places of the earth".[123]

Derart beschrieb Grünewald,	*In this fashion Grünewald,*
stillschweigend den Malpinsel führend,	*silently wielding his paintbrush,*
das Geschrei, das Grölen, das Gurgeln	*the scream, the wailing, the gurgling*
und das Geraune eines pathologischen	*and the shrieking of a pathological*
Schauspiels,	*spectacle*
zu dem er, und seine Kunst, wie er	*to which he and his art, as he must*
wohl wußte,	*have known,*
selber gehörten.	*themselves belong.*[124]

As I gazed at the central panel of the first set, I felt my eye being drawn away from the crucified Christ to the figures on the left: the swooning Mary, swathed in a great white robe, comforted by St John the Apostle. He wears a scarlet cloak and cradles her in his arms as tenderly as if she were an infant. It nearly took my breath away – quite literally. Or else I was under the spell of Max's lines.

... ein geisterhaft Abendwerden	*... a phantasmal encroachment of dusk*
mitten im Tag wie eine Ohnmacht	*in the midst of daytime like a fainting*
sich ausgoß ...	*fit ...*
Sie entfalten sich als die Rückseite	*... (These colours) unfold as the*
des Spektrums in einer anderen	*reverse of*
Beschaffenheit	*the spectrum in a different consistency*
der Luft, deren sauerstofflose Leere	*of the air, whose de-oxygenated void*
uns in der Atemnot der Figuren	*in the gasping breath of the figures*
des Isenheimer Zentralstücks schon	*on the central Isenheim panel is enough*
den Tod	*to portend our death by asphyxiation;*
durch Erstickung verheißt, wonach	*after which*
kommt	*comes the mountain landscape of*
die Berglandschaft der Beweinung...	*weeping...*[125]

In front of the Virgin, Mary Magdalene kneels in prayer. On the right stands John the Baptist, pointing at Christ with an elongated index finger and saying: *Illum oportet crescere, me autem minui*, "He must become greater, I must become less".

The panel is flanked by two wings. The one on the left shows St Sebastian the Martyr; above his head and beneath his feet, the plants struck me as being engaged in some kind of celestial debate. On the right wing is St Anthony himself, with light coming from an upper window through bullseye panes – curiously modern, like the ones Max describes in the breakfast room of the Hotel Columbus in his poem "In der schlaflos/verbrachten Nacht/auf

Sonntag den 16./Januar vorigen Jahres" ("In the sleepless/small hours/of Sunday the 16th/January last/year").[126]

In the second set, which barely features in "As the Snow on the Alps", the mood lifts. With the outer wings open, it shows, on the left, the Annunciation; and in the middle, a heavenly choir praises the Madonna and Child. In Grünewald's day, music was considered part of therapy, a means of restoring the unity of body and soul, re-establishing harmony with the stricken human being. In the foreground, one notably beatific angel plays a viola da gamba – the instrument no less blessed than its player: its C-holes and bridge form a comic smiling face. Other celestial beings, both fair and dark, are endowed with lustrous plumage – in particular, the green-feathered bird-angel with his large wings. He is, I guess, the *psychopompos* or soul-guide, responsible for escorting the souls of the dead to the beyond. The figure derives from Greek models rather than the Bible, his green body representing the colour of paradise, eternal life and the eternal homeland, a metaphor for rebirth into new life.[127]

The Madonna, like the one in Stuppach, radiates pleasure and playfulness. The right-hand wing depicts a Resurrection: Christ as a meteor, leaping up to heaven in a blaze of light.

The third set contains two side panels depicting scenes from the life of St Anthony: on the left, his meeting with the Hermit Paul of Thebes (clad in palm leaves) and on the right, the Temptation. Nightmarish creatures surround the saint; putrescence and monstrous deformity is given graphic expression. Max describes the panels in detail, followed by a vision of the apocalypse:

... in jenem irrealen und	*in that unreal and demented*
wahnwitzigen Getümmel,	*thronging*
das Grünewald um den von	*that Grünewald has developed*
einem grausigen	*around*
Monstrum am Schopf über	*St Anthony of the Temptation –*
den Boden Geschleiften	*dragged by the hair over the ground*

Heiligen Antonius der Versuchung
entwickelt hat.
Zuunterst in der linken Ecke kauert
der von syphilitischen Schwären
überzogene Leib eines Insassen
des Isenheimer Spitals...

... gegen die Mitte des Bildes
ineinander verkrebst, haifisch und
    lindwurm
artige Rachen, Zahnreihen,
    aufgeworfene Nasen,
aus denen der Rotz rinnt,
    flossenförmige,
kaltlappige Flügel, Haar und Hörner,
Haut wie nach außen gekehrtes
    Gekröse,
Auswüchse des ganzen Lebens,
in der Luft, zu Land und im Wasser...

... Der schwarze Vogel, der dem
    heiligen
Antonius zu seinem Platz in der
    Wüste
im Schnabel die Brotzeit bringt,
ist vielleicht der immer schon
näher an uns heranfliegende
mit dem gläsernen Herz,
von dem ein anderer heiliger Mann,
der letzten Tage verkündet,
er werde ins Meer scheißen,
so, daß es auskochen wird, daß

by a gruesome monster.
Low down in the bottom-left
    corner
cowers the body, covered with
syphilitic chancres, of an inmate
of the Isenheim hospital...

... towards the picture's centre,
crab-clawed together, shark- and
    dragon-like
maws, rows of teeth, pug noses
from which snot flows,
    fin-shaped
clammy limp wings, hair and
    horns,
skin like entrails turned
    outwards,
excrescences of an entire life,
in the air, on land and in water...

... The black bird that in
    its beak
carries a break-time
    meal
to St Anthony on his site
in the desert may be the one with
the heart of glass, the bird
flying ever closer to us,
of which another prophet
of the last days announces
that it will shit in the sea
so that the water boils itself out,

die Erde wackelt und die große Stadt	*that the earth trembles and the great city*
mit dem eisernen Turm im Feuer steht,	*with the iron tower stands in flames,*
der Pabst in einer Zille hockt	*whilst the Pope squats in a barge*
und die Finsternis kommt und	*and darkness comes and*
dort, wo das schwarze Kastl hinfällt,	*with it a yellow dust*
ein gelber und grauer Staub	*that covers the land.*[128]
das Land überdeckt.	

Visitors to the museum in August 2011 were informed that this panel had undergone recent restoration – certainly, the thoroughness of the cleaning had served to amplify the horror and grotesquery of the subject. Secretly, I couldn't help thinking it might have been better to have left it as it was.

V

There was a question that continued to exercise me after Christine and I had left Colmar: who was Matthias Grünewald and what had he meant to Max?

As one reads at the start of the second section of "As the Snow on the Alps", "little is known" of the life of the painter. There is no consensus as to when Grünewald was born, though it's generally believed to have been around 1475, in Würzburg. Max goes on to mention an account of 1675 by one Joachim von Sandrart who, whilst he hadn't been to Isenheim, had heard of the altarpiece and knew that for much of his life Grünewald had resided in Mainz where he had led "a reclusive, melancholy life".

This has a familiar ring about it. Like many of Max's later protagonists, Grünewald was a loner and a melancholic, of the type that came to be known in German as a *Sonderling*, an eccentric solitary. According to Claudio Magris, the figure of the *Sonderling* recurs "time and time again in German literature ... many of the heroes of Hoffmann and Jean Paul Richter are *Sonderlinge* ... all inspired by lacerating nostalgia and methodical rigour."[129] In this instance, I believe there's an even stronger identification between Max and his protagonist. In the preceding section of the poem, he describes a self-portrait by Grünewald, which he had discovered in the library at Erlangen:

... Selbstbildnis eines vierzig	*... a self-portrait ... of a painter aged*
	forty
bis fünfzigjährigen Malers.	*to fifty. Always the same*
Immer dieselbe	
Sanftmut, dieselbe Bürde der	*gentleness, the same burden*
Trübsal,	*of grief,*
dieselbe Unregelmäßigkeit der	*the same irregularity of the eyes,*
Augen, verhängt	*veiled*
und versunken seitwärts ins	*and sliding sideways down into*
Einsame hin.	*loneliness.*[130]

No doubt Max would have observed the portrait very closely; at the same time, it seems to be nothing short of a description of him himself – down to the details of age, disposition and temperament. It is a passage, I think, to be read alongside the final lines of a poem Max had written some nineteen years before, in 1967:

Man hinterläßt sein Porträt	*One leaves behind one's portrait*
Ohne Absicht	*Without intent* [131]

Grünewald is remembered in his native Würzburg by a nineteenth-century depiction of him on the Franconia Fountain in front of the Residenz and it was here in Würzburg that Christine and I had arrived the previous evening. The main reason for our visit was to view the work of another artist featured in Max's writing, the eighteenth-century Venetian painter Giovanni Battista Tiepolo.

We began our tour by walking round the Hofgarten of the Residenz, a garden in the formal, Baroque style. The air was damp and the sky grey. From the surrounding parkland drifted the sound of a brass band, rehearsing for their Sunday afternoon concert. Along the balustrades of the upper terrace, there was statuary – a lot of dogs, I noticed: children with a greyhound, a hunting dog straining at the leash of its master.

The main entrance hall of the Residenz is on such a scale that it's easy to get lost at the outset; you wander in and out of side-rooms, tending to miss the way to the grand staircase. When you do spot it and begin your ascent, it's as though you're climbing to the top of the world. The rise is deceptively gradual. The trough vault, unsupported by pillars, is a masterpiece of construction: twenty-three metres high at its maximum height and spanning an area of 540 square metres, the size of two tennis courts.

I'd read that passage in *Vertigo* many times – the passage where the narrator imagines Tiepolo, old and suffering from gout, making his way with his two sons from Venice to Würzburg:

I could not then and cannot now recall whether I was ever in the Krummenbach chapel as a child with my grandfather, who took me with him everywhere. But there were many chapels like that of Krummenbach around W., and much of what I saw and felt in them at the time will have stayed with me – a fear of the acts of cruelty depicted there no less than the wish, in all its impossibility, that the perfect tranquillity prevailing within them might sometime be recaptured. When the snow had eased off, I started on my way again, through the Bränte and along the Krummenbach as far as Unterjoch, where I ate bread soup and drank half a litre of Tyrolean wine at the Hirschwirt inn, to warm myself and prepare for the next stretch, which would be twice the distance. Perhaps prompted by the pitiful pictures in the Krummenbach chapel, my mind turned to Tiepolo once again, and the belief I had held for a long time that, when he travelled with his sons Lorenzo and Domenico from Venice across the Brenner in the autumn of 1750, he decided at Zirl that, contrary to the advice he had been given to leave the Tyrol via Seefeld, he instead made his way westward via Telfs, following the salt wagons across the Gaicht Pass, through the Tannheim valley, over the Oberjoch and through the Iller valley into the lowlands.

Had the artist taken another route after all? Might Tiepolo have stopped off near Wertach, where Max was born?

And I beheld Tiepolo, who must have been approaching sixty by that time and already suffered badly from gout, lying in the cold of the winter months at the top of the scaffolding half a metre below the ceiling of the grand stairway in the palace at Würzburg, his face splattered with lime and distemper, applying the colours with a steady hand, despite the pain in his right arm, onto the wet plaster of the immense, miraculous painting he was creating little by little. With imaginings such as these, and thinking about the Krummenbach painter who had, perhaps in the very same winter, toiled just as hard to represent the fourteen small Stations of the Cross as Tiepolo with his magnificent fresco, I walked on, the time being now about three o'clock, through the fields below the Sorgschrofen and the Sorgalpe, till I struck the road shortly before reaching the Pfeiffermühle. From there it was another hour to W.[132]

Just as many times, I'd read the passage in *The Emigrants* where Uncle Leo and Max Ferber are standing in the Residenz, gazing up at Tiepolo's ceiling:

Continuing his account of his visit to Würzburg in summer 1936, Ferber said that one day when they were strolling in the palace gardens Uncle Leo told him that he had been compulsorily retired on the 31st of December the year before and that, in consequence, he was preparing to emigrate from Germany, and was planning to go to England or America shortly. Afterwards we were in the great hall of the palace, and I stood beside Uncle, craning up at Tiepolo's glorious ceiling fresco above the stairwell, which at that time meant nothing to me; beneath the loftiest of skies, the creatures and people of the four realms of the world are assembled on it in fantastic array. Strangely enough, said Ferber, I only thought of that afternoon in Würzburg with Uncle Leo a few months ago, when I was looking through a new book on Tiepolo. For a long time I couldn't tear myself away from the reproductions of the great Würzburg fresco, its light-skinned and dark-

skinned beauties, the kneeling Moor with the sunshade and the magnificent
Amazon with the feathered headdress. For a whole evening, said Ferber, I
sat looking at those pictures with a magnifying glass, trying to see further
and further into them. And little by little that summer day in Würzburg
came back to me, and the return to Munich, where the general situation
and the atmosphere at home were steadily becoming more unbearable, and
the silence was thickening.[133]

Before daring to take my eye off the ground to look up, I had to steady myself
to get back my balance. What I now saw was just as Max had described: the
Amazon queen with her feathered headdress; the Moor with the sunshade;
the self-portrait of Tiepolo alongside the portraits of his sons; the portraits
of the stucco-artist and the architect Balthasar Neumann amongst European
dignitaries; the emperors, the beauty queens, the elephants, the dragons.
The figures in relief blended imperceptibly with the painted ones, giving the
illusion of going up and up.

The fresco is all about movement – everything is in flight. Centrally
placed, Apollo floats up into the heavens – a spiritual essence dwelling in the
upper air. The higher he mounts, the greater the sense of space.

VI

Our next port of call was the medieval town of Rothenburg, another of the stops on the tour with Christine's mother forty-eight years before. It was here that on 24 July 1963, the eve of my seventeenth birthday, we had checked into the Hotel Goldener Hirsch, of all the places we stayed at, the most glamorous.

This was what I wrote in my diary:

> ... we made our way on in very hot sunshine by way of country roads leading past swathes of cornfield, through thick, dark forests and tiny villages decked out with flowers ... 'til we got to Rothenburg ob der Tauber. Drove in under the arch at the entrance and along the main street ... cobbled, shops on either side, each with a wrought-iron sign hanging above the door ... Went and booked in at the most expensive hotel in town, the Hotel Goldener Hirsch ... our cases were carried upstairs ... by a porter who showed us to our rooms ... in mine, there was a telephone next to the bed and all the furniture matched, even the folding stool where you put your luggage. There was a washstand, too – in the room! – and good pictures. After we'd unpacked, we went downstairs for Eiskaffee [iced coffee] on the terrace overlooking the Tauber Valley ...[134]

What those pictures were and why I decided they were "good", I no longer remember. Canons of taste, including those applied to interior décor, are often the stuff of comedy. Max's writing is full of examples. Here is one such – in a poem dating from the 1990s:

Nachtblau	The carpet
gesprenkelt der Teppich	is spotted with midnight
kürbisfarben der samtene	blue the velvet
	curtain is claret the
Vorhang weinrot	sofa ultra
das Sofa ultramarin &	marine the bedspread
türkis die Blüten	calyx motif
Kelche auf dem Bett	turquoise with a
überzug die Bett	dizzying arabesque
umrandung eine	in lilac & violet
schwindelerregende	on the bedside rugs.[135]
Arabeske aus Lila	
& Violett.	

Christine and I had arrived in Rothenburg towards the end of the afternoon, as the holiday coaches were off-loading passengers at the doors of the hotels. The tourists were flocking in the lobbies and we began to think we were out of luck – everywhere seemed full.

We walked back along the main street and were on the point of giving up when we caught sight of a "family-run" hotel – a somewhat drab-looking establishment that also ran a bakery – close by the old city wall. We went in and asked. "Yes," said the woman at the counter, "there are still two rooms available." It was all rather gloomy, even a bit depressing: the creaky wooden staircase leading to the upper floor, the dark brown furniture in the bedrooms and the dark brown tiling in the adjoining shower-rooms.

Having parked the car in a side street, we pulled out our luggage and carried it back to the hotel. I was about to open the door when I looked up and saw the name of the street: Galgengasse (Gallows Lane). Would have suited Max, I reflected – or, at any rate, one of his other selves...

After settling in, we went off to get a meal and explore the town.

Independently of each other, Christine and I realised we'd been thinking along the same lines. There was no doubt Rothenburg had undergone big changes since we were last here – that was only to be expected; at the same time, there seemed to have been another kind of transformation – the like of which I'd not encountered anywhere else.

It was a phantasmagoria of kitsch, a Bavarian theme park. There were shops selling Christmas cribs all year round; chocolate snowballs – a "Rothenburg speciality"; signs in Gothic script to put around the home or on your garden gate; miniature carved wooden animals – the same sort as the ones Uli Raulff had sent me back in 1981; characters from Grimm – some hideous, others twee; and window displays featuring automata – shoemakers tapped, merry fiddlers fiddled, whilst hook-nosed witches stirred the contents of their cauldrons.

Harmless fun, perhaps. But there is also a dark side to Rothenburg – much darker. For Nazi ideologists, the town represented "the most German of German towns". Throughout the 1930s, the Nazi organisation known as the KdF – *Kraft durch Freude* ("Strength Through Joy") laid on regular day trips to Rothenburg from across the Reich, an initiative strongly supported by the inhabitants of the town, many of whom were sympathetic to National Socialism. In October 1938, to the approval of the Nazis and their supporters, Rothenburg had expelled its Jewish citizens.

On our way back to the hotel, alongside the Judengasse (Jews' Lane), we noticed a small garden with a memorial and gravestones – gravestones that had been moved there from the former Jewish cemetery on the Schrannenplatz.

* * * * *

Next day, having checked out and paid our bill, we made our way along the main street to look for the church containing a work of art we had also visited in 1963, Tilman Riemenschneider's carved altarpiece.

Riemenschneider, sculptor and woodcarver, was born ten years before Matthias Grünewald, in 1460. In the first part of *After Nature*, the two of them are granted an emotional link. Referring to the Lindenhardt Altar, Max has it that in his portrait of St Dionysius, Grünewald had paid tribute to Riemenschneider by giving the saint the face of his fellow-artist:

Es ist der heilige Dionysius,	*... It is St Dionysius,*
das abgeschlagene Haupt unterm	*his cut-off head under one arm.*
Arm.	*To him, his chosen guardian,*
Ihm, seinem erwählten Protektor,	*who in the midst of life carries*
der inmitten des Lebens seinen Tod	*his death with him, Grünewald gives*
mit sich führt, gibt Grünewald das	*the appearance of Riemenschneider,*
Ansehen	*whom*
Riemenschneiders, dem der	*twenty years later the Würzburg*
Würzburger Bischof	*bishop*
zwanzig Jahre darauf auf der Folter	*condemned to the breaking of his hands*
die Hände zerbrechen ließ ...	*in the torture cell ...*[136]

It's thought that Riemenschneider's *Altar of the Holy Blood*, in the Jakobskirche in Rothenburg, was created between 1501 and 1505. It is located upstairs at the west end of the church on a level with the organ loft.

Breathtaking in its intricacy, it was now at its best, lit by intermittent shafts of bright morning sunlight. Seated opposite the altarpiece, we could be meditative. With its emphasis on humanity, Riemenschneider's carving was in striking contrast to the experience of the previous couple of days: Grünewald's fear-inducing vision and Tieplo's "out-of-reachness".

On my way to bed the previous evening, I had picked up some brochures left out on the table on the first floor landing. Before turning off the light, I flicked through them and came across a booklet listing local accommodation, amongst which, I noticed, was the Hotel Goldener Hirsch. So it was still in existence, at an address on the other side of town.

Over breakfast, Christine and I had agreed that before leaving we'd take a walk along the old city wall – probably not go the whole way, but as far as necessary to get good views across the valley.

We had just come down from the wall and were sauntering along the street when I realised where we were: in the Untere Schmiedgasse (Lower Smithy Lane), right outside the Hotel Goldener Hirsch. By the front entrance was a sign proclaiming it as belonging to an exclusive chain of "small, elegant hotels". Not everything, it seemed, had changed for the worse.

VII

We continued our journey via Bad Windsheim – Windsheim, "the home of the wind", which features in all three parts of *After Nature*, thereby serving as a connecting motif.

In the first part, "As the Snow on the Alps", we learn how Grünewald rides to Windsheim in 1525 to collect "the crowning piece for an altar" from Jakob Seckler's workshop; it is here that he "falls into conversation" with the brothers Barthel and Hans Sebald Beham, etchers and draughtsmen who had been deemed heretics and therefore expelled from their native city of Nuremberg.

Windsheim is also the birthplace of Georg Wilhelm Steller, to whom Max devoted "And if I Remained by the Outermost Sea", the early draft of which he had sent me in 1983.

Steller was born in Bad Windsheim in 1709. In 1740, he had been appointed to join the Danish-Russian explorer Vitus Bering on an expedition to chart and investigate the North Pacific. On Monday, 20 July 1741, the expedition landed at Kayak Island in Alaska. Harsh conditions notwithstanding, Steller set about making detailed studies of the flora and fauna along with the topography of the island, using these observations as the basis of "his zoological masterpiece", *De Bestiis Marinis*.[137]

The next two years Steller spent exploring the Kamchatka peninsula before being recalled to St Petersburg. On the return journey, he caught a fever – one that was to prove fatal. He died in Tyumen, in Russia, in 1746; he was just thirty-seven.

En route to Windsheim, I had entertained visions of it as a health resort from another era – a fashionable spa where young women could take the waters or promenade in the public gardens on the arm of their cavalier. This was, of course, very wide of the mark. As we strolled into the town centre, I became aware of the ubiquitous presence of "Nordic walkers", many of whom were just then stopping off for a midday treat of seaweed rice crackers and frozen yoghurt.

It didn't take long to locate the Stellergasse, the site of Steller's modest birthplace. Other than that, the only memorial was a somewhat indifferent sculpture in front of the city hall dating from 2009. It featured a vast creature rearing up over a tiny human figure: Steller and his sea cow. A stone's throw away, there was something that, judging by the number of people now gathering round and staring up, was by far the greater tourist attraction. It was a huge sandstone statue of Roland, the medieval knight, dedicated as a war memorial in 1928. The juxtaposition of Roland, eight metres tall, and the diminutive Steller, spoke volumes: the hyperbolic representation of a fantasised medieval past and eighty-one years later, almost as an afterthought, the commemoration of a real-life man-of-science. By giving the latter a place in poetry, Max had restored a sense of proportion.[138]

In the third, most autobiographical part of *After Nature*, "Dark Night Sallies Forth", Windsheim features again as the place where Rosa Sebald first becomes aware that she is pregnant with her second child. To understand the full significance of this in terms of the poem, I would need to wait until we reached our final destination: Bamberg.

* * * * *

Christine and I had toyed with the idea of staying the night in Bad Windsheim but now decided in favour of an afternoon departure. We were hungry, though, and rice crackers and frozen yoghurt weren't an option. Being Monday, everything looked closed; after some fruitless searching, we eventually found ourselves being directed to the *Gaststätte* at the

Freilichtmuseum – an open-air museum exhibiting local archaeological finds and agricultural machinery – on the edge of town.

We treated ourselves to a proper rural brunch: generous slices of black bread and cold roast beef accompanied by freshly grated horseradish – surprisingly mild – and a glass of dark local beer. Had I had the courage, I might well have chosen something listed further down the menu: *Hausgemachte Bratensülze vom Spanferkel mit Musik, dazu herzhafte Bratkartoffeln* – "Home-made Brawn of Suckling Pig with Music [i.e. an oil, vinegar and onion dressing] accompanied by Nourishing Sauté Potatoes". The idea of oil, vinegar and onion constituting the essence of sweet sound, and that giant portions of fried potatoes would promote good functioning of the heart (in a health resort?) was news to me. Here, nevertheless, were echoes of something Max had published towards the end of his life:

Seit Jahr & Tag	*Unchanged for years*
unverändert das inter	*now these inter-*
regionale Küchenlatein	*regional catering*
das herzhafte Bistro ...	*clichés the full*
	buffet breakfast ...[139]

VIII

By late afternoon, we were within sight of Nuremberg. Having found a hotel near the city centre and deposited our bags, we set out on an initial exploration. It would appear that the last time I was here, in 1963, the stark fact of wartime devastation, let alone the scale of it, had completely passed me by. At seventeen, I had asked no questions.

Since 1945 the city has been almost entirely rebuilt; everything, including the three big city churches, had succumbed to the ravages of aerial bombing and was still, even now, sixty-six years later, in the process of painstaking reconstruction. Standing in the Hauptmarkt, the main square, one couldn't help but marvel at the extent of the work: this resurrection from the rubble is a thing of wonder.

Next morning, there was a fresh wind and rain in the air as we walked out past the flower sellers and into the square with the Lorenzkirche, the Church of St Laurence – at one time, the parish church for the southern district. Here as elsewhere, restoration work seemed to be a permanent feature. Intricate scaffolding encased the choir and soared up to the vault, making it into a kind of temple within a temple. Tiny figures, restorers and plasterers in spotless white overalls darted to and fro high above; down below, an organist was going through his paces, playing snatches of a prelude and fugue.

From the Lorenzkirche, we made our way across the river towards the Sebalduskirche, the church that had once served the northern district. In 1945 the Church of St Sebald had been almost totally razed to the ground. Dedicated to Nuremberg's patron saint, it is situated at the top of an incline within sight of the remains of the old city wall.

We had just reached the Sebaldplatz, the square around the church, and were about to go in through the west door when Christine stopped, turned towards me and fired a question: as a teenager, what *had* I been told about the war? she wanted to know. I was taken aback. It raised issues that, in all the fifty years we'd known each other, I hadn't thought about before – not like this, anyway.

Along with politics and sex, I told Christine, the war had been a "banned" topic at home. My mother had insisted that it be kept out of the conversation at all costs. It was only when I went sailing with my father that I'd managed to get an inkling of what had happened in the world during the years before my birth.

Always happiest when afloat, it was on the boat that my father felt free to reminisce; and when it came to talk of the war, he recalled it as having been "the best time of his life". Christine listened closely; apparently, my father had said the same thing to her – laying great emphasis on his *enjoyment* of having been a soldier and able to fight in a war. She commented that this was something she hadn't understood at the time; and it still mystified her.

I attempted an explanation: like my uncle, John Bradburne, my father had served with the Chindits in Burma; and, also like John, he'd been severely traumatised in the process. Over the years, I'd come to regard what he had said to me, as to Christine – that he'd had "a good war" – as what was expected of a British soldier at the time: emotional trauma must be underplayed; if possible, denied altogether. In addition to which, there had been my mother's aversion to any mention of her husband's wartime experiences, good or bad.

This added up to the realisation that I'd gone through adolescence and early adulthood in ignorance of recent history. Furthermore, a good deal of bewilderment as to the nature of parental prejudice had gone into the mix. How fortunate, then, that Christine and I, two young girls, one German and the other English, had met when and where we did: on Guernsey, an island far away from our respective families. Had our parents had any objection to this aspect of the holiday, they would have been powerless to do anything about it.

We were still outside the church, standing in the gentle drizzle, lost in thought. When she'd first come to stay with me, Christine went on, she had brought her viola. Yes, indeed, I said, interrupting her with a memory: she had played the Schubert Arpeggione Sonata with my mother at the piano. Much to her relief, Christine added, Mary had been a "kind" accompanist – unlike at home, where her father was generally very critical of her efforts. She and my mother had also played chess – a fairly even match for each other. At the end of one round, she recalled, she had trotted out a phrase in German "*Sieg Heil und fette Beute ...*", (literally, "Hail, victory and rich pickings ...") doubtless something learnt at school. Whereupon, my mother, who knew no German but would instantly have recognised the words of the Hitler salute, had issued a sharp reprimand, one that Christine had never forgotten: "That's enough, Christine, we want no more of *that!*"

One memory led to another – this next, a phrase Christine had learnt from her father. When the children had been expected to complete a task or achieve a goal – for example, not stop before they'd made it to the next milestone on a country hike – Werner had urged them on with the words, "*Das machen wir jetzt aber tüchtig – bis zur Vergasung!*" ("But now we're going to do things properly – carry on to the bitter end!").

"*Bis zur Vergasung*" is an expression meaning to carry on doing something "until it has been completed to one's satisfaction". The word "*Vergasung*" (literally, "gasification") is a term used in thermodynamics, referring to the process whereby, with the input of heat, material is converted from a liquid to a volatile aggregate state. During the First World War, with the introduction of poison gas, the phrase "*bis zur Vergasung*" was in common usage amongst foot soldiers – one might think of it as a form of gallows humour. In the context of the Second World War, National Socialism and the deportation of thousands to the gas chambers, however, it acquires a connotation of an entirely different order.

When Christine related this anecdote, it was most certainly not in its "neutral", scientific sense that I understood the phrase *"bis zur Vergasung"*. I was stunned – wanted not to have heard. Christine, too, was surprised by what she'd just said – adding that the story hadn't come back to her until fifteen years ago. It struck me that she had never mentioned it again, either; that is, not until now, here on the Sebaldplatz in Nuremberg. We struggled to counter disbelief, agreeing that of course, at the time, she'd been only a child with no idea of the significance of the phrase – let alone of the irony of its having been used by the physicist Heisenberg.

This conversation gave rise to a string of associations – associations that continued to preoccupy me. In a sense, army life had formed the backdrop to my childhood at Wellington College: I'd grown up alongside dozens of boys whose fathers and grandfathers had been dedicated to soldiering. I was now taken up with the notion of the psychological impact of the Second World War on men who were – or were about to become – fathers, and the far-reaching effects on their families and children:

Christine's father, Werner, born in 1901, and between 1939 and 1945, the key scientist leading the development of German nuclear weapons, privately remembered as a devoted, if somewhat distant, paterfamilias; my father, Peter, born in 1918, the youngest of three sons in his family and the only one to join the fighting, and who, on his return, took up schoolmastering at Wellington where he was under pressure not to talk about his experiences in anything other than glowing terms; and Max's father, Georg, born in 1911, a serving officer with the *Wehrmacht*, taken prisoner in France at the start of 1945, released two years later and then began work as a civilian official with the police in Sonthofen. Max had never been able to forgive his father – even now, I wasn't sure I had fully grasped the reasons.

We entered the Sebalduskirche.

IX

My first impression of the Sebalduskirche was that it exemplified extremes
– extremes of love and hatred, tenderness and violence. On the one hand,
there was the graphic depiction of hatred in the stone carvings, a hatred of
Jews; on the other, amongst the items to have survived the ravages of the
Second World War, was the shrine of St Sebald.

In *The Rings of Saturn*, along with a photograph of the sarcophagus, the
narrator gives a deeply personal account of his visit:

> *That evening, in Amsterdam, I sat in the peace of the lounge of a private
> hotel by the Vondel Park, which I knew from earlier visits, and made notes
> on the stations of my journey, now almost at an end: the days I had spent
> on … my visits to the Alte Pinakothek in Munich and to the grave of my
> patron saint in Nuremberg, of whom legend has it that he was the son of a
> king, from Dacia or Denmark, who married a French princess in Paris.
> During the wedding night, the story goes, he was afflicted with a sense of
> profound unworthiness. Today, he is supposed to have said to his bride, our
> bodies are adorned, but tomorrow they will be food for worms …*

In an interview of 1998, Max spoke of St Sebald as "a quite obscure saint"
about whom almost all we knew was legendary. In *The Rings of Saturn*, he
had described the most famous of these legends, the *Eiswunder* – the Miracle
of the Icicle:

> *Before the break of day, he fled, making a pilgrimage to Italy, where he
> lived in solitude until he felt the power to work miracles arising within*

him. After saving the Anglo-Saxon princes Winnibald and Wunibald from certain starvation with a loaf baked from ashes and brought to them by a celestial messenger, and after preaching a celebrated sermon in Vicenza, he went over the Alps to Germany. At Regensburg he crossed the Danube on his cloak, and there made a broken glass whole again; and, in the house of a wheelwright too mean to spare the kindling, lit a fire with icicles.

Then comes a sentence that provides what I think of as the overriding key to understanding what had informed Max's writing:

This story of the burning of the frozen substance of life has, of late, meant much to me, and I wonder now whether inner coldness and desolation may not be the pre-condition for making the world believe, by a kind of fraudulent showmanship, that one's own wretched heart is still aglow.

The narrative flows on, with more about the life of St Sebald and a description of the reliquary. As I could now appreciate with my own eyes, it is the most elaborate work – cast in bronze and depicting the stories in intricate detail. Amongst the carvings of holy men and monsters, flora and fauna, there's a portrait of the artist, Peter Vischer, in his working clothes.

... my namesake is said to have performed many more miracles in his hermitage in the imperial forests between the rivers Regnitz and Pegnitz, and to have healed the sick, before his corpse, as he had ordained, was borne on a cart drawn by two oxen to the place where his grave is to this day. Centuries later, in May 1507, the Patriciate of Nuremberg resolved to have a brass sarcophagus crafted for the holy prince of heaven St Sebolt by master smith Peter Vischer. In June 1519, when his twelve-year labours were completed, the great monument, weighing many tons, standing almost five yards high on twelve snails and four curved dolphins, and representing the entire order of salvation, was installed in the chancel

of the church consecrated in the name of the city's saint. On the base of the tomb, fauns, mermaids, fabulous creatures and animals of every conceivable description throng about the four cardinal virtues of Justice, Prudence, Temperance and Fortitude. Above them are mythical figures – Nimrod the hunter, Hercules with his club, Samson with the jawbone of an ass, and the god Apollo between two swans – along with representations of the miracle of the burning of the ice, the feeding of the hungry, and the conversion of a heretic.

The prose starts to soar:

Then come the apostles with their emblems and the instruments of their martyrdom, and, crowning all, the celestial city with its three pinnacles and many mansions, Jerusalem, the fervently longed-for bride, God's tabernacle amongst mankind, the image of an other, renewed life. And in the heart of this reliquary cast in a single piece, surrounded by eighty angels, in a shrine of sheet silver, lie the bones of the exemplary dead man, the harbinger of a time when the tears will be wiped from our eyes and there will be no more grief, or pain, or weeping and wailing...[140]

This from Max the agnostic, expressing himself in the language of divine inspiration. One should not be fooled, however. Later in *The Rings of Saturn*, the narrator visits the builder of the model of the Temple of Jerusalem, Alec Garrard – Thomas Abrams in the English version – who has this to say on the subject:

One of the American evangelists once asked me whether [the building of] the Temple was inspired by divine revelation. And when I said to him it's nothing to do with divine revelation, he was very disappointed. If it had been divine revelation, I said to him, why would I have had to make alterations as I went along? No, it's just research really and work, endless hours of work.[141]

"Endless hours of work." For Max, the creation of sentences and syntax, like the building of the model of the Temple, was the result of long, hard graft – an arduous, often painful process, in his own words "very closely linked ... to neurotic disorders ... a behavioral problem".[142]

X

The conversation before entering the church followed by what we had seen inside left Christine and me in contemplative mood. After a glass of apple juice at a nearby café, we walked on up the hill in silence. From the top, we had a bird's-eye view of the city.

Coming down again, we passed by the Albrecht-Dürer-Haus, an on-site reconstruction of the artist's birthplace. It overlooks a little square that contains a recent sculpture intended, I think, to reflect the spirit of Dürer's hare. I thought of Max and the importance to him of Dürer's other famous etching, *Melencolia* – Melancholy and her dog, surrounded by arcane accoutrements. I already had a postcard reproduction of *Melencolia* at home, but seeing as we were standing right next to Dürer's house, I went to the card-shop on the corner and bought myself another one as a souvenir.

It brought to mind the passage in *After Nature*, where Steller discovers the explorer Vitus Bering, whom Max describes as "deeply depressive", facing the final moments of his life:

Am 20. März des Jahres 1741
betritt Steller das langgestreckte
Blockhaus der Kommandantur von
    Petropawlovsk
an der Ostküste der Halbinsel
    Kamtschatka.
In einem fensterlosen, nicht mehr als
sechs mal sechs Fuß messenden

On 20 March 1741,
Steller stepped into the long
blockhouse of the Petropavlovsk
command post on the eastern
    shore
of the Kamchatka Peninsula.
In a windowless recess, no larger
than six feet by six, at the far end

Verschlag am hinteren Ende
des sonst auf keine Weise
   unterteilten
Innenraums dieses Gebäudes
findet er Bering, den Kommandeur-
   Kapitän,
an einem aus Planken
   zusammengenagelten
von weißfleckigen Land- und
   Seekarten
über und über bedeckten Tisch,
den neunundfünfzigjährigen Kopf
in die Fläche der rechten,
mit einem Flügelpaar
tätowierten Hand gestützt,
einen Stechzirkel in der Linken,
   bewegungslos sitzen
bei einem blakenden Licht.
Es braucht eine unheimlich
lange Zeit, denkt Steller,
bis Bering die Augen
aufmacht und hinschaut
zu ihm. Ein Tier
ist der Mensch, in tiefe
Trauer gehüllt,
in einen schwarzen Mantel,
mit schwarzem
Pelzwerk
gefüttert.

of the building's interior,
in no other way subdivided, he
   finds,
at a table of planks nailed
   together,
covered by land maps
and sea charts showing
vast tracks of whiteness,
Bering, the Commandant-
   captain,
his fifty-nine-year-old
head supported by his
right hand tattooed
with a bird's unfolded wings,
the left hand holding
a pair of dividers,
sitting motionless
in a flickering light.
It takes an uncannily
long time, Steller thinks,
for Bering to open
his eyes and look
at him. What is this
being called human?
A beast, shrouded
in deep mourning,
in a black coat
lined with
black fur.

The "bird's unfolded wings" tattooed on Bering's right hand have a special resonance. Wings and feathers reoccur at several points in *After Nature* – notably, as the emblem of forthcoming disaster worn by the "stunted Tatar with a red headcloth and a white slightly curved feather" in Section II of Part 3. Elsewhere, Max has the white feather as a mark of shamanic power (Herbert Achternbusch the Red Indian wears one); and wings are a means to ultimate liberation from earthly life – as in the lines from *Unrecounted* that were later to become Max's epitaph.[144]

* * * * *

This part of Nuremberg continues to remain home to a great many craft workshops, artists' studios, silversmiths, picture framers and the like. Christine and I continued on past the toy museum, after which you cross another of the bridges and enter the old quarter, a part of the city that had sustained a good deal less damage; the façades of the houses along the street are relatively intact. Turning back down towards the river, you come to the Maxbrücke, the oldest stone bridge in the city, built in honour of King Maximilian II of Bavaria. So, I mused, by walking over the Maxbrücke (Max Bridge), one could find one's way back to the Sebaldplatz (Sebald Place)...

It was here by the bridge that Christine stopped again, wondering what her mother would have said had she lived to see the changes that had been wrought on the city of Nuremberg. On reflection, she thought her mother, who had been "increasingly subject to depression", as she put it, would simply have "harked back to the good times before the war".

Elisabeth Heisenberg died in 1997, outliving her husband by twenty-one years. I'm inclined to the view that, whilst she might well have been filled with dismay at the style of the changes, her response would have had as much to do with the forces that had shaped her and the values she espoused as with her psychological disposition. Her brother – "Onkel Fritz" – was the economist E.F. Schumacher, the author of *Small is Beautiful: A Study of Economics as if People Mattered*.

I have a memory of Onkel Fritz. In my diary for 1963, I see that no sooner had we – Elisabeth, Christine and I – returned from our trip along the Romantische Strasse, than Onkel Fritz and his wife had turned up with their very young baby, needing a bed for the night. This had caused Elisabeth to go into a spin: whilst wanting to be welcoming, she had had to organise and re-arrange things at very short notice:

Saturday, 27 July 1963

Arrival home. Onkel Fritz plus wife and baby ... supper: about ten of us for the meal. Afterwards, Frau H. worried about unexpected guests and where they're going to sleep – we rushed round making beds etc. Couldn't get the linen drawer open – all right in the end ...

Sunday, 28 July 1963

All of us off in two cars to Ambach – to visit Christine's aunt [Edith] ... Tante Edith very surprised to see us ... after Schnapps and handshakes all round, we went out for lunch in a café garden where the Schumachers had reserved three tables. There were twelve of us. Wasn't daring enough for beer, so settled for Apfelsaft [apple juice] instead ... home by late afternoon. Long discussion between the men [Werner Heisenberg, Wolfgang (Christine's eldest brother) and Onkel Fritz] about politics and industry. I listened and tried to concentrate but kept forgetting the meanings of words in German, then remembered – though by then it was too late. Before supper, we all sat round until it was time for some music. Herr Prof. [at the piano] and Wolfgang [on violin] played a Mozart sonata ... Over supper, didn't understand the "typical English story" Onkel Fritz told us ... afterwards, when the table had been cleared, we gathered for more discussion over glasses of wine. Onkel Fritz talked all the time (though quite slowly) about central heating, the winter of 1962, Tristan da Cunha, signs of the Zodiac and stars etc. Frau H. kept an eye on my glass ...

In *Small is Beautiful*, published ten years later in 1973, Schumacher had put forward the argument that our present economic system was unsustainable; if we, the human race, continued to erode our natural resources without regard for the consequences, we were heading for disaster: future generations would suffer and the question of the best use of technology could not be considered to have been addressed. His work proved extremely influential, coinciding with the growth of interest in ecology and environmentalism – as it happens, subjects of great importance to Max, especially during the 1970s and 80s when he was establishing himself in Norfolk.

* * * * *

Christine and I walked back to join the main thoroughfare. Just beforehand, where the streets intersected, I noticed a plaque on the wall informing passers-by that this was the house to which Kaspar Hauser had been brought after being found wandering the streets of Nuremberg in May 1828. More associations: Kaspar the *Sonderling*, the *enfant sauvage*, who nowadays would probably be classified as autistic; and Peter Handke's play, focusing on the themes of language, homelessness and the search for identity, in which the Prompters subject Kaspar to "speech torture" as a means to his socialisation.

I was reminded of Wittgenstein's proposition in the *Tractatus*: "The limits of my language are the limits of my world"; and of Max's moving essay in which he describes Kaspar's ordeal as an attempt by others "to turn an individual who by ordinary standards is uncivilized into a respectable citizen".[145] It was in this essay, too, that Max had referenced several of my old heroes – the intellectuals of the 1960s and 70s who had dared break the rules: Michel Foucault; and David Cooper with his *Anti-Psychiatry* and *Death of the Family*.

I also found myself thinking back to the impact upon me of first watching Werner Herzog's film *The Enigma of Kaspar Hauser*[146] – most of all, its remarkable star, Bruno Schleinstein. Bruno S, as he was known, was not a professional actor; in real life, he had suffered abuse as a child and spent many years in psychiatric institutions. In fact, I recalled, he had died quite recently – a year ago to the day, on 11 August 2010.

* * * * *

As we had left the Sebalduskirche that morning, I'd caught sight of a notice pinned to the west door announcing a series of *Sommerliche Abendführungen* – summer evening guided tours, one of which was due to take place at six o'clock, entitled "St Sebald in St Sebald". I had made a note of it, with the idea of returning later.

Christine and I made our way back to the church and joined the group. There were about twenty of us; our guide, Gustav Roeder, was an elderly gentleman with a walking stick. He was entertaining and lively – at pains to emphasise that the legends surrounding the city's patron saint should be taken with a large pinch of salt. He began by pointing out the high number of images of the saint to be found within the church, explaining that Sebald had declined royal status in favour of living the life of a hermit; he is most often depicted with his pilgrim's hat and staff.

With regard to the shrine, apart from the snails and the dolphins on which it was supported, on the upper levels were the cherubs playing with dogs, the fabulous creatures. Commenting on the Miracle of the Icicle, Herr Roeder noted that the idea of ice being turned into fire had also been important for Goethe, who referred to it in *Wilhelm Meisters Lehrjahre*. Then there was the story of Sebald and the heretic – the heretic who'd had his eyes gouged out as punishment. In his goodness, Sebald was shown restoring the heretic his sight by offering him an eyeball – a detail that would surely not have escaped Max's attention. It prompted Herr Roeder to say to us now:

"Thus we can see that, amongst his many other accomplishments, Sebald was a gifted ophthalmologist!"

Before leaving, I went up to Herr Roeder and, explaining I was from England, asked whether he knew of "the writer W.G. Sebald" and *The Rings of Saturn*. He had heard of him, he said, but not read his work. I told him I was writing a book in memory of Max and happened to have with me a copy of the passage about the shrine. He accepted it graciously, wishing me well with my book. I later found out that at one time, Herr Roeder had been the editor-in-chief of the local paper, *Die Nürnberger Zeitung*.

*   *   *   *   *

W.G. Sebald – Sebald of Nuremberg. Some months later, it occurred to me that I had met this "other" Sebald on more than one occasion in another guise – and not just in *The Rings of Saturn*. Here, for instance, in the shape of Jacques Austerlitz, telling the narrator about that final day in Marienbad with Marie de Verneuil, when they had taken an evening walk to the pump-room at the Auschowitz Springs:

Marie moved closer to me and asked whether I had remembered that tomorrow was my birthday. When we wake up tomorrow, she said, I shall wish you every happiness, and it will be like telling a machine working by some unknown mechanism that I hope it will run well. Can't you tell me the reason, she asked, said Austerlitz, why you remain so unapproachable? Why, she said, have you been like a pool of frozen water ever since we came here? ... We stood there a couple of paces apart, like two actors on stage. The colour of Marie's eyes changed as the light dimmed. And once again I tried to explain to her and to myself what incomprehensible feelings had been weighing on me over the last few days; how I kept thinking, like a madman, that there were mysterious signs and portents all around me here; how it even seemed to me as if the silent façades of the buildings knew something ominous about me, how I had always believed I must be alone ... That evening in Marienbad, said Austerlitz, I could not admit to myself how right everything Marie said was ...[147]

XI

Our final port of call was Bamberg, which we reached via small roads, taking in a swathe of countryside around the town of Herzogenaurach (as distinct from Aurach, further south, near Ansbach).

Herzogenaurach, home of Adidas sports goods, is situated on the banks of the River Aurach, a tributary of the Regnitz. It had first been mentioned in a document under the name of Uraha in AD 1002 when Emperor Heinrich II had granted it to the archbishopric of Bamberg. It has had a chequered history, including transformation into a military air base in the 1930s.

By contrast, the surrounding wetlands are a pastoral idyll: dotted with fish-pools, water meadows and copses of deciduous woodland. I sensed Max would have been familiar with this – indeed, it bore striking comparison with parts of South Norfolk. Hanna Blösser, a friend of mine and a native of Bamberg, has told me that much of the region is now under conservation order; and that for many years, the marshland around Herzogenaurach had been used for the cultivation of carp. Apparently, one of the most celebrated local delicacies is fillet of carp with potato salad. That poem of Max's comes to mind again:

... der Schnitt	... the sliced cheese
käse der gekochte	the cooked ham
Schinken das Rührei	the scrambled eggs
die Nußnougatcreme	the nutty nougat
das Eintopfgericht	crème the stew of
des Tages die deftige	the day the hearty
Goulaschsuppe das	goulash the Nuremberg
Nürnberger Rostbrat	Bratwurst the potato
würstchen der Kar	salad the burger
toffelsalat die Frika	
delle mit Brötchen	with bread-roll
die Rinderroulade nach	grandma's beef
Hausfrauenart	olives ...[148]

It was in November 1993 that Max had presented me with a hardback copy of *Die Ausgewanderten* (*The Emigrants*) and when I first read it, I remember wondering how he had come by the name for his Mancunian emigrant. A few months later, at the beginning of 1994, he had brought round a copy of the cassette of a radio play he thought I might like to hear. The typeface of the title printed along the spine – *Max Aurach* – was immediately recognisable as that of the old typewriter Max had at home. "Is that you?" I asked him. To which he had responded with an enigmatic smile, as though unwilling to give anything away, "Yes – and no..." followed by a long pause, then, " ... in a way, I suppose, it is..."

In fact, the character in the story is a composite, inspired by two real-life people, one of whom was Max's landlord in Manchester during the sixties; the other, the London-based painter Frank Auerbach, about whom Max had read an article in a weekend colour supplement. By the time *The Emigrants* appeared in English translation in 1996, Max Aurach had assumed yet another identity. Auerbach hadn't wanted to be identified with a character in a book, however indirectly; and having no wish to cause upset, Max had changed "Aurach" to "Ferber".

* * * * *

As Bamberg was to be the last night of our journey, Christine and I had agreed to treat ourselves to extra comfort. We found what we wanted at the Barockhotel am Dom, the site of a house dating back to 1520, built for a canon of the cathedral, Willibald von Redwitz. In 1740, it had received the addition of a baroque façade and interior restoration, and was subsequently taken over as the headquarters for several generations of hop merchants. In 1975, the building had undergone complete modernisation, leading to its present use as a hotel.

It was late afternoon when we began our explorations by walking up the hill to the cathedral – another of the sights we had visited together in 1963. One of the star attractions for tourists is the life-size stone statue of the Bamberger Reiter (the Bamberg Horseman), dating from the first half of the thirteenth century. Located on a console at the north pillar of the St George choir, there has been much debate as to the identity of the Horseman. He is crowned yet unarmed; and, since the statue is in a church, it is thought to represent a specific king, perhaps one who was also a saint. Considered to be the first monumental equestrian statue since classical antiquity, it's also one of the first to depict a horseshoe. Beneath the horse's front hooves there's a sculptural representation of the Green Man, perhaps a symbol of the power of metal to suppress wildness and paganism.

The poet Stefan George, presumed to be the lover of Hugo von Hofmanns- thal and an ardent advocate of art for art's sake, wrote a poem about the Bamberger Reiter.[149] It would appear that the figure of the Horseman fitted in with George's notion of the *"geheimes Reich"* (literally," hidden empire"); and it's known that George's work influenced Claus von Stauffenberg, the would-be assassin of Hitler, whose cavalry unit, the *Bamberger Reiter- und Kavallerieregiment 17*, bore the name of the Bamberg Horseman.

As we gazed up at the Horseman, Christine commented that her mother had been very taken by him – she'd never understood why. I suggested it might have been to do with the Horseman's demeanour: fine-featured, sensitive, noble, aristocratic and romantic – qualities I imagined would have appealed to Elisabeth. Christine's response was interesting. "Not my type!" she said, somewhat tartly; and walked away, still preoccupied. A few moments later I found her waiting to talk to a churchwarden, who was standing in the side-aisle, offering information to tourists. We explained that we were interested in the identity of the Horseman. He eyed us closely, as though weighing up the kind of people he was dealing with. It seemed he hadn't caught on to the fact that I wasn't German; taking advantage of this, I urged him to say more. Affecting caution – "opinions varied on the point" – he told us that during the Third Reich, the Horseman had represented the ideal Aryan male; adding, with a flourish, that "the beautiful Uta of Naumburg, wife of Count Ekkehard II of Meissen who died in 1046" had stood for the female equivalent.

We left the cathedral and walked across the precinct to the Neue Residenz to find the rose garden still open. Inspecting the different varieties and picking out the ones with the best scent brought back memories to Christine – memories of the family garden in Göttingen where her father had planted roses: his favourites had been New Dawn and Gloria Dei.

On our way back into the town, we stopped at one of the gate towers by a bridge over the river and, looking up, saw two memorial plaques: one in honour of the Jews, the other to commemorate "those loyal men of Bamberg who had enlisted as soldiers and given their lives for their country ..." Christine said nothing; her face was a picture of scorn. Pretending to take a "neutral" stance with regard to the wording, I said I saw nothing unusual about it – the sort of thing one was likely to find on war memorials. But Christine was having none of it. Incandescent with rage, "*So ein Nazinest!*" she burst out with – "A right Nazi nest!"

Retracing our steps and going up a hill named the Katzenberg, we found a *Gaststube* where we sat outdoors and had supper: *Ochsenbrust* (beef brisket) along with a glass of Bamberg's local speciality, *Rauchbier*. Then, before returning to the hotel, we discovered another part of the town, including the house where E.T.A. Hoffmann had lived between 1809 and 1813. There was a theatre nearby, named in his honour, and in the neighbouring square, a small bronze of the characters from his famous story, "Kapellmeister Johannes Kreisler and the Tomcat Murr".

By now it was obvious: in stark contrast to Nuremberg, Bamberg had been largely untouched by enemy bombing; at the same time, I found it unsettling to think of this beautiful city as a "*Nazinest*". In the quiet of my room back at the hotel that evening, I thought more about what Christine had said and what it might have to do with Max and the stormy relationship with his father.

It was true that Georg Sebald had been absent for much of his son's childhood and that, when he was home, he was a strict disciplinarian. Echoes of Schreber *père et fils*. It then occurred to me that perhaps these weren't the only reasons for Max's negative feelings towards his father. Georg may not have been a Nazi – in 1947 he had been cleared of all involvement with the NSDAP. But in his son's view, he was a *Mitläufer* – roughly translated, a follower or fellow traveller – a passive collaborator in the Nazi regime who had continued to uphold the conspiracy of silence after the end of the war.

XII

Next morning, having taken advice from the hotel receptionist, we put on our boots and set off on a walk up the highest of the hills that enclose the city, the Altenburg, to the former Benedictine monastery at the top.

Halfway up, it was wooded and shady, with a nature trail. Stopping to read the information, I learnt something that I thought might help resolve the question about the trees mentioned by Max in *The Rings of Saturn* in his description of the grounds at Somerleyton Hall. There were two distinct species of tree to be found here in the Schatthangwald: the *Spitz-Ahorn*, the Norway maple, *Acer platanoides*; and the *Berg-Ahorn*, the sycamore, *Acer pseudoplatanus*, both of which had propeller-like winged seeds and might therefore be confused. What distinguished the *Spitz-Ahorn*, however, were its pointed leaves whereas the *Berg-Ahorn* had more rounded ones. Max refers to the *"seltene Sykomoren"* – translated into English as "rare oriental planes"...

> ... *the outermost extremities of which had bowed down as low as the lawn, securing a hold where they touched the ground, to shoot up once more in a perfect circle. It was easy to imagine this species of plane tree spreading over the country, just as concentric circles ripple across water, the parents becoming weaker and dying off from within as the progeny conquers the land about them...*[150]

As in families, so in plant life.

There was other interesting information to be had on reaching the top of the Altenburg and walking through into the monastery. Albrecht Dürer had visited it in the 1500s; and so had the itinerant alchemist Doctor Johann Georg Faust of Heidelberg, in February 1520. Three centuries later, in 1812, E.T.A. Hoffmann had established himself in a small "writer's hut" overlooking the valley, which he'd designed himself; it had about it something akin to a Wendy house.

* * * * *

The last part of our excursion took us back into town and along the riverbank of the Regnitz to the botanical garden, the so-called *Hain* ("grove") where Max's parents, Georg and Rosa Sebald, had had their photograph taken on 26 August 1943:

... Das ganze macht zunächst	*... The whole leaves an impression*
einen irgendwie undeutschen	*that is somehow un-German, the*
Eindruck, die Ulmen, Rüstern	*elms, the hornbeams and densely*
und dichtgrünen Koniferen	*green conifers in the background,*
im Hintergrund, das kleine	*the small pagoda-like building, the*
Pagodengebäude, der feine geharkte	*finely raked gravel, the hortensias,*
Kies, die Hortensien, Schilflilien,	*flag-irises, aloes, ostrich-plume*
Aloën, der Straußfederfarn und	*ferns and the giant-leaved*
der riesenblättrige Zierrhabarber.	*ornamental rhubarb.*[151]

The afternoon we were there, it seemed not much had changed – at least in terms of atmosphere: the gravel was still as finely raked, the plants as opulent – the late summer colours pulsated in the sunshine. Christine and I were content just to sit and enjoy the peace.

In the poem, however, the description of the idyllic scene swiftly gives way to a more sombre tone, a sense of something ominous about to happen. Georg and Rosa take leave of each other, he for Dresden and she to "her parents' home in the Alps". Rosa gets no further than Fürth, from where she sees "Nürnberg in flames", a sight about which later she is unable to remember any of her feelings. It is immediately after this that she discovers she is pregnant.

The child Rosa was carrying would be born on Ascension Day the following May, and christened Winfried Georg.[152]

XIII

The drive back to Göttingen passed remarkably quickly – taking us just over three hours. Over supper on the terrace that evening, we chatted about the experience of the past week: it had indeed been a rich one.

On my final morning, we took a walk through the park. We'd been to the Hainberg once or twice before and I was aware how much it meant to Christine. Whenever she came here, she said, she was reminded of her childhood, of where she used to play with her brothers and sisters.

The path led past a concrete structure, looking as if it'd seen better days. It was here, she told me, that she and her Girl Guide group had gathered each week. This started us on another conversation about her father, who, as a young man, had excelled himself as a scout leader. We went on to talk more generally about the British Scout and Girl Guide movements and how these compared with the German *Pfadfinder* – or, indeed, the *Wandervogel*, a movement that had had its roots in the German Romantic tradition.

It made me think of Goethe –

... I am a voluntary exile, a wanderer by design, unwise with a purpose, everywhere a stranger and everywhere at home, letting my life run its course where it will, rather than trying to guide it, since, in any case, I don't know where it will lead me...[153]

– and of the wanderer contemplating the vista in the painting by Caspar David Friedrich; of Schubert's song cycle, *Winterreise* –

Ich mußt' auch heute wandern	Today I go a-wandering
Vorbei in tiefer Nacht,	Through this deep, dark night
Da hab' ich noch im Dunkeln	I passed this tree in darkness
Die Augen zugemacht.	But did not care to look.
Und seine Zweige rauschten,	I heard the branches rustle
Als riefen sie mir zu:	As if they spoke to me
Komm her zu mir, Geselle,	Come here, my friend, come here
Hier find'st du deine Ruh'!	Where you will find your peace.
Die kalten Winde bliesen	Cruel winds were blowing
Mir grad' ins Angesicht;	Cold against my face
Der Hut flog mir vom Kopfe,	My hat blew off behind me
Ich wendete mich nicht.	But I did not turn back.
Nun bin ich manche Stunde	I'm now a long way distant
Entfernt von jenem Ort,	From that old linden-tree.
Und immer hör' ich's rauschen:	But still I hear it whisper:
Du fändest Ruhe dort!	Come here, find peace with me.[154]

– and then, of Max Sebald.

When I met Max in 1981, he had been at a critical juncture in his life. During the 1990s, versions of himself started to appear in his writing that strike me as direct descendants of that German Romantic tradition: Max the wanderer, the *promeneur solitaire* – as likely to be encountered on a steep track in Corsica or a path on Dunwich Heath as in a remote part of the Bavarian Alps.

Be that as it may, the abiding image I have of Max is different. Like the central figure of Tiepolo's ceiling in Würzburg, I can just make him out:

So wie ein Rochen schwebt in der Tiefe	As a stingray hovers deep down
des Meers, so glitt ich lautlos	in the sea, so soundlessly I glided,
kaum einen Flügel rührend	scarcely moving a wing,
hoch über die Erde hin ...	high above the earth ...[155]

Notes

1   Taken from W.G. Sebald, *Über das Land und das Wasser – Ausgewählte Gedichte 1964–2001*, Munich: Hanser Verlag, 2008, p.25. English translation by Iain Galbraith, *Across the Land and the Water*, London: Hamish Hamilton, 2011, p.21.

2   Originally published in Paris: Éditions de Minuit, 1957, translated into English by Jean Stewart, London: Faber, 1961.

3   Translated into English by R.J. Hollingdale, Harmondsworth: Penguin, 1971. In the original German: "Ebenso zieht sich durch Ottiliens Tagebuch ein Faden der Neigung und Anhänglichkeit der alles verbindet und das Ganze bezeichnet. Dadurch werden diese Bemerkungen, Betrachtungen ... und was sonst vorkommen mag, der Schreibenden ganz besonders eigen und für sie von Bedeutung. Selbst jede einzelne von uns ausgewählte und mitgeteilte Stelle gibt davon das entscheidendste Zeugnis."

4   See *The Rings of Saturn*, London: The Harvill Press, 1998, translated by Michael Hulse, pp.3–5.

5   Cited in "Die weiße Adlerfeder am Kopf: Versuch über den Indianer Herbert Achternbusch", *Manuskripte:*

Zeitschrift für Literatur No.79/83 edited by Alfred Kolleritsch & Günter Waldorf, Graz, 1983, p.77.

6   In Claude Lévi-Strauss, *La Pensée sauvage*, 1962, translated into English as *The Savage Mind*, London: Weidenfeld & Nicolson, 1966, reprinted Oxford: OUP, 2004, pp.19–20. Translator unnamed.

7   Taken from Alfred Döblin, *Berlin Alexanderplatz*, Frankfurt: Suhrkamp Verlag, 1980, p.24. My translation. In the original German: " ... die Hauptsache am Menschen sind seine Augen und seine Füße. Man muß die Welt sehen können und zu ihr hingehn."

8   From *Walter Benjamin Selected Writings*, Vol. 3, ed. Howard Eiland & Michael W. Jennings, Cambridge, Massachusetts: Belknap Press of Harvard, 2002.

9   From *Tristram Shandy*, 1759–67, Vol. V, Chapter 17.

10 *The Emigrants*, London: The Harvill Press, 1996, translated by Michael Hulse, pp.154–155.

11 *Un Coeur Simple* [*A Simple Heart*], written during 1876.

12 See Ulrich Raulff, "Glas. Silber. Staub." in *Kunstforum International* Vol. 43 (1/81), Mainz, 1981. My translation.

13 From "Ghost Hunter", an interview with Eleanor Wachtel, recorded on 16 October 1997 and reproduced in *The Emergence of Memory: Conversations with W.G. Sebald*, ed. Lynne Sharon Schwartz, New York: Seven Stories Press, 2007.

14 Vladimir Nabokov, *Speak, Memory*, Harmondsworth: Penguin, 1966.

15 From Thomas Bernhard, *Verstörung*, Frankfurt am Main: Suhrkamp, 1988 (1967), p.162. My translation. The book was first published in English translation in 1970 as *Gargoyles*.

16 Taken from John Berger's essay "Between Two Colmars", which first appeared in *The Guardian* in 1973 and was later included in the volume of essays *About Looking*, London: Writers and Readers Publishing Cooperative, 1980.

17 An essay written in 1998 and included in the collection *Logis in einem Landhaus*, Munich and Vienna: Carl Hanser Verlag, 1998. English translation by Jo Catling, *A Place in the Country*, London: Penguin, 2013.

18 *City of Women*, 1980.

19 From Virginia Woolf's review of the Golden Cockerel edition of the works of Sir Thomas Browne, published in *The Times Literary Supplement*.

20 The essays bear the full titles *Hydriotaphia. Urne Buriall; or, a Discourse of the Sepulchrall Urnes Lately Found in Norfolk*; and *The Garden of Cyrus; or, the Quincunciall, Lozenge, or Net-work of Plantations of the Ancients, Artificially, Naturally, Mystically Considered*, both published in 1658.

21 The essay bears the full title *Konstruktion der Trauer: Günter Grass und Wolfgang Hildesheimer*.

22 Sir Thomas Browne, *Religio Medici and Other Writings*, introduction by M.R. Ridley, London: Dent, Everyman's Library No. 92, 1965.

23 *The Earthquake in Chile* was written in late 1806 or early 1807; and *The Betrothal in Santo Domingo* in 1811.

24 From W.G. Sebald, *Schwindel. Gefühle.* Frankfurt am Main: Vito von Eichborn Verlag, 1990. English translation by Michael Hulse in *Vertigo*, London: The Harvill Press, 1999, p.44.

25 Taken from Chapter 63 of *In Patagonia*, London: Jonathan Cape, 1977.

26 Ernst Herbeck's work was collected and edited by Leo Navratil; and published in 1977 as *Alexanders poetische Texte*, Munich: Deutscher Taschenbuchverlag.

27 See W.G. Sebald, *Vertigo*, London: The Harvill Press, 1999, translated by Michael Hulse, pp.38–42.

28 Taken from Robert Burton, *The Anatomy of Melancholy*, edited with an introduction by William H. Gass, New York: New York Review of Books, 2001.

29 *The Diaries of Franz Kafka 1910–23* ed. by Max Brod, translated by Martin Greenberg with the cooperation of Hannah Arendt, Harmondsworth: Penguin Books, 1964. In the original German "Die Furcht ist das Unglück, deshalb ist nicht der Mut das

Glück, sondern Furchtlosigkeit ...
Furchtlosigkeit, ruhende, offen
blickende, alles ertragende. Zwinge
dich zu nichts ... und wenn du
dich nicht zwingst, umlaufe nicht
immerfort lüstern die Möglichkeiten
des Zwanges ..."

30 Oskar Negt and Alexander Kluge,
Geschichte und Eigensinn, Frankfurt:
Zweitausendeins, 1981, p.380. My
translation.

31 *On Love: Aspects of a Single Theme* by
the Spanish liberal philosopher, Ortega
y Gasset (1883–1955), translated into
English by Tony Talbot in 1957.

32 "Zwischen Geschichte und
Naturgeschichte. Über die literarische
Beschreibung totaler Zerstörung"
published in *Orbis litterarum* 37 (1982),
later included in the posthumous
volume *Campo Santo*, Munich: Carl
Hanser Verlag, 2003, translated into
English by Anthea Bell, London:
Hamish Hamilton, 2005.

33 In the original German: "'... Wir
kommen aus dem Dunkel und gehen
ins Dunkel, dazwischen liegen
Erlebnisse, aber Anfang und Ende,
Geburt und Tod, werden von uns nicht
erlebt, sie haben keinen subjektiven
Charakter, sie fallen als Vorgänge ganz
ins Gebiet des Objektiven, so ist es
damit.' Dies war des Hofrats Art und
Weise, Trost zu spenden ..." Translated
into English by H.T. Lowe-Porter,
London: Martin Secker & Warburg
Ltd, 1927.

34 Taken from the opening of the third
scene of *Minetti* by Thomas Bernhard

in *Stücke 2*, Frankfurt am Main:
Suhrkamp, 1988. My translation.

35 The 1982 film *The Magic Mountain*,
based on the novel by Thomas Mann,
directed by Hans W. Geissendörfer.

36 "Die weiße Adlerfeder am Kopf:
Versuch über den Indianer Herbert
Achternbusch" in *Manuskripte:
Zeitschrift für Literatur* No.79 edited by
Alfred Kolleritsch & Günter Waldorf,
Graz, 1983.

37 From *Unerzählt:33 Texte und 33
Radierungen*, Munich: Carl Hanser
Verlag, 2003. The book, published
posthumously, contains a series of
elliptical "micro-poems" written by
Max along with etchings by his close
friend, the artist Jan Peter Tripp. The
book was translated into English by
another of Max's friends, the poet
Michael Hamburger, and published
as *Unrecounted*, London: Hamish
Hamilton, 2004. The lines in question
appear on p.73, beneath the picture of
Samuel Beckett.

38 William Shakespeare, *A Midsummer
Night's Dream*, 1594, Act V, scene 1.

39 *A Radical Stage: Theatre in Germany
in the 1970s and 1980s*, ed. W.G.
Sebald, Oxford, New York, Hamburg:
Berg Publishers Ltd, 1988, a volume
comprising papers from a colloquium
held at the University of East Anglia in
Spring 1987.

40 See "Max Ferber" in *The Emigrants*,
London: The Harvill Press, 1996,
translated by Michael Hulse, p.171.

41 From W.G. Sebald, *Die Ringe des
Saturn: Eine englische Wallfahrt*,
Frankfurt am Main: Vito von Eichborn

Verlag, 1995. English translation by
Michael Hulse in *The Rings of Saturn*,
London: The Harvill Press, 1998,
pp.37–38.

42 The quote is taken from Canto 17
"Schwacher Trost" of *Der Untergang
der Titanic – eine Komödie* [*The Sinking
of the Titanic – a Comedy*], Frankfurt am
Main: Suhrkamp Verlag, 1978.
My translation.

43 Born in Bavaria in 1929, Hans Magnus
Enzensberger was destined to become
one of the leading intellectuals of his
generation.

44 A line taken from the libretto for *Peter
Grimes*, Act II, scene 2. Benjamin
Britten's opera was first performed on
7 June 1945, one month after the end
of the war in Europe. The libretto was
written by Montagu Slater, derived
from George Crabbe's "poem in 24
letters", *The Borough*.

45 " ... the night of 19th/20th May saw
the last German air raid over England
until WW2. That evening ten Gothas
and three Giant bombers spent two
hours wandering in over Kent and
Essex to be met by an incredible
number of anti-aircraft shells and
patrolling fighter aircraft. Six German
aircraft were shot down ..." from
Derek Faulkner's *Letters from Sheppey:
Airmail*, blog post for Saturday, 19
February 2011, available at http://
www.lettersfromsheppey/blogspot.
co.uk/2011/02/airmail.html.

46 Taken from W.G. Sebald, *Über das
Land und das Wasser – Ausgewählte
Gedichte 1964–2001*, Munich: Carl
Hanser Verlag, 2008, pp.77–78. English

translation by Iain Galbraith, *Across the
Land and the Water*, London: Hamish
Hamilton, 2011, pp.123–124.

47 See *The Rings of Saturn*, London:
The Harvill Press, 1988, translated by
Michael Hulse, pp.38–40.

48 From W.G. Sebald, *The Natural History
of Destruction*, London: Penguin Books,
2003, translated by Anthea Bell,
pp.74–75.

49 From Werner Heisenberg's *Diary
15 April-15 May 1945*, a 14-page
typewritten manuscript, together
with a drawing of Urfeld and its
surroundings. Contrary to its title, the
diary ends on 3 May 1945. This excerpt
is my translation, a modified version of
that by Heisenberg's daughter-in-law,
Irene Heisenberg. The complete text is
available on the website http://werner-
heisenberg.unh.edu/diary.htm.

50 Christine Mann, née Heisenberg, was
born at the end of June 1944 – in other
words, six weeks after Max Sebald.

51 See "Moments musiceaux" in *Campo
Santo*, London: Penguin Books, 2006,
translated by Anthea Bell, p.195.

52 From "Die Dunckle Nacht Fahrt Aus",
the third part of *Nach der Natur*,
Nördlingen: Greno Verlagsgesellschaft,
1988, Section II, pp.76–77/"Dark Night
Sallies Forth", Part 3 of *After Nature*,
London: Hamish Hamilton, 2002,
translated by Michael Hamburger,
pp.86–87.

53 A description of the Scottish novelist,
William McIlvanney, at the end of
Chapter 7 of *Stone Voices: The Search
for Scotland*, London: Granta Books,
2002.

54   My translation. In the original German: "Frauen kommen in dem Stück wenig vor, sind aber gerade deshalb von zentraler Bedeutung. Es muss Sorge getragen werden, dass ihr 'Erscheinen' in der Männergesellschaft immer von einer fast greifbaren 'Aura' begleitet wird."

55   In *Illuminations: Essays and Reflections*, translated by Harry Zohn, edited with an introduction by Hannah Arendt, New York: Schocken Books, 2007, pp.217–251.

56   See Susanne K. Langer, *Philosophy in a New Key: A Study in the Symbolism of Reason, Rite, and Art*, Cambridge, Massachusetts: Harvard University Press, 1979 for a discussion of the two modes.

57   "Helle Bilder und dunkle – Zur Dialektik der Eschatologie bei Stifter und Handke" appeared in *Manuskripte 84*, June 1984 and subsequently in *Die Beschreibung des Unglücks: Zur österreichischen Literatur von Stifter bis Handke* Salzburg & Vienna: Residenz Verlag, 1985.

58   Published as "Preussische Perversionen: Anmerkungen zum Thema Literatur und Gewalt, ausgehend vom Frühwerk Alfred Döblins" (1983) in *Internationale Alfred Döblin-Kolloquien Basel 1980 New York 1981 Freiburg im Breisgau 1983*, ed. Werner Stauffacher, Berne, Frankfurt a.M. & New York: Peter Lang.

59   From "Und Blieb Ich am Aussersten Meer", the second part of *Nach der Natur*, Nördlingen: Greno Verlagsgesellschaft, 1988, Section

XIX, p. 66/"And if I Remained by the Outermost Sea", Part 2 of *After Nature*, London: Hamish Hamilton, 2002, translated by Michael Hamburger, p.74.

60   See *The Rings of Saturn*, pp.18–23 and 271–274. Also Jorge Luis Borges *El libro de los seres imaginarios*, Buenos Aires: Fce-Breviarios, 1969, translated into English as *The Book of Imaginary Beings*, London: Jonathan Cape, 1970.

61   See *The Emigrants*, London: The Harvill Press, 1996, p.32.

62   This and subsequent citations are from *The Diary of John Evelyn*, Vol. I, Everyman's Library No. 220, ed. William Bray, London: J.M. Dent, 1907.

63   In the *Diary*, Evelyn records that he sat to Walker on 1 July 1648 and that the portrait was intended to accompany a treatise on marriage he'd written for his young wife, Mary Browne. (Originally, the painting showed him holding a miniature or medal of his wife, later substituted by a skull bearing a motto in Greek "Repentance is the beginning of Wisdom"; and a quotation from Seneca in Latin on the importance of preparing for death.) The portrait was purchased by the National Portrait Gallery in 1992, with help from The Art Fund, The National Heritage Memorial Fund and The Dame Helen Gardner Bequest.

64   In *Über das Land und das Wasser – Ausgewählte Gedichte 1964–2001*, Munich: Carl Hanser Verlag, 2008, p.59. *Across the Land and the Water – Selected Poems 1964-2001*, London: Hamish Hamilton, 2011, translated by Iain Galbraith, p.95.

65 See *Schwindel. Gefühle.* pp.297–299 and *Vertigo*, London: The Harvill Press, 1999, translated by Michael Hulse, pp.261–263.

66 Volumes 53 and 54.

67 The Holy Bible, King James Version, Cambridge: CUP, Psalm 90, verse 10.

68 "The Garden" originally appeared in Andrew Marvell's *Miscellaneous Poems*, 1681.

69 Taken from W.G. Sebald, *Über das Land und das Wasser – Ausgewählte Gedichte 1964–2001*, Munich: Carl Hanser Verlag, 2008, p.7. English translation by Iain Galbraith *Across the Land and the Water*, London: Hamish Hamilton, 2011, p.3.

70 The conference proceedings were later to appear in book-form as *Die Erloschene Seele: Disziplin, Geschichte, Kunst, Mythos,* edited by Dietmar Kamper and Christof Wulf, Berlin: Dietrich Reimer Verlag, Reihe Historische Anthropologie, 1988. It contains my essay, translated as "Die Beseelung des Gartens – Der Garten als Widerspiegelung der Sensibilität: Ein Versuch den Genius Loci zu finden."

71 From W.G. Sebald, *Schwindel. Gefühle.* Frankfurt am Main: Vito von Eichborn Verlag, 1990. English translation by Michael Hulse in *Vertigo*, London: The Harvill Press, 1999, p.52.

72 From *Austerlitz*, Munich and Vienna: Carl Hanser Verlag, 2001. English translation by Anthea Bell, London: Hamish Hamilton, 2001, p.304.

73 Taken from Hugo von Hofmannsthal *The Lord Chandos Letter and Other Writings*, selected and translated by Joel Rotenberg, New York: New York Review Books, 2005.

74 From the poem "Am 9 Juni 1904" in *Über das Land und das Wasser – Ausgewählte Gedichte 1964-2001*, Munich: Carl Hanser Verlag, 2008, p.70/"On 9 June 1904" in *Across the Land and the Water – Selected Poems 1964–2001*, London: Hamish Hamilton, 2011, p.117.

75 Published in the collection of essays *Die Beschreibung des Unglücks: Zur österreichischen Literatur von Stifter bis Handke* [*The Description of Misfortune*], Salzburg & Vienna: Residenz Verlag, 1985. Also in *Fin du siècle Vienna*, Proceedings of the Second Irish Symposium on Austrian Studies held at Trinity College, Dublin, 28.2–2.3.85, ed. G.J. Carr & Eda Sagarra, Dublin: Trinity College, pp.143–60.

76 On 3 June 1924 in Dr Hoffmann's sanatorium in Kierling, near Vienna.

77 In the original French: "L'empire des femmes est beaucoup trop grand en France, l'empire de la femme beaucoup trop restreint." In Stendhal *De l'amour – Fragments divers 132*, Paris: Éditions Garnier Frères, 1959, p.288. My translation.

78 Excerpt from "Echoes from the Past: A Conversation with Piet de Moor" published in *Knack* magazine, Brussels, 6 May 1992, translated from the Dutch by Reinier van Straten and reproduced in *Saturn's Moons: W.G. Sebald – A Handbook*, edited by Jo Catling and Richard Hibbitt, London: Legenda, 2011, pp. 350–354.

79 See "Beyle, or Love is a Madness Most Discreet", in *Vertigo*, London: The Harvill Press, 1999, translated by Michael Hulse, pp.18–19.

80 Ibid., pp.20–21.

81 See Joseph Cuomo "A Conversation with W.G. Sebald" in *The Emergence of Memory: Conversations with W.G. Sebald*, edited by Lynne Sharon Schwartz, New York: Seven Stories Press, 2007, pp.97–98.

82 From Idris Parry's essay, included in *Speak Silence*, Manchester: Carcanet Press Ltd., 1988.

83 From W.G. Sebald, *Die Ringe des Saturn: Eine englische Wallfahrt*, Frankfurt am Main: Vito von Eichborn Verlag, 1995. English translation by Michael Hulse in *The Rings of Saturn*, London: The Harvill Press, 1998, p.80.

84 See *The Emigrants*, London: The Harvill Press, 1996, p.167.

85 Bayer's novel, *Der Kopf des Vitus Bering*, was published posthumously in 1965.

86 Daniel Paul Schreber's *Memoirs of My Nervous Illness* was edited and translated into English by Ida MacAlpine and Richard A. Hunter in 1955. Originally published in German as *Denkwürdigkeiten eines Nervenkranken*, Leipzig, 1903.

87 See "Summa Scientiae – System und Systemkritik bei Elias Canetti" ("Summa Scientiae – System and Critique of System in Elias Canetti"), first published in 1983 and contained in *Die Beschreibung des Unglücks*, Salzburg & Vienna: Residenz Verlag, 1985, pp.93–102. See also Elias Canetti, *Crowds and Power* translated from the German by Carol Stewart, London: Victor Gollancz, 1962.

88 See William G. Niederland, *Folgen der Verfolgung: Das Überlebenden-Syndrom Seelenmord*, Frankfurt am Main: Suhrkamp Verlag, 1980.

89 See *"Ich fürchte das Melodramatische" Ein Gespräch mit Martin Doerry und Volker Hage* ("I fear the melodramatic" *A Conversation with Martin Doerry and Volker Hage*) reproduced in W.G. Sebald *"Auf ungeheuer dünnem Eis" Gespräche 1971 bis 2001* ("On extremely thin ice" *Conversations 1971 to 2001*) edited by Torsten Hoffmann, Frankfurt am Main: Fischer Taschenbuch Verlag, 2011, p.204. My translation.

90 From W.G. Sebald, *An Attempt at Restitution* (*Ein Versuch der Restitution*), November 2001, included in the posthumous volume *Campo Santo*, Munich: Hanser, 2003, translated into English by Anthea Bell, London: Hamish Hamilton, 2005, pp. 209–210.

91 See *The Emigrants*, London: The Harvill Press, 1996, pp.230–231.

92 See *Austerlitz*, London: Hamish Hamilton, 2001, pp.172–174.

93 Paragraph 203. Taken from the bi-lingual edition of *Philosophical Investigations*, edited by G.E.M. Anscombe and R. Rhees, translated by G.E.M. Anscombe, Oxford: Basil Blackwell, 1958.

94 In the original German: "Wie schlecht ich als passionierter Leser ohne die österreichische Literatur auskommen könnte, das ist mir erst letzthin wieder aufgegangen, als ich im Zug zwischen München und Frankfurt aus lauter

Langeweile und Unachtsamkeit ein Stück aus dem derzeit in der F.A.Z. erschienenden Fortsetzungsroman eines namhaften westdeutschen Autors las, was mir ein solches Gefühl der Übelkeit verursachte, daß ich in den Speisewagen gehen und einen Schnaps trinken mußte." In *Manuskripte: Zeitschrift für Literatur* No.89/90 edited by Alfred Kolleritsch & Günter Waldorf, Graz, September 1985. My translation.

95   See *Austerlitz*, London: Hamish Hamilton, 2001, p.3.

96   Frans Post (1612-1680). The original painting is in the Mauritshuis in The Hague. Itamaracá is an island and city in Pernambuco, Brazil, whose name means "stone shaker".

97   This is how George Steiner ended his lecture, *An Exact Art*, given in Norwich on 26 April 1994.

98   From Claudio Magris *Microcosms*, (*Microcosmi*), London: The Harvill Press, 2000, translated by Iain Halliday, p.123.

99   See *Campo Santo*, London: Hamish Hamilton, 2005, translated by Anthea Bell, p.36 ff. See also, *Wandernde Schatten: W.G. Sebalds Unterwelt*, marbacherkatalog 62, edited by Ulrich von Bülow, Heike Gfrereis and Ellen Strittmatter, Marbach am Neckar: Deutsche Schillergesellschaft, 2008, pp.129–224; and Gustave Flaubert *La Légende de Saint Julien L'Hospitalier*, 1876.

100 Fr John Dove SJ *Strange Vagabond of God: The Story of John Bradburne*, Dublin: Ward River Press, 1983.

101 See "Die hölzernen Engel von East Anglia: eine individuelle Bummeltour durch Norfolk und Suffolk" originally published in *Die Zeit*, 26 July 1974 and reproduced in *Saturn's Moons: W.G. Sebald – A Handbook*, edited by Jo Catling and Richard Hibbitt, London: Legenda, 2011, pp. 319–322.

102 From *The Emergence of Memory: Conversations with W.G. Sebald*, edited by Lynne Sharon Schwartz, New York: Seven Stories Press, 2007, p.95.

103 See David Crystal *By Hook or by Crook: A Journey in Search of English*, London: HarperCollins, 2007, PS p.2 "Bees and Fires: Travis Elborough talks to David Crystal".

104 Ibid. Chapter 8 "The Robot's not Working: Risbury", pp.136–137.

105 From *Nach der Natur – Ein Elementargedicht*, Nördlingen: Greno Verlagsgesellschaft, 1988, Part Three, "Die Dunckle Nacht Fahrt Aus", Section IV, p.83/*After Nature*, London: Hamish Hamilton, 2002, translated by Michael Hamburger, Part Three "Dark Night Sallies Forth", Section IV, p.95.

106 See *Logis in einem Landhaus – Über Gottfried Keller, Johann Peter Hebel, Robert Walser und andere*, Munich and Vienna: Carl Hanser Verlag, 1998, p.5. English translation by Jo Catling, *A Place in the Country*, London: Penguin, 2013.

107 "Threnody", dedicated to Max, was the final song in my song-cycle *In This Trembling Shade*, set to music by the composer Andrew Griffiths for mezzo-soprano to lute accompaniment. It was given its first performance at the Royal

Northern College of Music on 20 June 2007.

108 Including, specifically, a review of *The Emigrants*, "Butterfly memories" in *The Independent on Sunday*, 14 July 1996, by my friend Neal Ascherson.

109 The essay was to be included in the catalogue accompanying an exhibition of the work of Jan Peter Tripp held in Öhningen, a town on the western edge of Lake Constance. It was published in the international edition of the *Neue Zürcher Zeitung*, 23 September 2000 and reprinted in *Campo Santo*, London: Hamish Hamilton, 2005, translated by Anthea Bell, pp.174–178.

110 See "Venezianisches Kryptogramm: Hofmannsthals *Andreas*" in *Die Beschreibung des Unglücks*, Frankfurt am Main: Fischer Taschenbuch Verlag, 1994, p.73.

111 English translation by W.H. Auden and Elizabeth Mayer, London: Collins, 1962.

112 From "Max Ferber" in *The Emigrants*, London: The Harvill Press, 1996, translated by Michael Hulse, p.224.

113 "The butterfly man" is a figure that turns up at several points in *The Emigrants*. He can be taken as a reference to Vladimir Nabokov, the author of *Speak, Memory*; or more generally, to symbolise "memory".

114 From "Ambros Adelwarth" in *The Emigrants*, London: The Harvill Press, 1996, translated by Michael Hulse, pp.144–145.

115 Kafka's short story "The Hunter Gracchus" ("Der Jäger Gracchus") was written in the first half of 1917 and

published posthumously in *Beim Bau der Chinesischen Mauer*, Berlin, 1931. This excerpt is from a translation by Ian Johnston.

116 Taken from "An einem Herbstsonntag 94" in *Über das Land und das Wasser – Ausgewählte Gedichte 1964–2001*, Munich: Carl Hanser Verlag, 2008, p.90/"One Sunday in Autumn 94" in *Across the Land and the Water – Selected Poems 1964–2001*, London: Hamish Hamilton, 2011, translated by Iain Galbraith, p.145.

117 Taken from "K's Auswanderung" in *Über das Land und das Wasser – Ausgewählte Gedichte 1964–2001*, Munich: Carl Hanser Verlag, 2008, p.44/"K's Emigration" in *Across the Land and the Water – Selected Poems 1964–2001*, London: Hamish Hamilton, 2011, translated by Iain Galbraith, p.68.

118 Javier Marías, *Your Face Tomorrow 1: Fever and Spear* (2002), London: Vintage, 2006, p.283, translated by Margaret Jull Costa, p.283.

119 Taken from "In der Nacht auf " in *Über das Land und das Wasser – Ausgewählte Gedichte 1964–2001*, Munich: Carl Hanser Verlag, 2008, p.100/"On the Eve of" in *Across the Land and the Water – Selected Poems 1964–2001*, London: Hamish Hamilton, 2011, translated by Iain Galbraith, p.157.

120 Idris Parry *Speak Silence*, Manchester: Carcanet Press Limited, 1988, p.258.

121 From "Wie der Schnee auf den Alpen", the first part of *Nach der Natur*, Nördlingen: Greno Verlagsgesellschaft, 1988, Section VI, p.22/"As the Snow on the Alps", Part 1 of *After Nature*,

London: Hamish Hamilton, 2002, translated by Michael Hamburger, Section VI, p.24.

122 From *The Emigrants*, London: The Harvill Press, 1996, translated by Michael Hulse, pp.170–171.

123 The phrase is taken from Joseph Conrad's novella, *Heart of Darkness*, first published in 1899.

124 *Nach der Natur/After Nature*, p.24 (26).

125 Ibid, p.27 (30–31).

126 From "In der schlaflos" in *Über das Land und das Wasser – Ausgewählte Gedichte 1964-2001*, Munich: Carl Hanser Verlag, 2008, p.84/"In the Sleepless" in *Across the Land and the Water – Selected Poems 1964-2001*, London: Hamish Hamilton, 2011, translated by Iain Galbraith, p.136.

127 See also *Austerlitz*, p.74 ff. and p.250.

128 *Nach der Natur/After Nature* pp. 23, 25 (25, 27–28).

129 In Claudio Magris *Danube*, London: The Harvill Press, 1989, p.68.

130 From "Wie der Schnee auf den Alpen", the first part of *Nach der Natur*, Nördlingen: Greno Verlagsgesellschaft, 1988, Section I, pp.7–8 /"As the Snow on the Alps", Part 1 of *After Nature*, London: Hamish Hamilton, 2002, translated by Michael Hamburger, Section I, p.6.

131 Taken from "Giuliettas Geburtstag" in *Über das Land und das Wasser – Ausgewählte Gedichte 1964-2001*, Munich: Carl Hanser Verlag, 2008, p.28/"Giulietta's Birthday" in *Across the Land and the Water – Selected Poems 1964-2001*, London: Hamish Hamilton, 2011, translated by Iain Galbraith, p.24.

132 From *Vertigo*, London: The Harvill Press, 1999, translated by Michael Hulse, pp.179–181.

133 From *The Emigrants*, London: The Harvill Press, 1996, translated by Michael Hulse, pp.184–185.

134 An excerpt from my diary for July–August 1963.

135 Taken from "Zimmer 645" in *Über das Land und das Wasser – Ausgewählte Gedichte 1964-2001*, Munich: Carl Hanser Verlag, 2008, pp.86–87/"Room 645" in *Across the Land and the Water – Selected Poems 1964-2001*, London: Hamish Hamilton, 2011, translated by Iain Galbraith, pp.139–140.

136 From "Wie der Schnee auf den Alpen", the first part of *Nach der Natur*, Nördlingen: Greno Verlagsgesellschaft, 1988, Section I, p.8/"As the Snow on the Alps", Part 1 of *After Nature*, London: Hamish Hamilton, 2002, translated by Michael Hamburger, Section I, pp.6–7.

137 See "Und Blieb Ich am Aussersten Meer", the second part of *Nach der Natur*, Nördlingen: Greno Verlagsgesellschaft, 1988, Section XIX, p.66/"And if I Remained by the Outermost Sea", Part 2 of *After Nature*, London: Hamish Hamilton, 2002, translated by Michael Hamburger, Section XIX, p.74.

138 See also Part 1, Chapter XIX of *Ariadne's Thread*.

139 From "Seit Jahr & Tag" in *Über das Land und das Wasser – Ausgewählte Gedichte 1964-2001*, Munich: Carl Hanser Verlag, 2008, p. 95/"Unchanged for years" in *Across the Land and the*

Water – Selected Poems 1964–2001, London: Hamish Hamilton, 2011, translated by Iain Galbraith, pp.151–152.

140 From *The Rings of Saturn*, London: The Harvill Press, 1999, translated by Michael Hulse, pp.86–88.

141 Ibid, p.245.

142 See "Ghost Hunter" an interview with Eleanor Wachtel, recorded on 16 October 1997 and reproduced in *The Emergence of Memory: Conversations with W.G. Sebald*, ed. Lynne Sharon Schwartz, New York: Seven Stories Press, 2007, p.60.

143 From "Und Blieb Ich am Aussersten Meer", the second part of *Nach der Natur*, Nördlingen: Greno Verlagsgesellschaft, 1988, Section X, pp.48–49/"And if I Remained by the Outermost Sea", Part 2 of *After Nature*, London: Hamish Hamilton, 2002, translated by Michael Hamburger, Section X, p.55–56.

144 See "Die Dunckle Nacht Fahrt Aus", the third part of *Nach der Natur*, Nördlingen: Greno Verlagsgesellschaft, 1988, Section II, p.77/"Dark Night Sallies Forth", Part 3 of *After Nature*, London: Hamish Hamilton, 2002, translated by Michael Hamburger, Section II, p.87–88. See also Part 1, Chapter XIV of *Ariadne's Thread*.

145 Peter Handke, *Kaspar*, 1967. Max's essay, "Fremdheit, Integration und Krise: Über Peter Handkes Stück *Kaspar*" ("Strangeness, Integration and Crisis: On Peter Handke's play *Kaspar*") had first appeared in 1975 in *Literatur und Kritik* 10 and was later included in the posthumous collection

Campo Santo, translated by Anthea Bell, London: Hamish Hamilton, 2005.

146 *The Enigma of Kaspar Hauser*, directed by Werner Herzog, 1974.

147 From *Austerlitz*, London: Hamish Hamilton, 2001, translated by Anthea Bell, pp.303–304.

148 From "Seit Jahr & Tag" in *Über das Land und das Wasser – Ausgewählte Gedichte 1964–2001*, Munich: Carl Hanser Verlag, 2008, p.95/"Unchanged for years" in *Across the Land and the Water – Selected Poems 1964–2001*, London: Hamish Hamilton, 2011, translated by Iain Galbraith, pp.151–152.

149 The text of Stefan George's poem "Bamberg" appeared in the first edition of *Der siebente Ring* (Berlin: Blätter für die Kunst, 1907) as follows:
Du Fremdester brichst doch als echter
spross
Zur guten kehr aus deines volkes flanke.
Zeigt dieser dom dich nicht: herab vom
ross
Streitbar und stolz als königlicher Franke!
Dann bist du leibhaft in der kemenat
Gemeisselt – nicht mehr Waibling oder
Welfe –
Nur stiller künstler der sein bestes tat –
Versonnen wartend bis der himmel helfe.

150 From *The Rings of Saturn*, London: The Harvill Press, 1999, translated by Michael Hulse, p.37.

151 From "Die Dunckle Nacht Fahrt Aus", the third part of *Nach der Natur*, Nördlingen: Greno Verlagsgesellschaft, 1988, Section I, pp.72–73/"Dark Night Sallies Forth", Part 3 of *After Nature*, London: Hamish Hamilton, 2002,

translated by Michael Hamburger, Section I, p.83.

152   See also Part One, Chapter XVII of *Ariadne's Thread*.

153   Johann Wolfgang von Goethe *Italian Journey 1786–1788*, translated by W.H. Auden and Elizabeth Mayer, London: Collins, 1962.

154   From "Der Lindenbaum" by Wilhelm Müller, the fifth song in the *Winterreise* cycle. My translation.

155   From "Die Dunckle Nacht Fahrt Aus", the third part of *Nach der Natur*, Nördlingen: Greno Verlagsgesellschaft, 1988, Section VII, p.96/"Dark Night Sallies Forth", Part 3 of *After Nature*, London: Hamish Hamilton, 2002, translated by Michael Hamburger, Section VII, p.109.

Permissions

Excerpts from *Across the Land and the Water, The Natural History of Destruction, Austerlitz, Campo Santo* and *After Nature* by W.G. Sebald

Reprinted by permission of The Penguin Group

Quotations from *Campo Santo* © 2003, The Estate of W.G. Sebald.

Quotations from *After Nature* © 1988, Eichborn AG, Frankfurt am Main.

Excerpt from *Elective Affinities* by Johann Wolfgang von Goethe

Reprinted by permission of The Penguin Group

Excerpts from *The Rings of Saturn, Vertigo* and *The Emigrants* by W.G. Sebald

Published by The Harvill Press

Reprinted by permission of The Random House Group Limited

Excerpt from *In Patagonia* by Bruce Chatwin

Published by Jonathan Cape

Reprinted by permission of The Random House Group Limited

Excerpt from *The Diaries of Franz Kafka*

Reprinted by permission of The Random House Group Limited

Excerpts from *Your Face Tomorrow* by Javier Marías

Published by Vintage

Reprinted by permission of The Random House Group

Excerpt from *Microcosms* by Claudio Magris

Published by The Harvill Press

Reprinted by permission of The Random House Group

Excerpt from *Danube* by Claudio Magris

Published by The Harvill Press

Reprinted by permission of The Random House Group

Excerpt from *Stone Voices* by Neal Ascherson

Reprinted by permission of Granta Books